Players and performances in the Victorian theatre

Players and performances

IN THE
VICTORIAN THEATRE

George Taylor

Manchester University Press
Manchester and New York

distributed exclusively in the USA and Canada by St. Martin's Press

Copyright © George Taylor 1989

Published by Manchester University Press
Oxford Road, Manchester M13 9PL, UK
and Room 400, 175 Fifth Avenue,
New York, NY 10010, USA

Distributed exclusively in the USA and Canada
by St. Martin's Press, Inc.,
175 Fifth Avenue, New York, NY 10010, USA

British Library cataloguing in publication data
Taylor, George
    Players and performances in Victorian theatre.
    1. England. Theatre, 1850-1905
    I. Title
    792'.0942

Library of Congress cataloging in publication data
Taylor, George, 1940–
    Players and performances in Victorian theatre / George Taylor.
        p.   cm.
        Includes bibliographical references.
        ISBN 0-7190-3167-2
        1. Theater—Great Britain—History—19th century.
    2. Actors—Great Britain.   I. Title
    PN2594.T39   1989
    792'.0941'09034—dc20   89-36251

ISBN 0 7190 3167 2 *hardback*

Typeset by Koinionia Ltd, Manchester

Printed in Great Britain
by Courier International, Tiptree

Contents

List of illustrations   *page vi*
Preface: The purpose of playing   *vii*

1 Tradition and change in the Victorian theatre   *1*

2 *The Corsican Brothers* by Dion Boucicault   *23*

3 A theatre of feeling   *30*

4 *Richelieu* by Edward Bulwer-Lytton   *51*

5 The comedian: comic or actor?   *62*

6 *Our American Cousin* by Tom Taylor,
   adapted by E. A. Sothern   *80*

7 French naturalism and English ensemble   *92*

8 *Caste* by T. W. Robertson   *108*

9 The conventions of melodrama   *119*

10 *Jack Sheppard* by J. B. Buckstone   *134*

11 The psychology of acting   *144*

12 *Trilby* by Paul Potter, after Du Maurier   *162*

13 Shakespearian interpretation   *173*

14 *Hamlet* by William Shakespeare   *192*

Notes   *205*
Further reading   *231*
Index   *233*

Illustrations

PLATES

   I Long-run machinery: *The Corsican Brothers* by Dion Boucicault,
      1852   *page 219*
  II The classical image: Macready and Faucit   220
 III A versatile mimic: *Patter v Clatter* by Charles James Matthews, 1836   221
 IV A traditional comic costume: Three actors as Paul Pry   222
  V The Yankee and the Toff: *Our American Cousin* by Tom Taylor, 1858   223
 VI Cup-and-saucer ensemble: *Caste* by Tom Robertson, 1862   224
VII Cross-dressing in melodrama: Mrs Keely and Madame Celeste   225
VIII Sacred or profane? *The Sign of the Cross* by Wilson Barrett, 1896   226
 IX La vie bohémienne: *Trilby* by Paul Potter, 1895, and *Drink*   227
      by Charles Reade, 1879
  X Shakespearian heroines: Ellen Terry and Ada Rehan   228
 XI 'Elizabethan' settings: *Taming of the Shrew*, 1844, and *Hamlet*, 1900   229
XII *Hamlet*, 1897: Forbes Robertson and Mrs Patrick Campbell   230

FIGURES

1 The start   *page 32*
2 'Horror'   *39*
3 Andrew Ducrow   *48*
4 Frederick Robson   *74*
5 Jack Sheppard   *137*
6 'Zones of Gesture'   *151*
7 Henry Irving reciting   *195*

Acknowledgements

Plates II (a), IX (b), X (a), XII (a and b) and cover illustration: The John Rylands University Library, Manchester (Brook Collection).
Plates IV (a), VI (a), X (b) and XI (a and b): The Theatre Museum (Guy Little and Gabrielle Enthoven collections).

Preface:
The purpose of playing

The purpose of this book is not to chart chronologically the development of the acting profession in Victorian England, nor yet to analyse details of theatrical production, but to consider what actors thought they were doing on stage – the purpose of their playing. To do this I have adopted a combination of approaches: the anecdotal account of particular moments and effects in the theatre; the examination of contemporary analyses of the actor's art, from philosophical discussions to technical handbooks; the consideration of how changes in social and economic conditions, and in cultural and scientific thinking, influenced, and were reflected by, theatrical performances. It is a wide net to cast, but, although a concentration on any one of these approaches might lead to fascinating new insights, my overall intention is to convey the richness and variety of the Victorian stage, and not to lose in theoretical analysis that sense of enjoyment which was the overriding purpose of all Victorian entertainers.

Although many shared the high sense of moral propriety typical of the age, and often desired to use plays to educate and edify, there were no actors comparable to the political agitators of our own century, nor, although Macready and Irving may have spoken of their theatres as 'Temples of Art', was there any concept of theatre as a self-conscious ritual, or that the 'way of the actor' had anything in common with that of the priest or mystic. Nevertheless, although actors believed their first duty was to entertain, many performers brought a seriousness of purpose, a physical and mental discipline, and a depth of emotional commitment to their art that might surprise those for whom Victorian Drama means pantomime and melodrama, and Victorian Acting means 'over-the-top'.

In order to do justice to the evocative details as well as the wide range of my study, I have alternated chapters of general discussion with more sharply focused descriptions of specific productions. However, general topics often need anecdotal illustration, and detailed analysis throws up wider issues than just what happened 'on the night'. So, despite my attempts to categorise and subdivide, both kinds of chapter tend towards discursive, rather than definitive, analysis. I do not appologise for this, merely regret that space has forbidden my pursuing even more disparate aspects of the subject. I do hope, however, that my account raises questions, and suggests avenues for further research. But above all, my purpose has been the same as the actors – to entertain.

Players and performances

My interest in the subject goes back many years, and I would like to acknowledge the inspiration I drew from Stephen Joseph and Peter Thomson, who were officially my teachers, and from the enthusiasm that they provoked in those who were originally my fellow students: Christopher Baugh, Knight Mantell, Robin Estill and Chris Meredith, all of whom shared what was then considered to be a rather eccentric interest in nineteenth-century theatre. More recent colleagues, whose contributions have been more direct on the research and writing of the present volume, include David Mayer, Kenneth Richards, Vivian Gardiner, Michael Holt, and Susan Rutherford. I would also like to thank David Wiles for his advice after reading early drafts. I have received assistance from several libraries in England, and, with the valuable aid of a British Academy travel grant, in America. My research was also greatly assisted by two periods of study-leave granted by the University of Manchester. Finally, I would like to thank John Banks and Manchester University Press for their much appreciated help.

In memory of
George Percy Taylor

1

Tradition and change
in the Victorian theatre

Henry Irving attempted Hamlet for the first time at the Theatre Royal, Manchester in 1864. At twenty-six he was a professional of eight years' standing, having worked in theatres throughout Scotland and Northern England. All these were 'stock companies', which could present a different play each night, because they had a stock of actors able to perform with seldom more than a single rehearsal, a walk-through of the play to establish from which side they were to make their entrances. There were no directors as we know them today, and, the essential ordering of the moves was made by the stage-manager. His prompt-copy was usually the only complete version of the text, and actors had to learn their parts from 'sides' of their own lines and cues. In these conditions the only guidance for a young actor in technique and interpretation was advice from more experienced actors, and his observation of how others had played the role.

Irving had seen Samuel Phelps play Hamlet at Sadler's Wells when he first visited a professional theatre at the age of twelve. Henry's parents had sent him to one of the Sadler's Wells actors, William Hoskins, to eliminate his stutter and West Country accent. When he was seventeen, Hoskins arranged an interview with Phelps, who offered him a lowly post in the company, but Irving decided to start his career in the provinces. He hoped that he would be launched, like many beginners, in a major role, advertised in the bills as 'for the first time on any stage', but the manager of the Sunderland Lyceum could not see star quality in the gawky young man with a peculiar voice. Irving had to work his way up. In the first three seasons he played 428 different supporting roles.

An old Irish prompter once told a new member of a stock company: 'Get on the stage when you see they want you; get them off, and then get off yourself.'[1] Such advice seems rather casual today, but similar directions might have been given to an Italian Commedia dell' Arte troupe, who improvised from scenarios that provided little more than the cues for 'getting on' and 'getting off'. Lack of rehearsal did not mean that there was chaos on stage, but that the particular skill of the stock actor, like that of the Italian comedian, was to improvise his moves, if not his lines, according to the basic rules of stage positioning, so that the action could flow smoothly and effectively.

Although most nineteenth-century provincial theatres had leading actors of their own – often the manager and his family, like the Crummles in *Nicholas Nickleby* – they were expected to provide instant support for visiting stars from London, who toured provincial theatres in the summer months. As stars seldom stayed more than a week, and performed different roles each night, detailed rehearsal was impossible. In the early years of the century all Edmund Kean wanted from Edward Stirling, the second lead in *The Iron Chest* at Croydon in 1829, was explained in the dressing room:

> 'In the Library scene, sink gradually on your right knee, with your back to the audience. When I place my hand on your head to curse, mind you keep your eyes fixed on mine'. Stirling: 'Is that all, sir?' Kean: 'Yes – do whatever you like after that; it will be all the same to me.'[2]

Robert Elliston, however, sent more precise instructions when he planned to perform *The Venetian Brothers* at Bath. From the company as a whole he required 'correct and rapid acting – everyone knowing where they are to stand, and giving supernumerary or other aid to the general effect – I shall order a book to be marked and sent to you by this post, and in it as many directions as can be crowded', but his leading lady was given more detailed instructions:

> Take care when Michalli is killed that it is so near the side scene he may stagger off... *You* turn round quick and stand in an attitude of *terror*, Abelino scarcely knowing at first whether he shall approach you, and remain fixed, his arms (the dagger still in his hand) toward you, which increases your fear – Then the cry of 'This way, this way' takes place – he must press you rapidly to his breast, half choked in his utterance, and when he leaves you, do you, even after your father comes on, remain for a moment or two fixed, as a statue representing *horror*; then recovering *shriek* out '*He* was here – *he*' 'What saidst thou? Can it be?' – after this pause an instant – '*No, no, my eyes deceive me*' – quick – half belief half doubt – I am deceived if you don't make a great line of this.[3]

The precise nature of this conventional style of acting will be discussed later, at present we need only note that the actress was presumed to know exactly how to represent an 'attitude of terror' and a 'statue of horror' without the benefit of the detailed rehearsal that such a passionate scene would receive today.

In the 1820s and 1830s, however, theatre productions in London were becoming more elaborate in their setting, dressing and 'getting up'. When, in 1832, Macready visited Bristol, he had to send instructions on the technical and scenic details of his new production of Byron's *Sardanapalus:*

Now – to make it easy, and diminish expense, – instead of the bungling manner it was done in London... Let there be a sort of Persian or Egyptian style of arch at the 2nd Wing – in the Hall of Nimrod, from which a curtain is festooned so as to fall and meet in the centre, and shut in the Banquet &c. By this means, as I will show, the erection of the pile *[Sardanapalus's funeral pyre]* takes place *behind it, out of sight of the audience*, which allows the use of one painted piece with trick flaps to fall and show itself on fire... I hope the Scene Painter & Carpenter will understand this, for it will save money, time, trouble & add greatly to the effect.[4]

Like Elliston, Macready sent ahead his own prompt copies, and the list in this letter shows the Bristol theatre was expected to support all his current roles: Macbeth, Lear, Hamlet, Virginius, William Tell, Richelieu, Werner and Sardanapalus. As for the Bristol actors, he wrote to the manager before his 1836 visit:

Pray get the study as as forward as possible – for it will be a very hard fortnight – It is not enough to desire the various books to be given out – but the pieces should all be cast at once, and the books & parts given out to be used, and care to be taken to see that they are used, and the books received back and sent out to others to be written from – if you do not see that proper exertion is made, the whole engagement will fall to the ground – for the novelties cannot be done.[5]

On this occasion the two 'novelties', *The Provost of Bruges* and *Ion*, were each allocated a two-hour rehearsal. If preparations at the prestigious Theatre Royal, Bristol were so perfunctory, it is not surprising that Macready had difficulty in lesser theatres, such as at Sheffield, where he performed *William Tell* in 1834: 'I acted very ill, but should not have been so bad but for the shamefully neglectful and imperfect state of the play... Ulric did not know two consecutive lines of the last three acts.'[6]

One suspects that Macready was often ill-served by such companies because he was not popular with supporting actors, whom he regularly bullied and abused in frustration at their shortcomings. Charles and Ellen Kean, on the other hand, were more considerate, and, although Kean was even more concerned than Macready with settings and complicated crowd scenes, he managed to stretch the stock system to its limit. John Colman described a nine-day engagement, with nightly changes of programme, in Belfast in the mid-1840s:

These works could never have been got through at all, save for the fact that Mr & Mrs Kean did not require to rehearse their own scenes – i.e. scenes which were entirely confined to themselves – and had not the majority of the company been experienced and accomplished actors. It was a terrible drudgery, however, for everyone, from the stars downwards. Our rehearsals commenced daily at ten, and lasted until four, and sometimes even later. By the time we got home to dinner, and had arranged our 'properties' etc. it was almost time to get back again to commence the performance. It was a labour of love, however, to do whatever we could to help the Keans, not only because it was our duty, but because they made our duty delightful, by their grace and charm of manner. [7]

Stock theatres were better organised to support the performances of a lone star, like Edmund Kean, than to recreate the elaborate productions of his son Charles.

By 1864 Irving had been involved in many performances of Hamlet and had performed the parts of Osric, Guildenstern, Horatio, Laertes, Claudius and the Ghost to a whole range of wandering Hamlets, including Charles Dillon, Barry Sullivan and Edwin Booth. Now he felt he was ready to attempt the great role itself. It had not been suggested by the management, but was his own choice for his seasonal benefit. It was inevitable that an ambitious young actor faced with a great role should be torn between two impulses; one was to make a striking impact by his originality, the other was to follow the stock system, in which he had been trained, and act according to the accepted model. Irving would, of course, have to keep to the general structure of the usual Manchester production, as benefit performances were mounted without any rehearsal at all. The rest of the cast would expect him to make the same 'points' as previous Hamlets, or, at least, to restrict his originality to the same key passages, where they might anticipate a pause, a gesture or a bit of byplay. In the event, Irving stuck to tradition; though this did not mean that he skimped his private preparation. One night, when he was not performing, he travelled to Birmingham to consult W. H. Chippendale, a most experienced Polonius, who had first performed the part in 1819 with Edmund Kean. Being the oldest actor 'in the business', in that he knew the stage-business of the part, Chippendale could demonstrate points from all the famous Hamlets of the century, and no doubt Irving attempted to incorporate some of them into his own performance.

Irving's first Hamlet, then, was a product of the stock theatre, and it is not surprising that, as the thin, angular actor, with his odd husky voice, was hardly the critics' idea of a stock Hamlet, they were lukewarm in their reviews and recommended that he stuck to his usual range.

The house knew well Mr Irving's ability in the light drama and scarcely expected an ideal Hamlet from him... At times Mr Irving found it difficult to avoid the gait and mien of comedy, or rather fell into them from long usage. Such things were to be expected and they are not mentioned disparagingly.[8]

In fact it was hardly a performance to attract the notice of a theatre historian, were it not that Irving played Hamlet so successfully at his second attempt, ten years later, on 31 October 1874. By then he was leading actor at the London Lyceum, and this time the originality of the performance was to prove a nail in the coffin of the stock company system. Obviously Irving was more experienced and mentally better equipped – although some critics could never accept his voice and physique in the great tragic roles – but now he was not concerned solely with his own performance, but with the production as a whole, and how the other characters related to each other and particularly to Hamlet himself. There was a deep romantic love between the Prince and Ophelia, and the closet scene was played with unusual intimacy, demanding a special subtlety from the Gertrude of Mrs Pauncefort. Without a fully rehearsed cast Irving's own performance would not have worked. To an extent, this may have been true of earlier performers, like Macready, Charles Kean or Phelps, but Irving was determined not to compromise his vision by trailing a solo performance round the provinces. His Hamlet could only be played with the Lyceum company – and the theatre played it for 200 nights![9]

The ten years between Irving's 1864 Hamlet and that of 1874 had seen a crucial change in the organisation of the British theatre: a watershed to be remembered when considering all other developments. The differences between the stock company and the permanent long-run company not only effected the style of performances but the whole structure of the acting profession. Of course these changes cannot be attributed to Irving alone, and indeed many performances could be cited to illustrate the transformation that took place during the 1860s. For instance, that of James Anderson's Macbeth (27 April 1860), which came at the end, rather than at the beginning, of a distinguished career. It had no more intrinsic value than Irving's first Hamlet and indeed lasted for only twelve nights, which was hardly a long run, but it was long enough for the manager of the Princess Theatre, Augustus Harris, to prepare an original *mise-en-scène*. The experience undermined all Anderson's traditional values.

Unfortunately I was weak enough to allow [Harris] to try new effects with scenery and machinery, which all proved abortive, and destroyed legitimate acting. In the 'murder scene', when Macbeth disappeared into Duncan's chamber, the witches were seen in a transparency high up in the castle wall, making triumphant gestures at the success of their wicked teachings. The platform on which they stood, however, gave way, and they all came to ground, receiving more or less injuries; indeed, one of them died a few weeks afterwards. I need scarcely say this novel and dangerous effect was never repeated. Banquo, instead of rising from a trap in the stage and taking his place in Macbeth's chair, appeared in a transparent pillar, where the light necessary to show him off set his wig on fire, and they were obliged to shut him up before Macbeth could exclaim, 'Hence, horrible shadow! Unreal mockery, hence!' The unnatural thirst for novelty and the new readings of Shakespeare is the curse of the modern stage. The scene-painter and machinist have eclipsed the actors; and the actors themselves, ignoring what was done by Garrick, Kemble, Kean and Macready, and fearing to be called conventional, invent new readings and 'business', from Hamlet to the Second Gravedigger.[10]

As far as Anderson was concerned the only tradition upheld at the Princess was that of the disasters that always seem to accompany the 'Scottish Play'.

Anderson had been a first-rate stock theatre actor. He had started his career in 1811, at the age of two, playing the baby in Sheridan's *Pizarro*. By twelve he was a fully-fledged professional, and in 1837 a respected member of the Covent Garden company. He played with Macready, Phelps and Charles Kean, and in the 1850s, having bankrupted himself trying to manage Drury Lane for two years, he became a touring star on his own account. He retired in 1874, aged sixty-three, a few weeks after Irving's second Hamlet. During the 1880s he watched the progress of Irving at the Lyceum and saw the Bancrofts bring their new 'society drama' to the Haymarket. In his memoirs he wrote perceptively of developments since his retirement:

The change that has taken place in things theatrical within the past few years is something wonderful. The influence of modern forces – gas, electricity, telegraphy, steamships, and railways – have made a strange and detrimental impression on the drama and the stage. All is now hurry-scurry, bustle and haste; melodrama and burlesque have taken the place of tragedy and comedy; poetry and romance are voted slow; and actors speak with such rapidity of utterance as to give one the idea that they are rushing to catch an express train. I was tired, and longed to be out of the crowd... The legitimate drama is many fathoms deep, and poor Shakespeare, if not drowned, is at least a great way under water.[11]

As well as the technological advances listed by Anderson, other developments in mid-Victorian society help explain this revolutionary change. In the early years of the reign, at least up to 1848 – the year of the European revolutions and the culmination of the Chartist agitation

– there had been very real class-conflict in England, and it had found expression in the theatre as well as in the press and on the streets. Several recent studies have pointed out the political content of early East End and Surrey-side melodramas.[12] The well-to-do, educated classes felt a sense of danger, which kept them away, not only from the rougher theatres, but from the two great Patent Houses. Despite separate entrances for boxes, pit and gallery, there was a threat not only from lower-class theatre-goers, but from the thieves and prostitutes who thronged the streets and alleys of the Covent Garden district. In the eighteenth century this disreputable area had been unavoidable for all classes, lying as it did between the two worlds of the commercial City and the fashionable Town, but in the nineteenth century there were new worlds which seldom met: the slums of the East End and the middle-class suburbs of the West and North, where they would rather read about the underworld in Dickens than risk a visit to it themselves.

In the late forties and fifties, however, reforms in local government led to new schemes for public health and public order. Better policing and paving, lighting and licensing all helped to make London streets safer after nightfall. The Great Exhibition of 1851 was a revelation in this respect, in that great numbers from all classes came together peacefully for instruction and entertainment.[13] The Queen and Prince Albert, whose coach had been stoned earlier in the reign, were now greeted by a population apparently united in its loyalty. Of course, the social and economic inequalities remained, but the fear that had dominated the Hungry Forties had been dissipated, and Disraeli and his Young Englanders were beginning to impress even the Tory party with the possibility of an alliance between the Two Nations. By the 1860s, and particularly after the 1867 Reform Bill, there was a new feeling of social compatibility, which was reflected in attitudes towards the theatre.

In the sixties theatre-building was renewed for the first time since the proliferation of Minor Houses in the twenties and thirties. Some were specifically designed for a new middle-class audience, with decorous orchestra stalls replacing the unruly pit, while in the provinces the old Theatres Royal were replaced by large touring houses. The moral and social censure of the theatre, made by puritans and utilitarians alike, decreased, but, although these changes seem to reflect a new sense of democracy in the country, they were in fact part of a continuing class division. The middle classes were taking the theatre over. More music-halls were being built in the sixties and seventies than legitimate theatres, and it was to these that the lower classes, who had once terrorised the galleries, were expected to go. Michael Baker in his indispensable study of the profession, *The Rise of the Victorian Actor*, describes how the

1866 Select Committee on the Theatre evoked considerable argument from the actors themselves as to their social, educational and cultural distinction from the sort of popular entertainers who in earlier days would have belonged to the same stock company. Implicit in the arguments brought before the Committee was a conviction that:

> The demonstrably proletarian associations of the halls would foster the 'wrong' sort of actor. The playwright Tom Taylor voiced these fears when he spoke of burlesque, the staple fare of the halls, as encouraging a 'lower class of actors' in the profession. Horace Wigan, actor-manger of the Olympic, concluded that for actors to perform in the halls would compromise the advance in dignity and status which they had achieved over the preceding thirty years.[14]

Historians have argued that it is arbitrary and misleading to isolate the reign of Victoria as a self-contained period, as there was an unmistakable watershed in the middle of the reign. But the very fact that it encompassed a wholesale transformation of British society gives the period a unity that is ideal for analysis. The change from stock system to long-run was indeed revolutionary from the actor's point of view, but it was a change that took a whole generation. Because it is impossible to pinpoint exactly the moment of change, or even of equilibrium, it is necessary to study a period that extends from thirty years before to thirty years after the moment where one feels the rift-line to be. If that rift took place around 1865-70, as James Anderson alleged, and Irving's career suggests, then the reign of Victoria does indeed seem to be a meaningful period.

Most theatre historians of the nineteenth century have concentrated on playwriting and the repertoire, and it is obviously true that the changes from legitimate drama to popular melodrama, and from melodrama to society plays, were very important. However, I intend to maintain my focus on the theatre as the province of the actor rather than the playwright, and in this respect the production in 1860 of Dion Boucicault's *The Colleen Bawn* was of particular significance. Its text may have been more sophisticated than earlier melodrama, its characterisation more naturalistic and its social awareness more specific, but I believe its chief importance was that Boucicault, in his role as actor-manager, rather than author, used its popularity to organise production companies specificly for a long run. It played for 230 consecutive nights at the Adelphi, and Boucicault claimed that by this run and his subsequent touring productions, he had created 'a new order of theatrical affairs':

I engaged four or five excellent performers. They were carefully rehearsed and prepared to perform the principal characters, but the play was to be the 'star'. This proposition was fiercely opposed by managers, but I steadily refused *The Colleen Bawn* to be played under any other conditions, and they yielded. The result was an unprecedented success. I sent three similar groups on the road and the golden harvest of that year, including my own takings in London, amounted to more than $200,000 clear profit, the largest, I believe, ever taken up to that date.

Of course this policy did not transform the profession all at once, but Boucicault claimed that by the time he was writing (1883), 'Provincial managers found at last that so many fully equipped entertainments were emerging yearly from London they could dispense with the engagement of a resident company altogether and fill their seasons with these roving troupes.'[15] However there were more intrinsic reasons than the phenomenal success of one or two plays why the theatre was transformed.

It is impossible to estimate exactly the number of theatres in London when Victoria came to the throne in 1837, as the unlicensed Minor Houses merged imperceptibly with other entertainment establishments in the capital, such as concert halls, public house free-and-easies, and backstreet penny-gaffs. Allardyce Nicoll names sixty-five theatres which were providing some sort of entertainment in 1837, but the list of thirty-four in the *Revels History of English Drama* is probably more accurate for theatres specifically involved in presenting drama. Leman Rede in *The Road to the Stage* listed twenty-one London theatres, plus six 'occasionals', and claimed there were forty to fifty provincial theatres, though statistical evidence is even more unreliable when applied to the provinces. In 1833 John Miller had drawn up a list of ninety-five theatres for the Dramatic Authors' Society, but most of these functioned for only a few weeks in the year, usually coinciding with local race meetings or the assize courts, when outsiders would have been expected in town.[16] Nearly all provincial theatres belonged in circuits of some five to ten theatres, and were served by itinerant stock companies. Some of these, like the Jackmans of Northampton, or the Robertsons of Lincoln, were drawn from a single family, others, like the Bristol, Edinburgh or Manchester Theatres Royal, could maintain themselves in a metropolitan centre with little or no touring, and employed a range of actors comparable to the larger London theatres. Finally, there were several tiny troupes of actors, thrown together in barns or fairground booths, whose existence can properly be described as vagabond. Peter Paterson, in *Glimpses of Real Life* (1864), considered himself a fairly successful stroller when he earned thirty shillings a week, but gave up when he could earn no more than six. James Grant, writing of the penny-gaffs in 1838, said that many performers earned only five shillings a week, which left them near starvation.[17]

It is even more difficult to estimate the full number of actors in the early Victorian period. Leman Rede suggests there were some three thousand in 1836, 'who thoroughly knew the business', but had no real evidence on which to base this figure. Even today Equity membership is hardly a reliable guide to the real size of a profession which offers irregular employment, is informal in its recruitment, and imprecise in its distinction between actors and other performers. Michael Baker has turned to the census returns and suggests a 'conservative estimate' of 1,357 actors and actresses in 1841, which rose to 3,592 by 1861, and to 7,321 by 1891. The later figures cover entertainers and dancers as well as legitimate actors, and the proliferation of music-halls in the second half of the century is obviously reflected in these numbers. Baker points out that these figures, although probably too low overall, indicate a general expansion and a significant change in the ratio of men to women: in 1841 there were about three actors to each actress, in the 1850s it was two to one, and by 1891 the actresses were just in the majority.[18]

In such an expanding and varied industry there must have been many different artistic and commercial policies at any one time, as well as changes over the years. The physical size and facilities of theatre buildings also had a direct influence on acting, and, before considering the details of acting methods, these physical and organisational circumstances need examining. The Haymarket, the Olympic and Sadler's Wells were all excellent theatres in their different ways, and at each of them first-class acting was to be found. The Haymarket tended to look backwards to the traditions of the eighteenth century, the Olympic was a bold experiment, and Sadler's Wells, under Samuel Phelps, was considered, at first, to be a new departure, but was eventually regarded as a bastion of tradition.

Before the passing of the Theatre Regulating Act in 1843, the only theatres legally entitled to present 'legitimate' drama were the Patent Houses: Drury Lane, Covent Garden and the Haymarket. From the point of view of 'legitimate' acting, the Haymarket was the most consistently successful of the three. To a great extent this was because its scale suited the traditions of eighteenth-century stock theatre performance. The Haymarket's patent rights dated back to 1766, when Samuel Foote had been allowed to organise summer seasons, primarally of comedies, whilst the two older 'Winter Houses' were closed, and this comic tradition survived well into the nineteenth century. Around 1800 Drury Lane and Covent Garden had been considerably enlarged in response to increasing demand, but this had not benefited the acting. Both the statuesque style of Kemble and the exaggerated vehemence of Kean had, to an extent, been prompted by having to act in what Sarah Siddons described as a 'wilderness'. By the 1830s both theatres were finding it difficult to fill their three to four thousand seats. Macready did his best to maintain the classics and create a new legitimate repertoire, but Alfred Bunn, who in 1833 was managing both theatres, recognised, more realistically, that the only thing to draw sufficient audiences were spectacular melodramas and pantomimes, or the operatic talents of Malibran, the dancing of Taglioni and the virtuosity of Paganini. Bunn relied on a policy of presenting stars for short fashionable seasons, and had little time for fostering the lasting qualities of a permanent stock company. In his autobiography, the manager boasted that at least fifty per cent of his programmes had included Shakespeare and legitimate plays, but these were only part of an evening's entertainment dominated by spectacular and musical afterpieces.[19] At Drury Lane on 27 April 1836 Bunn had insisted that Macready perform the first half of *Richard III*, to be followed by excerpts from the musical spectaculars, *Chevy Chase* and *The Jewess*. Macready was enraged by this rag-bag programme and when, leaving the stage, he saw Bunn in his office counting the night's takings, he assaulted the manager, crying 'You damned scoundrel! How dare you treat me in such a manner!' Bunn suffered a sprained ankle, and Macready withdrew from Drury Lane stricken with remorse. He completed the season at Covent Garden, eventually taking over its management from Osbaldiston. However two seasons as his own manager were enough to convince even Macready that Covent Garden, like Drury Lane, was just too large to survive economically on a purely legitimate repertoire, and in 1839 he contracted to play four nights a week at the Haymarket.[20]

During the period from the death of Samuel Foote in 1777 the Haymarket saw few changes of management. George Colman the Elder, who had bought the patent from Foote, was succeeded by his son in 1794, who ran the theatre until 1817. In that year he handed management over to his brother-in-law David Morris, who rebuilt the theatre in 1821. Unlike Covent Garden and Drury Lane, the capacity was kept under a thousand and the apron stage with proscenium doors was retained. Morris continued the same stock company policy as the Colmans, although by now the season lasted all year and the company was no longer made up of actors laid off from the Winter Houses. In 1837 one of his regular actors, Benjamin Webster, took over, and during the early years of Victoria's reign he championed traditional acting, at least in comedy. However in 1843 Webster redesigned the theatre to introduce orchestra stalls in front of the pit benches, 'by a curtailment of the useless portion of the stage in front of the curtain, and advancing Orchestra and Lights near the Actors and Scenic Effects'.[21] As well as the 'useless' apron stage, the proscenium doors were also removed. Thus even the Haymarket changed with the times, and these alterations must have affected performing styles. In 1853 Webster handed over to the comedian J. B. Buckstone, who was manager until 1879.

With managers lasting for an average of twenty years each, and who were either related to each other or drawn from the existing company, it is not surprising that there was a consistency of policy and of company membership. The normal Haymarket programme followed the eighteenth-century pattern of a five-act play, usually a comedy, followed by a two-act afterpiece, usually a farce. Some were perennial favourites like the plays of Sheridan, others were new pieces specially written to the requirements of the company and its chief comedians. One of the most successful was *Paul Pry*, which in 1825 had starred the nonchalant William Farren and the lugubrious John Liston, yet even this hit had an initial run of only fourteen nights before joining the general repertoire of alternating pieces. Liston had been a member of the Haymarket company for twenty years at the time of *Paul Pry*, and in the Victorian period other actors were similarly dedicated. W. H. Chippendale was to be there from 1853 to 1879, while Henry Howe started with Webster's management in 1837 and remained until 1879. He could eventually claim that 'I have played every part in the male role in some of the pieces produced on its stage. For instance in "The Lady of Lyons" I began with *First Officer*, then I played *Gaspar, Beuseant, Claude Melnotte* and now *Colonel Damas*.'[22] Like Chippendale he ended his career in Irving's Lyceum company, for, although Irving was dedicated to the long-run, he also appreciated the stalwart value of 'table-leg' actors.[23]

It is not surprising that while the Patent Houses were forced to adopt the repertoire of the Minor Houses in order to fill their cavernous auditoria, and the Minor Houses were legally banned from the legitimate drama, the Haymarket was considered the custodian of traditional standards. 'It is the only theatre now where we can catch a glimpse of the good old comedy', wrote the *Examiner* in 1835.[24] Westland Marston praised Webster's management more highly than his skill as a performer: 'He had assembled a company of actors so numerous as well as brilliant, that the accidental absence of one star could at once be substituted by another.'[25] Unlike his fellow managers, Webster cared little for scenery and effects. His productions were often considered scruffy, re-using inappropriate stock scenery. Indeed, Macready wrote of the theatre that 'dirt, slovenliness, and puffery make up the sum of its character'.[26] But this was to misjudge Webster's priorities, who 'in his time paid more money to actors and authors and behaved more liberally to them, than any of his compeers'.[27]

Macready arrived at the Haymarket in 1839 after failing to maintain legitimate drama at Covent Garden, but the style in which he wanted to produce serious plays made new demands on the Haymarket. Macready wanted the support of specific actors, well rehearsed in their roles, and he brought with him Mrs Warner, Helen Faucit, Samuel Phelps and Precilla Horton. For two years at Covent Garden he had got used to spending more on the dressing and setting of his shows than Webster was prepared to allow him. So, to an extent, Macready remained a visitor at the Haymarket, just as if he had been touring the provinces. In October 1839 he introduced *The Sea Captain* by Bulwer-Lytton, who had provided him with *Richelieu* and *The Lady of Lyons*, but it was well below the standard of the two earlier plays. Indeed none of the plays that Macready produced under Webster's management succeeded, until 1840, when Bulwer provided them with a play more suited to the Haymarket tradition – the modern satirical comedy *Money*.

Bulwer and Macready wanted special settings and costumes, but Webster could not see the point of them in a modern-dress comedy. When he protested at the expense, they threatened to offer the play to Mme Vestris, who had taken over Covent Garden after Macready's departure in 1838. Webster had always considered Vestris as a dangerous rival and was stung to write bitterly to Macready.[28] He began by objecting to the high and mighty attitude that Macready brought to most of his professional dealings: 'Your contempt for me as an actor and manager is made painfully apparent by your word and manner.' He reminded Macready that 'the pieces introduced by you are always attended with great expense and in five act matters I have not had one attractive novelty since the first season'. Macready had insisted on the engagement of actors from outside the company and extra scene painters and costumes. 'Now all these points as far as my means will allow and even beyond I have most cheerfully acceded to, and endeavoured to study your every wish till at last my patience is literally exhausted, as my pocket will soon be if I do not make a stand against these continued unproductive outlays.' And now Macready was threatening to send Bulwer's play to Covent Garden, 'a theatre directly opposed to the one in which you are receiving one hundred pounds per week at least for ten months of the year'. Although he left a door open for reconciliation, Webster concluded that unless the two of them could 'work amicably and zealously together with perfect confidence in each other, and I must reluctantly confess my faith in your friendship to me is shaken by last night's threats, I feel that it would be far better for me to jog on comfortably in my old and humble, but profitable, way, than to endure this continued scene of splendid misery which will probably end in loss'. The quarrel was patched up and *Money* successfully presented in December 1840, but this letter illustrates most vividly the strain that was put on a highly competent manager by the demands of an actor who wanted his productions to be more thoroughly prepared than in the 'old and humble, but profitable, way' of Ben Webster and his stock company.

But what of Mme Vestris, to whom the play had been offered? Macready had confided to his diary that 'it is not a fitting spectacle – the national drama in the hands of Mme Vestris and Mr Charles Mathews'.[29] In his view the old Patent Houses had a national duty to present tragedy, and Vestris and her husband Mathews were a light comedy team of what Edwardians were to refer to as 'matinee idols'. But Vestris was not just a comedienne. As manageress of the Olympic Theatre throughout the 1830s she had championed a completely new kind of drama. Originally a singer, her voice, though sweet and expressive, did not have the power for an operatic career, and she gravitated towards musical afterpieces. In 1820 she had her first success at Drury Lane in *Giovanni in London*, a burlesque of Mozart's opera with Vestris as the Don *en travestie*. From then on Vestris was considered more of a 'personality' than an actress or singer. Part of her appeal was sexual – her legs became the toast of Regency London – but she was not vulgar. She played burlesque roles with elegance and charm, displaying a rather patronising attitude towards the trivial nonsense she condescended to perform. Moreover, although she was performing in illegitimate burletta, she appealed to a fashionable audience, who ignored not only other Minor Houses, but the Patent Houses themselves.

In 1831, tired of being relegated to afterpieces, she decided to create her own theatre, and leased the Olympic. Of course, she had to avoid the legitimate repertoire but she shunned the formless melodrama and variety bills of the Surrey, the Coberg or Astleys. She employed J. R. Planché to provided a new kind of elegant burletta. Planché was not only a witty punster and parodyist, but an antiquarian scholar, who in 1823 had revolutionised the dressing of Shakespeare with his historically accurate designs for Charles Kemble's *King John*. At the Olympic he provided Mme Vestris with burlesques set in several periods of history, from the Classical *Olympic Revels* to the Restoration *Court Beauties*, in which Vestris brought on her own pet King Charles spaniels. At the Olympic tasteful refinement was grafted on to traditional triviality.[30] In 1835 she hired the elegant and educated Charles Mathews, who became as much a favourite with female spectators as Madame was with the men. In 1838 they married – in deference to the puritanical attitudes of

America, where they were to tour that year. As consummate publicists they knew when to adapt the slightly risqué image, that had appealed during the Regency, to become more respectable in the Victorian period.

In appealing to a fashionable audience Vestris anticipated something of the society theatres of the 1870s. The auditorium was kept clean, tidy and well appointed; her prices were high (4s boxes, 2s pit, and 1s gallery) thus pricing out the rowdy lower-class 'gods'; and the evening's entertainment finished by eleven o'clock, rather than dragging on into the early hours as at other theatres, which attracted half-price trade by a multiplicity of attractions.[31] Although it could be described as a stock company, as the programme changed each night, the actors were not expected to turn their hands to all and sundry; the style of entertainment – burletta, musical-comedy and farce – was limited, and, as pieces remained in the repertoire for some time, they were well prepared and rehearsed. As a producer Vestris already had something of the long-run mentality:

> When not on the stage, [she] was constantly in her private box, watching the performance, noticing the slightest imperfection, and seeking to increase effects instead of allowing them to be gradually destroyed by time and carelessness. Many of our Christmas pieces were thoroughly re-dressed twice during their run, and consequently as brilliant on the last as on the first night of their performance.[32]

Her actors were so well and regularly paid that she was able to do away with the system of benefit performances. As benefits depended on the improvisatory skills of a stock company, the Olympic was becoming something of a specialist troupe.

Gradually the sophistication and careful preparation of the Vestris/Planché burlesques began to affect her style of presenting regular comedies, and this became particularly apparent when she took over Covent Garden in 1839. She opened with *Love's Labour Lost*, in acknowledgement of the responsibility of a Patent House towards the classics, and followed it with revivals of Sheridan. In these, if the ensemble acting was not as good as at the Haymarket, they were more accurately dressed and set. But Vestris's most influential production was her counter-attraction to the Haymarket's *Money*: Dion Boucicault's first play *London Assurance* (4 March 1840). In some ways this play seems like a late flowering comedy of manners, but in others, and especially in its production and acting style, it anticipated the society plays of the later nineteenth century. Costumes were bought from the most fashionable tailors and the box-sets were furnished in meticulous detail. According to *The Times* the production 'was sustained by nearly every actor in the company, and each part [was] one which the sustainer would, of his own free will, have chosen... [The] plot might seem but meagre to sustain a piece in five acts, but the author has contrived... to keep his audience in a roar from the beginning to the end'.[33] Instead of the rather broad style of Macready and the Haymarket company in *Money*, *London Assurance* was acted by Mathews, William Farren, Louisa Nesbitt and Vestris herself with vivacity and charm.

Boucicault soon gave up comedy to write melodrama, introducing to the genre a restraint in characterisation and dialogue, which came to be associated with the 'gentlemanly' style of Charles Kean at the Princess Theatre (see Chapter 2). Charles Kean benefited from the passing of the 1843 Regulating Act in a way that was impossible for Vestris. She had been associated too long with the burlesque theatre, and her attempts at legitimate comedy had been made at Covent Garden, a theatre that was, despite the success of *London Assurance*, really too large for the subtle playing of herself and Mathews.

Despite the passing of the Theatre Regulating Act, the 1840s and 1850s did not see a boom in legitimate drama, rather the reverse. Existing theatres continued to develop their own specialisations. The Adelphi, the Surrey and the Britannia were quite content with the houses they were getting for melodrama, and, as the Patent Houses were struggling to draw audiences with a legitimate repertoire, there was little incentive to set up new legitimate companies. In 1844, for instance, Ben Webster took over the Adelphi with Mme Celeste, and he maintained its melodrama policy. In 1853 he even deserted the Haymarket to concentrate on this second theatre. It was, in its own way, just as much a stock company, but in the melodrama line rather than in traditional comedy. Henry Morley's description of the typical 'Adelphi drama' reflects precisely the static nature of its style:

> There should be in their drama mystery, villainy, comic business, smugglers, caves, crossing of swords, firing of guns, lost daughters, mysteriously recovered, shrieking their way into their fathers' arms, hair-breadth perils, executions, reprieves. Mr O. Smith should be a villain; Mr Keeley should have his comic genius, especially in the depiction of mortal terror, well brought out; Mr Webster should have a part to make a study of quite his own vein; Mr Leigh Murray should have a gentleman's part; Madame Celeste should have something melodramatic and picturesque which would enable her to display all the great power that is in her; and Miss Woolgar should be enabled also to bring into play nearly the whole range of her skills. Other actors were to be equally well-fitted... The Adelphi audience is fitted to perfection with its play, and every actor fitted to perfection with his or her part.[34]

Melodrama, almost by definition, is based on cliché. The same stock characters endure the same emotional distresses and achieve the same happy resolutions. It is not surprising that the melodramatic actor was steeped in tradition: he knew which points always told, and which jokes always got a laugh.

The proliferation of theatres in the 1830s, and their conflict with the theatre monopoly, has been described by Michael Baker as *seeming* to be a movement towards theatrical 'free trade', but in fact

> the measure of 1843 was solidly protectionist in spirit, effectively replacing a monopoly with a system which, albeit more broadly based, was nonetheless highly restrictive. Indeed, the dramatic halt to theatre-building in central London for the following two decades and more is partly explained by the rigorous conditions which continued to govern the licensing of new play-houses.[35]

The 1843 reform was not intended to change the style, repertoire, or even management of the already well established minor theatres, but to supress the 'underground' theatres of the penny-gaff and the strolling barn-stormer, by insisting that for a theatre to be licensed it had to be permanent and purpose-built. Like the famous repeal of the Corn Laws in 1845, the Theatre Act was passed to benefit the managerial class more than the theatrical 'hands' (the actors), or even the consumers (the audiences). Baker describes the managers and leading actors of the time as 'the theatrical equivalent of the rising middle-class activists, who in the course of the early nineteenth century sought to assert their social and political supremacy' (p. 143). He points out that even managers born into theatrical families were educated by their parents to take up more respectable careers. On the night of his first triumph at Drury Lane Edmund Kean had boasted that he could 'now send Charley to Eton'; Macready had been to Rugby and was intended for law or the church; Charles Mathews, after Merchant Taylors', considered architecture; and Samuel Phelps began his career in journalism. Some managers, like Webster, Davidge and Osbaldiston, who ran the Adelphi, Coberg and Surrey Theatres, were commercially minded entrepreneurs, and hoped, like any self-respecting Victorian businessman, to give good value for money so as to reap a fair profit; but some others, like Macready, Charles Kean and Phelps, were cast in the more idealistic Victorian mould. They considered themselves as artists, with a duty towards the culture of their country comparable to that of Tennyson, Carlyle or Dickens.

Yet, in a way which was more typical of the visual artists than the writers of the high Victorian period, these actor-managers seemed more concerned with honouring and restoring the culture of the past, than with commenting on contemporary society. Just as the Gothic style was the only one deemed worthy of the new Houses of Parliament, so only

Shakespeare – or 'revivals' in the Shakespearian style by Knowles, Bulwer and Talfourd – were deemed worthy by Macready for his classical repertoire. Some of these plays, like the Palace of Westminster itself, had political content concealed behind their Gothic or Classical veneer, as we shall see when considering Macready's performances of *Virginius* and *Richelieu*. Macready himself was too egotistical and intolerant of those who lacked his own dedication and talent to get fully involved in the business side of theatre management. He had an almost Quixotic dedication to the Patent Houses as the home of the National Drama, and refused to act in an illegitimate theatre until after the passing of the Theatre Act (he appeared at the Princess and the Surrey in 1845-46). This meant that Macready was never fully in command of his own company, and was forced to rely on a stock system which he ultimately despised. Charles Kean's brave management of the Princess, 1850-59, remarkable for its meticulous antiquarian settings and well-drilled crowd scenes, was an artistic success in the revivalist spirit, but it could only be financed by gruelling summer tours undertaken by Kean and his wife.[36]

Of the three major tragedians of the mid-century only Phelps can be said to have been a truly successful manager. His acting of individual roles may not have been as widely acclaimed, but that was not his style; he was an ensemble actor, not a star who insisted on holding centre-stage like Macready, with whom he acted for many years. In 1843 Macready's management of Drury Lane folded, and (partly because the Patent House monopoly had not prevented the failure) the Theatre Act was passed. From the disbanded company Phelps and Mrs Warner were invited by Thomas Greenwood, lessee of Sadler's Wells, to establish a suburban legitimate company. They opened on 27 May 1844: 'Macbeth will be the first performance, the *legitimate* will be the order of the day... we trust the Islingtonians will support so bold and arduous a novelty.'[37] They did so for eighteen years.

In the late forties and fifties Sadler's Wells was the only London theatre really upholding the traditions of the legitimate repertoire. No other Minor House considered the policy financially viable, and, although Kean continued to present Shakespeare at the Princess's, he did so with a new emphasis on spectacular production rather than the traditional acting ensemble; and before long he adopted a long-run policy. Henry Morley considered Phelps to be the more artistic manager:

> It is not because of anything peculiar in the air of Islington, or because an audience at Pentonville is made of men differing in nature from those who would form an audience in the Strand, that Shakespeare is listened to at Sadler's Wells with a reverence not shown elsewhere. What has been done at

Islington could, if the same means were employed, be done at Drury Lane. But Shakespeare is not fairly heard when he is made to speak from behind masses of theatrical upholstery, or when it is assumed that there is but one character in any of his plays, and that the others may be acted as incompetent actors please.[38]

One reason for the success of the Wells was that it appealed to a new audience, which was to prove particularly loyal. Mention has been made of the unsavoury reputation the theatre area had with the suburban bourgeois; the Wells was to become their theatre. Although some critics adopted a rather patronising tone: 'there sit our working-classes in a happy crowd, as orderly and reverent as if they were in church',[39] they were more accurately described as 'the most respectable portion of the immediate neighbourhood'.[40] The prices (Circle 3s/2s; pit 1s; gallery 6d) were more in line with those of the Surrey Theatre than the Olympic, yet the Wells remained profitable throughout Phelps's management.

The company was not particularly brilliant, but it had the solid virtues of the best provincial stock companies. Although in 1844 'the closing of the great theatres enabled him to secure the services of an unrivalled troupe of experienced and admirable artists at small salaries', in later years the theatre was to become 'almost the only school of acting in the metropolis'. In this too it resembled the provincial theatres, where most actors started, but inevitably some of the 'birds trained in his nest took wing westward as soon as he had taught them self-sustainment'.[41] Because many of his company of thirty-five to forty actors were beginners, they took instructions from the manager, and Phelps's productions were remarkable for careful ensemble playing, a concentration on the clear delivery of the text, and the avoidance of complicated and gimmicky business.

His whole programme followed stock company traditions. In 1855, when Charles Kean ran the Princess's production of *Henry VIII* for one hundred nights, Phelps presented ten different Shakespeare plays for an average of ten nights each; nine non-Shakespearian plays averaged four performances each, with fifteen for one new play, Angelo Slous's *Hamilton of Bothwellhaugh*. Another illustration of the policy is that the 133 performances of his favourite role, Macbeth, were spread over fourteen seasons out of the eighteen he was at the Wells. Even when a new production met with success he refused to let it run for as long as possible,[42] which surprised *The Theatrical Journal*: 'We wonder that in consideration of the great success it received, it has only been played twice a week.'[43] Phelps himself usually performed only four nights a week: 'From his long acquaintance with the locality Greenwood knew that no attraction would at that period pull the Islington public into Sadler's

Wells on Friday and Saturday (now the best nights of the week).'[44] The actor would go off for a long weekend's fishing.

Phelps was respected by his middle-class audience, and he adopted a middle-class lifestyle, sending his children to private schools and his sons to university. He may not have had the fashionable patronage of Macready or Kean, but in many ways he was the more typically Victorian, and many families visited his theatre, who kept away from both the stylish West End and the uncouth melodrama houses. In 1862, when his wife contracted cancer, Phelps gave up management, 'slipping out of sight with neither flummery nor fuss, and so modestly takes his leave of us that we have scarce the opportunity to say how much we liked him'.[45] For the rest of his career he toured the provinces and made occasional London appearances, but he did so on his own terms without the extravagance or the aggravation of the Keans' later tours. On his death in 1878, William Archer recognised that Phelps, as an actor, was

> the last, and by no means the least, not only of a generation, but of a dynasty of actors – the Shakespearian dynasty – founded by Burbage, and stretching in an unbroken line from Betterton downwards. For two hundred years the stage was at no time without its two or three 'legitimate' actors, – men who had been trained in the classic drama, who could move with ease and dignity through the whole poetic repetory; to whom the march of sonorous iambics was as little a mystery as the modulation of the hexameters to the ancient rhapsodists... Phelps trod the stage in the buskins of Burbage; but to whom has he bequeathed it?

Nothing could more clearly indicate that in the 1870s a drastic change had come over the British theatre. It was not just a change of repertoire, with Boucicault, Taylor and Reade making melodrama respectable, and Robertson giving comedy a new contemporary relevance, nor just a change in theatre organisation from stock to long-run, but a change in the very nature and purpose of theatrical performance. At the start I associated this with the coming to maturity of Henry Irving; Archer felt the same when he contemplated the passing of Samuel Phelps: 'though he lived to see Mr Irving almost in the plenitude of his power, he would probably have been more at home with Burt and Mohun at the Cockpit than on the Lyceum stage'.[46]

The implications of this ending of 'a dynasty of acting' will be one of my main themes, but before considering descriptions of either the stock or the long-run style, one or two conjectures may be postulated. Without careful rehearsal, the stock actor needed a repertoire of gestures and movements, which he could call on almost instinctively, to give point and effect to the recitation of lines that he had hurriedly learnt or revised. As actors had little chance to work together in rehearsal, and thus had to rely on a traditional pattern of moves and business, it was easier for an actor, wishing to display originality, to concentrate on individual characterisation than on the relationship *between* characters. Thus the stock style emphasised individual expression rather than social interplay, and the outward expression of feeling, through gesture and vocal technique, rather than the gradual revelation of motives over a number of acts, or the exploration of environmental factors, which set the characters in a social context. This is borne out by the plays written for this type of theatre. Comedies of manners had declined at the turn of the century, coinciding with the erosion of the patent monopolies, and maintained a home only at the Haymarket. The romantic drama of the pre-Victorian nineteenth century – gothic melodrama and historical romance – tended to concentrate on the extraordinary personality of a single hero, or villain, which demanded the emotional display of a single star actor rather than the interplay of an ensemble. The stock system was ideally suited to service such a star. Thus throughout the first half of the century the Georgian ensemble was replaced by star actor-managers surrounded by merely competent supporting actors, from whom little originality was to be expected. Melodrama too implied a systematisation of the stock company: the categorising of heavy and romantic leads, low comedians, soubrettes, walking gentlemen, etc., indicates a team designed for efficient productivity rather than creative originality. The prolific turnover of new plays also suggests an industrialisation of the theatrical process.

If characterisation were thus restricted, and opportunities for interplay were more mechanical than organic, it is not surprising that emphasis was thrown on to the extravagant expression of passion in circumstances of extreme provocation: solo cadenzas of fervent rapture, frenzied remorse or mental prostration. The techniques of this passionate acting will be the subject of the next chapter, and it will be seen that its appeal was particularly strong in the Romantic Period. The development of the star/stock system which typified the first half of the century was one that was technologically conducive to such an emphasis, while the breakdown of that system was to lead, later in the century, to a shift in emphasis towards social interaction in the drama, and psychological subtlety in acting.

The other major development was the increasing complexity of production techniques: settings, effects, furniture and properties. The romantic soloist could spout quite satisfactorily in front of a splendid backcloth, but once a group of actors found themselves in the realistic environment of a box-set, or even the complicated machinery of a Boucicault. sensation scene, they had to plan their movements round the furniture, and time their business to fit the effects. Rehearsals were necessary to make the settings work, long-runs were necessary to recoup the cost of the scenery, and 'ideal' casting according to personality rather than type began to be introduced. It was a gradual process, but many of its implications can be seen in the first performance to be described in detail, Charles Kean's *Corsican Brothers*, a piece that illustrates, as well as any, how influences of tradition and of change affected the theatre of the mid-Victorian period.

2

The Corsican Brothers
by Dion Boucicault

Princess Theatre, 24 February 1852

Twin brothers	FABIEN DEI FRANCHI LOUIS DEI FRANCHI	Mr Charles Kean
	CHATEAU-RENAUD	Mr Alfred Wigan
	BARON DE MONTGIRON	Mr James Vining
	ALFRED MYNARD	Mr G. Everett
The heads of two	ORLANDO	Mr Ryder
Corsican families	COLONNA	Mr Meadows
	SAVILIA DEI FRANCHI	Miss Phillips
	EMILIE DE LESPARRE	Miss Murray

Act I

Fabien dei Franchi at home in Corsica feels premonitions of danger threatening his twin brother Louis, who is Paris. In the evening, after making peace between two feuding local families, he has a vision of his brother's death in a duel.

Act II

A flashback to the start of Louis dei Franchi's fatal quarrel in Paris. Louis protects the honour of Emilie de L'Esparre from being compromised by her ex-lover Chateau-Renaud, a renowned womaniser and duellist. They fight in the Forest of Fontainbleau, Louis falls and assures his second that his brother will avenge his death. He has a vision of Fabien in Corsica.

Act III

Fabien tracks down Chateau-Renaud to same clearing in the forest. After a prolonged and vicious duel Chateau-Renaud is killed. Fabien has a final vision of his brother's ghost.

It is not always easy to tell whether the success of a particular performance was due to the individual originality of an actor, who just happened to catch the mood of the times, or whether the style was somehow determined by prevailing cultural fashions. Many critics considered that Charles Kean was breaking new ground in his production of *The Corsican Brothers*, both in his own style of acting, and in the new type of drama. Even if Kean's own motive for change was to react against his famous father, he did seem to catch the spirit of the times. The Victorians' taste was for the edifying, the scientific and the organised, rather than the passionate and rebellious fashions of the Regency, which had idolised the erratic genius of the elder Kean. Charles certainly strove to cultivate a reputation for respectability, scholarship and industry. Because he lacked his father's power to embody the passion and poetry of Shakespeare's heroes, he dedicated his considerable organisational skill to mounting the plays with the pedantic accuracy of an academic antiquarian. This contributed significantly to the change from Romantic to Naturalistic styles of acting. Kean's acting was most praised in quieter, intellectual roles, like Hamlet, Wolsey and Richard II; in *Macbeth*, *Henry V* and *King Lear* the scenery, pageantry and general effect had to prevail over his artificially agitated emotion and his cold-in-the-nose delivery of the verse. Critics complained that poetry was being sacrificed to the scenery, but a newly-rich middle-class public, anxious for education, was flattered by the extravagance with which Kean honoured the national bard. It was so obviously 'culture', so obviously 'correct'.

Inevitably this popularity, and the scale of his preparations, led Kean to adopt the long-run rather than stock system, and the 1855 production of *Henry VIII* was the first Shakespeare play to be performed for one hundred consecutive nights. Banquets and balls, a coronation and a christening were the main attractions, but it was also an intellectual treat to see Holbein's portraits brought miraculously to life in all their historical detail. Even more culturally edifying was *The Winter's Tale*, in which not only were the Sicilian settings precisely defined as 'fourth century B.C. Syracuse', but Bohemia was transformed into 'Bythinia', so as to afford 'an opportunity of representing the costumes of the inhabitants of Asia Minor at a corresponding period, associated so intimately with Greece, professing the same form of paganism, and acquiring additional interest from close proximity to the Homeric kingdom of Troy'.[1] While most of Kean's directorial effort went into drilling the supers, all the cast had to fit into the visual ensemble. They were not allowed to fall back on their stock company conventions and clichés. Ellen Terry, appearing for the first time as an eight-year-old Mamillius, recorded the care with which Charles Kean and his wife rehearsed their cast far into the night:

During the rehearsals Mr Kean used to sit in the stalls with a loud-mouthed dinner-bell at his side, and when anything went wrong on the stage, he would ring it furiously, and everything would come to a stop, until Mrs Kean, who always sat on the stage, had set right what was wrong... No woman ever gave herself more trouble to train a young actress than did Mrs Kean.[2]

However, young Ellen noted a revealing complaint from John Ryder, a 'heavy' actor, whose physical bulk and vigorous style in such roles as Macduff, Buckingham and old Orlando in *The Corsican Brothers* contrasted well with the neat precision of his manager: 'D'ye suppose he employed me for my powers as an actor? Not a bit of it! He employed me for my damned archiological figure!'[3]

Charles Kean also applied these production techniques to modern plays, such as *The Corsican Brothers*, preparing the 1852 production with the same concern for accuracy of time and place as he brought to Shakespeare. The script was by Dion Boucicault, from a French dramatisation of the original Alexandre Dumas story. The play looked both backwards, to the supernatural Gothic tradition, with ghosts and visions, and forwards, to the society drama, with the compromising of an innocent woman's reputation, and, although it could not pretend to any great intellectual depth, it was skilfully constructed. Its careful production and controlled acting generated a genuine theatrical excitement, which was all too often missing from Kean's worthy Shakespeare productions.

The scenery was not just picturesque; it accurately conveyed the social setting of the play. The first scene was a Corsican castle and it included a comic squabble between two rival families. This sub-plot suggested that vendettas were undertaken by real islanders, not just by the *banditti* of Gothic melodrama. Next, the auditorium of the Paris Opera was reconstructed so that the stalls and boxes of the Princess seemed to be mirrored in its own proscenium, and a masked ball evoked the gaiety of *la vie Parisienne*. Finally, the scene shifted to the Forest of Fontainebleau, the actual venue for notorious duels as reported in the newspapers (see Plate I). To this apparent social and geographical accuracy was added a pseudo-scientific justification for the novel flashback construction, and for the ghosts and visions, which were staged using the ingenious 'Corsican Trap', the 'Sink and Rise', and gauze effects.[4] The identical twins, Fabian and Louis dei Franchi, were conceived as sharing telepathic communication and thus not only were their visions of each other given theatrical justification, but a psychological validity.

In fact, most of these aspects of the play merely confirmed the prejudices of the middle-class spectators. The vengeful dago and the sinful *demi-monde* were titillating stereotypes to the chauvinist London audience. However, the 'new style' of acting by Kean and his company gave the drama an impression of reality that was genuinely disturbing, as in George Henry Lewes's description of the final duel:

> Fabian and Chateau-Renaud fight; during the pause, the latter leans upon his sword and breaks it. Fabian, to equalise the combat, snaps his sword also, and both then take the broken halves, and fastening them in their grasp by cambric handkerchiefs, *they fight as with knives.* This does not read as horrible, perhaps; but to see it on the stage, represented with minute ferocity of detail, and with a truth on the part of the actors, which enhances the terror, the effect is so intense, so horrible, so startling, that one gentleman indignantly exclaimed *un-English!*[5]

Chateau-Renaud, the aristocratic villain, was played by Alfred Wigan, who for some years had specialised in stage Frenchmen. In 1842 his Alcibiades Blague in Jerrold's *Gertrude's Cherries* had been

> Personated with a closeness to the original, both in appearance and manner, that it is evidently the result of observation and study... Frenchmen have been so grossly caricatured on the English stage, that a true and finished portrait embodied from life, even to the bronze of the cheek, and the cut of the hair, is the more appreciated.[6]

He gave a similar meticulous performance in *The Corsican Brothers*:

> One of the most unique, perfect and powerful performances the stage has ever witnessed. I never heard him tell Montgiron in the last scene to prepare his mother for the news of his death without a strange sense of painful but sympathetic emotion. Then the fight with Kean was a superb exhibition of sword play.[7]

The excellence of Alfred Wigan in this play suggests the sort of casting-to-type that was to become normal under the policy of the long-run. Although he had been fairly satisfactory as Faulconbridge in *King John*, the conclusion of a stalwart stock actor, John Colman, was that, although 'he was an admirable and accomplished actor, his resources never carried him with advantage out of the coat and trousers of the nineteenth century'.[8] The critic Westland Marston agreed that he 'abounded in the delicate sensibility which often confines actors to the portrayal of a few parts suited to their own individualities'.[9]

Charles Kean too might have been criticised for a similar lack of range, but just as the old stock types of drama were no longer wholly acceptable, so new techniques of acting were being developed. Kemble, Siddons, Edmund Kean and even Macready had brought the same style to different roles, but it had been universally recognised as the classic-heroic style appropriate to leading actors, and a subtle differentiation between roles had not been expected. Now, in a more meticulous production, such as *The Corsican Brothers*, audiences expected each part to be filled appropriately, and that, if a new character was to be played for months on end, it should be subtly different from the actor's last performance.

The method that both Wigan and Kean used for this character differentiation was to accumulate detailed 'by-play'. Kean's performance of the identical twins in The Corsican Brothers was obviously a test case for such a technique, but a further description of Alfred Wigan indicates the change in style more clearly. Having left the Princess in 1854, Wigan performed in *Still Waters Run Deep* by Tom Taylor at the Olympic, and the *Times* described how

> Everything like commonplace exaggeration is shunned, and the language is made to approximate as much as possible to that of real life. He does not aim at violent contrast between the supposed dolt and the man of proved intellect, but he allows the impression of superiority to be gradually conveyed, and makes his audience feel he has a right to the position he acquires in the end.[10]

As the title of the play suggests, the actor did not reveal the 'truth' of his character all at once, but gradually revealed it by hints and suggestions, by the planting of carefully prepared 'telling details'. A Liverpool critic in 1862 emphasised this use of detail:

> No man on the stage, perhaps, has such an infinite power of varying his personality as Mr Wigan, and no man is more exactly every character he plays; but his strong point is *minuteness*... The critic can *discern*, in that general result of perfect assumption which delights the public in Mr Wigan, an infinity of detail and finish. The artist has the part always, as it were, in his hand... and making everything of it that exact imitation of details can accomplish under the direction of a sound conception.[11]

Comparing this testimony to Wigan's versatility with John Colman's accusation of limited specialisation, one realises that it was the special quality of the style that Colman was deploring. It was a meticulous, restrained and modern style, suited to the repertoire of Tom Taylor and Dion Boucicault, but unsuited to the improvisational hurly-burly of the stock theatre tradition. In this respect Wigan was ahead of many of his contemporaries.

With Charles Kean himself, however, we can perceive the transition from the old style to the new actually being accomplished, particularly in *The Corsican Brothers*. George Henry Lewes, who had long criticised Kean's performances in Shakespeare, recognised a new style of acting and welcomed it, although rather grudgingly, as he considered that melodrama 'appealed to the lowest faculties':

> Charles Kean, after vainly battling with fate so many years, seems now, consciously or unconsciously, settling down into the conviction that his talent does not lie in any Shakespearian sphere whatever, but in melodrames...

Charles Kean plays the two brothers; and you must see him before you will believe how well and *quietly* he plays them; preserving a gentlemanly demeanour, a drawingroom manner very difficult to assume on the stage, if one may judge from its rarity, which intensifies the passion of the part, and gives it a terrible reality. Nothing can be better than the way he steps forward to defend the insulted woman at that supper; nothing can be more impressive than his appearance in the third act as the avenger of his brother. The duel between him and Wigan was a masterpiece on both sides; the Bois de Boulogne itself has scarcely seen a duel more real or more exciting. Kean's dogged, quiet, terrible walk after Wigan, with the fragment of broken sword in his relentless grasp, I shall not forget.[12]

Westland Marston reported that Lewes had noticed a change in Kean's style during the first Princess season, in *The Templar* by Angelo Slous: 'A keen, if somewhat fastidious critic – the late Mr G. H. Lewes, no warm admirer of the actor – observed to me "Charles Kean is changing his style into a natural one. He will convert me yet".' Marston himself suggested that it was in his own play, *Anne Blake* (1852), that Kean 'seemed to sacrifice the abandon, of which he was capable, to a desire to conform to the usages of the drawingroom'. It was a performance of 'admirable keeping, and of a manly, if, at times repressed force, which made its way to the heart, through all the impediments of everyday customs and attire'.[13] Like Wigan in *Still Waters Run Deep*, Kean hinted at emotion, rather than displayed it. This 'repressed passion' was evident too in *The Corsican Brothers* – 'the quiet and menacing intensity of his acting' – and in *Pauline*, a similar French melodrama, 'the effect of passion at white heat was strangely enhanced somehow by the realism of modern costume and the nonchalance of modern manners'. *Pauline* too had a duel scene, and Marston's account reveals how the telling detail communicated more sharply than any conventional gesture:

> In the duel-scene in this piece he held the house breathless. By the conditions of the duel, the result must be fatal to one of the combatants. Thus the silent, concentrated quietude with which Charles Kean prepared for the encounter; the way in which he combined the merciless determination of fixed hatred with the refined ease and placidity of the man of society; the air of calm acquiescence in his fate when he removed from his lips the blood-stained handkerchief which betrayed his mortal wound, – all these details, if less ambitious than those of his acting in tragedy proper, far surpassed them generally in dramatic suggestiveness, incisive power, and freedom from artifice.[14]

Of course there was artifice, but it was the artifice of suggestion and selection rather than the traditional virtuosity of the Romantic style. The modern reader will not find it difficult to appreciate these qualities of detail, they are still, after all, the principal technique of our own naturalistic acting. Rather, it is the Grand Manner that seems alien to us now, and we are not surprised that critics like Lewes seemed to welcome its passing. However, when he looked back on Charles Kean's father, Lewes rated Edmund 'incomparably the greatest actor I have ever seen' and 'a genius', but not an instinctive or impulsive genius:

> He was an artist, and in Art all effects are regulated. The original suggestion may be, and generally is, sudden and unprepared – 'inspired', as we say; but the alert intelligence recognises its truth, seizes on it, regulates it. Without nice calculation no proportion could be preserved; we should have a work of fitful impulse, not a work of enduring art. [Edmund] Kean vigilantly and patiently rehearsed every detail, trying the tones until his ear was satisfied, practising looks and gestures until his artistic sense was satisfied; and having once regulated these he never changed them. The consequence was that, when he was sufficiently sober to stand and speak, he could act his part with the precision of a singer who has thoroughly learned his air. One who often acted with him informed me that when Kean was rehearsing on a new stage he accurately counted the number of steps he had to take before reaching a certain spot, or before uttering a certain word; these steps were justly regarded by him as part of the mechanism which could no more be neglected than the accompaniment to an air could be neglected by the singer. Hence he was always the same; not always in the same health, not always in the same vigour, but always the master of the part, and expressing it through the same symbols.[15]

These 'symbols of his art', as Lewes refers to them more than once, were clearly not the 'telling details' that Charles Kean and Alfred Wigan introduced as by-play, and, although Edmund's own career falls outside our period, it is to an analysis of these 'symbols' that the next chapter is dedicated.

3

A
theatre of feeling

Throughout the early Victorian period, there were two ideal models against whom all serious actors were measured, Sarah Siddons and Edmund Kean. Siddons died in 1831, though she had retired from the stage as early as 1812, two years before Kean's first Drury Lane triumph. Kean died in 1833, though his artistry had been in decline for several years due to drink and debauchery. Nevertheless such was the quality of Siddons as Lady Macbeth and Kean as Othello, Shylock and Giles Overreach, that for at least a generation all tragedians were measured against their legendary performances. Even Macready, the undisputed leader of the profession in 1837, was considered as an intelligent amalgam of their two styles, rather than an original genius in his own right. This may be unfair to his innovations in production techniques, but when compared as an actor to Edmund Kean, many would have agreed with George Henry Lewes that he was 'only a man of talent'.[1] The measuring of contemporary actors against the idols of the past was perhaps inevitable in stock theatre, where actors were denied the rehearsals in which to pursue originality of interpretation. Even Kean had been described as a second Garrick, with no less an authority than Garrick's widow remarking on the similarity of both appearance and technique.[2] The Kembles, on the other hand, had been recognised as innovators, with a greater sense of the artistic whole than the passionate immediacy of either Garrick or Kean.

But at this distance in time, what can we understand of these actors' techniques? What artistic assumptions did they make, and what were the effects they wanted? What was the purpose of their playing? First and foremost they wished to communicate *feeling*, what they called 'passions', by which were meant not only affective states of mind such as anger, fear or desire, but all mental activities, such as sensation, perception and recognition. Of course, such feelings have always been the stock in trade of actors, but in the late eighteenth century, arising from the study of the physiology of perception by such philosophers as Locke, Berkley and Hume, there was a particular awareness of the animated responses of the conscious mind to stimuli provided by sensory perception. The holistic influences of social environment or historical tradition were not considered as important as immediate circumstances in determining the distinction between personalities or the subtle variety of motivation within the individual.[3] Audiences were thrilled by the immediacy of David Garrick and Edmund Kean *perceiving* something that overwhelmed them with feelings of terror or triumph, of surprise or satisfaction. The technique they used to communicate this sense of sudden perception was the 'start'.

The classic example of a start dates from almost a hundred years before our period, when it had seemed a stroke of genius, rather than a hackneyed cliché. David Garrick's performance of Hamlet seeing the ghost of his father was recorded in detail in terms of both technique and effect. Georg Christoph Lichtenberg, a German visitor to London, described how

> Suddenly, as Hamlet moves towards the back of the stage slightly to the left, and turns his back on the audience, Horatio starts, and saying: 'Look, my lord, it comes,' points to the right, where the ghost has already appeared and stands motionless, before any one is aware of him. At these words Garrick turns sharply and at the same moment staggers back two or three paces with his knees giving way under him; his hat falls to the ground and both his arms, especially the left, are stretched out nearly to their full length, with the hands as high as the head, the right arm more bent and the hand lower, and the fingers apart; his mouth is open: thus he stands rooted to the spot, with legs apart, but no loss of dignity, supported by his friends, who are better acquainted with the apparition and fear lest he should collapse.[4]

As actors made more use of this technique of recoiling in surprise from whatever they perceived, there was a tendency, seen first in portraits of Garrick but by the early nineteenth century becoming almost universal in pictures of actors, to adopt a 'knees-bend' stance, similar to that of a pugilist, swordsman or modern tennis player, so that the actor could start with maximum effect in any direction. To us it seems contrived and over-demonstrative, but Lichtenberg's own response to Garrick's start was that 'his whole demeanour is so expressive of terror that it made my flesh creep even before he began to speak'. Nor was the German the only one to experience a feeling of terror. In a delightful passage in *Tom Jones*, Henry Fielding describes how the susceptible Partridge was affected by Garrick's performance. It is a fictitious account, but it reveals Garrick's artistic intentions most clearly, and also the sensibility expected of the ideal, naive auditor. Partridge would not believe that the actor playing Hamlet's father was a ghost, despite Jones's explanations:

> 'No, no, sir, ghosts don't appear in such dresses as that, neither.' In this mis-
> take... he was suffered to continue till the scene between the ghost and
> Hamlet, when Partridge gave that credit to Mr Garrick, which he had denied
> to Jones, and fell into so violent a trembling, that his knees knocked against
> each other... 'I perceive now it is what you told me... Yet if I was frightened, I
> am not the only person... if that little man there upon the stage is not fright-
> ened, I never saw any man frightened in my life!'... And during the whole
> speech of the ghost, he sat with his eyes fixed partly on the ghost and partly
> on Hamlet, and with his mouth open; the same passions which succeeded
> each other in Hamlet, succeeding likewise in him.[5]

Figure 1. 'The Start'. The reaction suggested for Macbeth's 'Hence horrible shadow'
in Gustave Garcia's handbook *The Actor's Art*, 1888

Sensibility was a quality that both actors and auditors were expected
to share in this period of the 'Sentimental' and 'Romantic Movements':
the faculty of empathising with the feelings of another when one's own
interests are not directly involved. In his *Treatise on the Art of Playing;
The Actor* of 1750, John Hill defined sensibility as

A disposition to be affected by the passions... that pliantness of disposition by means of which the different passions are made easily to succeed to one another in the soul... All the art in the world can never supply the want of sensibility in the player; if he is defective in this essential quality, all the advantages of nature, all the accomplishments he may have acquired by study, are thrown away upon him; he will never make others feel what he does not feel himself, and will always be as different from the thing he is to represent, as a mask from a face.[6]

I do not intend, as yet, to pursue this definition into the area of Diderot's *Paradox of Acting*, which argued that sensibility was not actually necessary for an actor imitating emotion, and that the secret was to maintain a cool head in order to be able to give the *impression* of a warm heart. The significance of Hill's description, at this point, is that the purpose of the player was to 'make others feel', and it was precisely this ability that was singled out in one of Garrick's obituaries: 'If he was angry, so was you: if he was distressed, so was you: if he was terrified, so was you: if he was merry, so was you: if he was mad, so was you. He was an enchanter, and led you where he pleased.'[7] Joseph Donahue in his *Dramatic Character in the Romantic Age* finds the same emphasis on making an audience share the subjective feelings of the performer in the drama of the period as it developed towards melodrama. Plays were written concentrating on 'affective scenes' of pathos and excitement, in which the responses of the characters were more important than the narrative logic of the plot, and he argues that:

Despite wide differences in their personal styles, Garrick, Kemble and Kean belong with equal right to the 'Romantic School' because their emphasis on interpreting character was orientated towards their presentation of subjective response. The aesthetic impression derived from such an emphasis is that the character is by nature individual and so his response to a given situation is necessarily unique. Consequently the audience identifies sympathetically with the character, sees the world through his eyes, and ultimately finds the meaning of the play inseparable from, and in fact the same as, the meaning of that character's responses.[8]

This emphasis on emotional responses, and the defining of character according to feeling, encouraged the exaggeration of emotion out of proportion to the ostensible motives of the dramatic scene, though some actors applied a more thorough, even scientific, analysis to dramatic characters, in terms of sensibility and 'ruling' passions. Of the two histrionic giants, Kean and Siddons, it was the actor who tended to indulge in excessive passion, and the actress who revealed the unifying power of the Ruling Passion.

In John Hill's definition of the actor's art he described the mental process as one of 'different passions succeeding one another in the soul,' and it was the tendency of actors to think in terms of *different* passions, each of which had its specific physical manifestations, that led to the technique most readily attributed to Edmund Kean, that of making points. A 'point' was a particular theatrical moment when the actor, by making a gesture, striking an attitude, or changing the tone of his voice created the impression of a new passion, whether it was a moment of sudden recognition – a start – or a gradual change of emotion – a transition. Making points was something Garrick had done, but Kean was to make his particular speciality, the one that distinguished him most clearly from the Kembles. When William Hazlitt saw Kean perform Shylock at Drury Lane in January 1814, he described how he performed each passion distinctly and vigorously, even at the expense of consistency of characterisation. It was the immediacy of his reactions that was impressive, rather than that the emotions were necessarily appropriate to the character. Hazlitt wanted Kean to reveal Shylock's ruling passion for revenge, but instead the actor gave a virtuoso display of starts, points and transitions:

> There was a lightness and vigour in his tread, a buoyancy and elasticity of spirit, a fire and animation, which would accord better with almost any other character than with the morose, sullen, inward, inveterate, inflexible malignancy of Shylock. The character of Shylock is that of a man brooding over one idea, that of its wrongs, and bent on one unalterable purpose, that of revenge. In conveying a profound impression of this feeling, or in embodying the general conception of rigid and uncontrollable self-will, equally proof against every sentiment of humanity or prejudice of opinion, we have seen actors more successful than Mr Kean; but in giving effect to the conflict of passions arising out of the contrasts of situation, in varied vehemence of declamation, in keenness of sarcasm, in the rapidity of his transitions from one tone and feeling to another, in propriety and novelty of action, presenting a succession of striking pictures, and giving perpetually fresh shocks of delight and surprise, it would be difficult to single out a competitor.[9]

However, Kean was not restricted only to the sprightly start or the vehement rant. Leigh Hunt, who resented such effects as 'trickery', noticed certain more restrained, individualised responses, such as when Richard III rubbed his hands together in vulgar glee at his own cunning, or when, before the final battle, he paused reflectively, drawing lines on the ground with the point of his sword. These were not stock oratorical gestures, but original means of revealing the inner feelings of the character, not quite 'stage business', but unique and individualised gestures that gave the performance what Hunt described as a 'noble familiarity'.[10] George Henry Lewes, who clearly recognised the conscious artistry with which Kean prepared his points, also remembered long afterwards his ability to give a temporal shape to his depiction of individual passions, not only the spontaneous start, but the 'subsiding emotion':

> Although fond, far too fond, of abrupt transitions – passing from vehemence
> to familiarity, and mingling strong lights and shadows with Caravaggio force
> of unreality – nevertheless his instinct taught him what few actors are taught
> – that a strong emotion, after discharging itself in one massive current, con-
> tinues for a time expressing itself in feebler currents. The waves are not
> stilled when the storm has passed away. There remains the ground swell
> troubling the deeps. In watching Kean's quivering muscles and altered tones
> you felt the subsidence of passion. The voice might be calm, but there was a
> tremor in it; the face might be quiet, but there were vanishing traces of the
> recent agitation.[11]

The problem with playing each passion of the moment, whether
strongly or subtly, was that what was shown was not always what was
felt. Few actors, or even physiognomists, of the time realised this; they
tried to discover, define and fix all the physiological expressions of inner
feeling. Macready recorded amusingly how George Frederick Cooke

> volunteered to exhibit to a young man sitting opposite to him the various
> passions of the human heart in the successive changes of his countenance.
> Accordingly, having fixed his features, he triumphantly asked his admirer,
> 'Now, sir, what passion is that?' The young gentleman with complacent con-
> fidence replied, 'That is revenge, Mr Cooke', 'You lie, sir! It's love!' was
> Cooke's abrupt rejoinder.[12]

Either Cooke could not express, or the young man could not read, the
signs and signals of the passion. To an extent the actors of the period –
perhaps of any period – relied on an artificial vocabulary of grimaces,
gestures and tones of voice, which playgoers had learnt to recognise. On
the other hand, what might have been lacking in Cooke's demonstration
was the context within which the expression could have been placed, and
thus interpreted.

The ability to create such a psychological context, a communication
of the whole rather than of the moment, was the particular skill developed by the Kembles. They also interpreted character in terms of feelings, but looked for the motivating emotion, the 'ruling passion', that
gave the characterisation unity and a through-line of development.
Hazlitt had felt that Kean's Shylock had lacked unity, but when he compared Kemble's Hamlet to his Coriolanus he observed the opposite quality:

> It has always appeared to us, that the range of characters in which Mr
> Kemble more particularly shone, and was superior to every other actor, were
> those which consisted in the development of one solitary sentiment or exclu-
> sive passion... where all the passions move round a central point, and are gov-
> erned by one master-key... So in Coriolanus, he exhibited the ruling passion
> with the same unshaken firmness, he preserved the same haughty dignity of
> demeanour, the same energy of will, and unbending sternness of temper

throughout... In such characters, Mr Kemble had no occasion to call to his aid either the resources of invention, or the tricks of the art: his success depended on the increasing intensity with which he dwelt on a given feeling, or enforced a passion that resisted all interference or control... In Hamlet, on the contrary, Mr Kemble in our judgement unavoidably failed from a want of flexibility, of that quick sensibility which yields to every motive, and is borne away with every breath of fancy... he played it like a man in armour, with a determined inveteracy of purpose, in one undeviating straight line.[13]

As well as analysing his characters in terms of a single ruling passion, Kemble structured his whole performance so that the single line of increasing intensity reached a specific climax in one grand moment of passion. Macready recorded that Kemble's Cato was 'listened to with respectable, almost drowsy attention. But like an eruptive volcano from some level expanse, there was one burst that electrified the house'.[14] Similarly in Macbeth, Kemble showed that the tragedy lay in the hollowness of the rewards gained by a ruling passion of ambition, and the climax of the performance was not the murder, nor the confrontation with Banquo's ghost, where Garrick and Kean had displayed their starts and transitions, but the despair towards the end. Hazlitt wrote of the later scenes, 'He displayed great energy and spirit: and there was a fine melancholy retrospective tone in the manner of delivering the lines "my way of life has fallen into the sear, the yellow leaf"... His action in delivering the speech "To-morrow and to-morrow", was particularly striking and expressive.'[15] Macready, who saw Kemble's farewell performance of Macbeth, also noted:

> Through the whole first four acts the play moved heavily on: Kemble correct, tame, and effective: but the fifth, when the news was brought 'The queen, my lord is dead', he seemed struck to the heart; gradually collecting himself, he sighed out 'She should have died hereafter'. Then, as if with inspiration of despair, he hurried out, distinctly and pathetically the lines 'Tomorrow and tomorrow and tomorrow...' rising to a climax of desperation that brought down the enthusiastic cheers of the closely packed theatre.[16]

Kemble built up to the emotional climax by following what Stanislavsky was to call a 'through-line of development', although in using this phrase Stanislavsky implied a continuous line of motivation – 'I want': Kemble's continuity was one of emotion – 'I feel'.

If Macbeth was not Kemble's finest part, his personality being better suited to the stoical Cato or the haughty Coriolanus, Sarah Siddons's performance of Lady Macbeth became legendary. Although she analysed the role in a similar way, showing how the single passion of ambition led ultimately to despair and destruction, the effect was more impressive than her brother's.[17] To an extent this was because of her greater acting skill, but also because the role is more single-minded and offers more opportunities for emotional intensity:

> When the actress, invoking the destroying ministers, came to the passage –
> 'Wherever in your sightless substances You wait on nature's mischief', the
> elevation of her *brows*, the full *orbs* of sight, the raised shoulders, and the hol-
> lowed hands, seemed all to endeavour to explore what yet were pronounced
> no possible objects of vision. Till then, I am quite sure, a figure so terrible
> had never bent over the pit of a theatre.[18]

As for the final sleep-walking scene, Siddons's own emotional climax,
the intensity was such that Sheridan Knowles, when asked by Edwin
Forrest for his memory of the scene, replied in terms reminiscent of
Partridge's overwhelmed sensibility: 'Well, sir, I smelt the blood! I swear
I smelt the blood!'[19] It was this infectious nature of extreme mental torment that Siddons shared with Edmund Kean. Madness on stage
inspired a sympathetic madness in the audience, as when Kean performed the insane jealousy of Massinger's Sir Giles Overreach:

> Scream after scream reverberated thro the solemn stillness of the house – a
> stillness now broken by the confusion caused by the removal of hysterical
> women; Lord Byron was seized with a sort of convulsive fit; the pit rose en
> masse; all parts of the house followed its example; and as hats and handker-
> chiefs were waved with unparalleled enthusiasm, thunders on thunders of
> applause swept over the theatre.[20]

Although both Siddons and Kean died before Victoria came to the
throne, their influence continued through those who had acted with
them, and in the memories of audiences and critics. Some, like William
Robson, looked back to the dignity and control of Kemble and Siddons,
scorning the point-making of Edmund Kean:

> While Mr Kean continues to keep his bad voice at perpetual stretch, stamp
> his foot, sneer with his eyes and lip when he should smile, falls in the midst of
> a burst of passion from the loudest tones to audible whispers, one of the vilest
> of stage tricks, plays to his audience instead of the characters of the piece, and
> speaks with such unintelligible rapidity, I can see no reason to join the cry
> which has placed him, in the opinion of the general, at the top of his profes-
> sion. Kean was a vulgar actor.[21]

As many less able actors of the early Victorian period merely copied such
tricks, Kean's influence was not entirely beneficial. However, it was an
influence that lasted many years, and the starts, attitudes and transitions
that he used to communicate the intensity of dramatic passion were
reproduced, not only by the stars of minor houses, where pantomimic
gesture was necessary in the dumb-show of burlettas, but by more ambitious actors, such as his son Charles, prior to his adoption of 'gentlemanly naturalism', and Macready, who inherited techniques from both Kean

and Kemble.

Handbooks of acting reproduced detailed instructions of how the passions ought to be portrayed, and, although most claimed to be based on the observation of life, many descriptions seem to owe more to behaviour on stage than in the street. *The Thespian Preceptor* of 1810 describes

> DESPAIR, as in a condemned criminal *(George Barnwell)* or one who has lost all hope of salvation *(Cardinal Wolsey)* bends the eye-brows downward, clouds the forehead, rolls the eyes, and sometimes bites the lips, and gnashes with the teeth. The heart is supposed to be too much hardened to suffer the tears to flow; yet the eye-balls will be red and inflamed. The head is hung down upon the breast; the arms are bended at the elbows, the fists clenched hard, and the whole body strained and violently agitated. Groans expressive of inward torture, accompany the words appertaining to his grief; those words are also uttered with a sullen, eager bitterness, and the tone of his voice is often loud and furious. When despair is supposed to drive the actor to distraction and self-murder, it can seldom or ever be over-acted.[22]

The whole of this treatise indicates a confusion between the reproduction of 'reality' and the conventions of performance. Having insisted that 'the actor should speak as if he felt every word', the author describes prescriptively how 'in every climax... the voice should rise, and the concluding part of the climax be delivered with the loudest note'. Having described how certain actors use false rhetorical gestures, 'at the first sentence with their right hand, and the second with the left, continue to alternate through each speech... others who continually shake a single figure; some two fingers; some the whole hand... The arms akimbo is also often thought the attitude of grandeur, instead of, as it really is, the certain sign of vulgar and inflated imbecility', he goes on to detail the correct gestures to express 'the passions and emotions of the soul... Dismissing with approbation is done with a kind aspect and tone of voice; the right hand open, gently waved towards the person: with displeasure, beside the look and tone of voice which suits displeasure, the hand is hastily thrown out toward the person dismissed, the back part toward him; the countenance at the same time turned away from him.'[23]

Similarly, George Grant's *Science of Acting* (1828) argues that the gestures of acting are not those of oratory, and yet lays down specific and highly artificial rules: 'The hands should be in sight of your eyes, and so corresponding with the motions of the head, eyes and body, that the audience may see the concurrence, every one to signify the same thing', and when discussing speech he quotes the highly conventional Colley Cibber: 'The voice of a singer is not more strictly tied to time and tune, than that of an actor in theatrical elocution.' As for the interplay of actors, Grant insists that 'to preserve what is termed stage effect, actors

Figure 2. 'Horror' as depicted in Henry Siddons, *Practical Illustrations of Rhetorical Gestures*, 1822

should never approach nearer to each other, than that by extending their arms, they might be enabled to take hold of hands.'[24] These books were primarily inspired by the decorum of Kemble's classical style, as was the most influential early nineteenth-century handbook *Practical Illustrations of Rhetorical Gesture and Acting*, translated from the German of J. J.Engel by Henry Siddons, Sarah's eldest son, in which, once again, each passion was given its own physical expression in attitude and action. Siddons, like Grant, recognised the danger 'that everything which is executed by *prescribed rules* will be *formal, stiff, embarrassed, and precise*', but argued that acting is like dance, in which the steps need to be practised until 'habit becomes a kind of nature'.[25] As a true Kemble, he was very aware of the artistic nature of an actor's representation, and he used his mother's performance as an example to make his point:

> There are but two counsels to give the actor... first, that he ought to seize all occasions of observing nature, even in those effects which are unfrequent in their occurrence; and, in the second place, that he should never lose sight of the main end and grand design of his art, by shocking the spectator with too

coarse or too servile an imitation.

If the first actress now on our stage had never been present at the bed of a dying person, her acting, under such circumstances, might probably have lost one of its most natural and affecting traits... At the moment when her soul is supposed to be just ready to quit her body, she gives signs of a slight convulsion, but this is apparent only at the ends of her fingers: she nips up her robe; and the arm, in that action, suddenly seems numbed and powerless...

With regard to the second piece of advice, I would give one rule... that the agonies and approach of death ought not to be represented with all the horrors which attend these dreadful moments in nature. The judicious player will soften down these horrors. His head should have more the appearance of a man sinking to a sound sleep than of a person convulsed with strong agonies; the voice should be broken and altered, but not so as to give the effect of a disgusting rattling: in a word, an actor ought to acquire a manner of his own, in representing the last sigh of expiring mortality. He should give such an idea of death *as every man would wish to feel at that crisis...*

My added emphasis indicates, once again, how it was presumed that all acting should inspire an identity of sensation in the audience. In criticising actors who exaggerated 'naturalness' in their performance of extreme emotion, Henry Siddons may have been thinking of Edmund Kean and Eliza O'Neill.

Contemplate... the abominable grimaces and unnatural distortions in which some players indulge themselves... I have myself seen a *Macbeth* die in convulsions, which were certainly very naturally imitated, but at the same time have thrown the spectators into convulsions of laughter... I do not know what evil genius persuades so many of our performers, the female in particular, that it is so exquisite a manoeuvre to be perpetually rolling themselves on the ground. A lady acting Juliet, or any other character of that description, will sometimes fall on the boards with such violence, when she hears of the death or banishment of her lover, that we are really alarmed, lest her poor skull should be fractured by the violence of the concussion.[26]

Apart from this theatrical decorum, Siddons pays little attention to how scale and style might indicate individuality of character, but deals with the passions as if they were of universal application, and goes no further into the causes of emotion than to attribute them to immediate stimuli of an almost Pavlovian kind: 'The present moment is real – the future uncertain... Sentiment, always conformable to the situation, constantly shews itself just as it is:- feeble or impetuous at its birth; imperious in its progress; mastered sometimes, or half extinguished; hid for a moment, to re-appear with greater force hereafter.'[27] As Joseph Donahue explains, this concentration on individual passions, and their physical manifestations, implies that a dramatic character is

plunged into the immediate situation, he has no time to meditate on his reactions; they burst forth at the instant they are formed in the mind, impelling him into the future. Subsequent moments, drawing forth repeated demonstrations of his responsive nature, reveal the struggle of the mind with the varying forms of passion. Only these moments, as they occur, are real. Siddons' idea of the magical illusion of reality on the stage presupposes that this reality consists entirely of a sequence of 'moments', each revealing the character's nature by eliciting a reaction 'conformable to the situation'.[28]

Since the seventeenth century increasing emphasis had been placed on the physiological origin of emotion. In his account of the psychology of acting, *The Player's Passion*, Joseph Roach describes how Descartes's *Les passions de l'âme* (1649) had analysed the nervous system as a kind of hydraulic machine, by which perceptions, sensations and emotional reactions automatically stimulated each other by the flow of 'animal spirits'.[29] This explained the instantaneous nature of the start, and the precision with which physiognomists described the outward expression of internal sensations. Descartes had argued that the rational mind could override these bodily reflexes, but later Romantic artists stressed the power of emotion to overwhelm censorious reason; some writers, following Rousseau, associated impulsive feelings with the action of the soul, instinctively creative and sympathetic, others, following de Sade, recognised their destructive and pathological nature.

Scholars of a scientific rather than philosophical bent continued to submit the expression of emotion to a process of observation and analysis, thus developing theories of neurology and psychology. Charles Bell brought aesthetics and science together in his *Anatomy and Expression, as Connected with the Fine Arts* (1804) which developed the thesis that 'the muscles were the soul in action'. He observed that the eyes roll upwards in sleep, death and trance-like ecstasy, and then argued:

> So, in intercourse with God, although we are taught... that the Almighty is everywhere, yet, under the influence of this position of the eye, which is no doubt designed for a purpose – we seek Him on high... See, then, how this property of our bodily frame has influenced our opinions, and belief; our conceptions of the Deity – our religious observances – our poetry, and our daily habits.

Similar attempts to find a correspondence between physical expression, mental states and received religion tended to concentrate more and more on the actualities of physiology than on abstract ideas conceived in the mind, or on spiritual states inspired by the external agency of God. Charles Bell noted that:

> It is curious that expression appears to precede the intellectual operation... the expression is in fact the spontaneous operation and classification of the muscles which await the development of the faculties to accompany them... It may be too much to affirm, that without the cooperation of these organs the

frame the mind would remain a blank; but surely the mind must owe something to its connection with an operation of the features which precede its own conscious activity.[30]

By the end of the century the same observation was to lead William James to propound, in his *Principles of Psychology* (1890), the most extreme materialist James/Lange theory of emotion, that 'the bodily changes follow directly the *perception* of the exciting fact, and our feeling of the same changes as they occur *is* the emotion'.[31] Our heart does not beat faster because we are afraid; 'fear' is the name we give to the increased pulse-rate. It was thus scientifically respectable, as well as an aesthetic convention, to identify the internal mental state with its external physical expression.

During the 1820s two 'pseudo-scientific' studies became widely publicised in Britain: the Physiognomy of Johann Kaspar Lavater and the Phrenology of Franz Joseph Gall. Although neither discipline is tenable today, and indeed both were disputed at the time, their significance, as widely-held explanations of character and behaviour, is not only of particular importance in the study of actors, whose task is to artificially represent character and behaviour, but, as Roger Cooter argues in *The Cultural Meaning of Popular Science* (1984), we can gain an insight into the social and moral thinking of the age, if we can 'determine how and why some conceptions of reality acquire the mantle of objective scientific truth and enter into the domain of common sense, while others come to be regarded as arrant nonsense.'[32] Lavater, a Swiss Calvinist minister, wrote his *Physiognomical Bible* in 1772 and it was translated into English by Thomas Holcroft, the playwright and political radical, in 1789. As well as recording how facial muscles reflect, or respond to, each of the passions, Lavater tried to define how appearances reveal the underlying personality, or 'ruling passion', of individual characters. Some of his descriptions were of long-held stereotypes, such as a receding chin indicating stupidity; others strike us as more fanciful, for example: 'Thin eyebrows are an infallible sign of apathy and flabbiness.' This observation was still being quoted in the 1880s, not only by Gustave Garcia, professor of declamation at the Royal Academy of Music, but by the distinguished Italian psychologist Paolo Mantegazza.[33]

Like Physiognomy, Phrenology also tried to reveal character by examining appearances. Its discoverer (or inventor), the Viennese physicist Franz Joseph Gall, suggested that the shape of the skull was determined by the shape and size of the brain, that mental faculties each had a specific place or 'organ' within the brain, and thus, by feeling or measuring the bumps of the head, character and disposition could be discovered. This 'philosophy' was popularised in Britain in the 1820s, particularly by George Combe, whose *Constitution of Man* (1828) has been compared in its influence on the development of liberal capitalist ideology to such seminal texts as Tom Paine's *Rights of Man*, John Stuart Mill's *Political Economy* and Samuel Smiles's *Self Help*. According to Roger Cooter, 'long before "Darwinism" the sluice-gates had been opened for the lay application of scientific materialism to all manner of social, moral, political and evolutionary thought... a qualitative leap in the understanding of human psychology, when, Adam Smith-like, he [Gall] elaborated a division of mental labour.'[34] Attacked as atheistical, phrenologists appealed at first to radicals, Benthamites and Chartists, but by the 1840s the doctrine was reconciled to, at least, the Free Churches, and established doctors took to 'reading the bumps'. An advert from 1846 indicates the practical appeal of the 'science':

> In every step of life we ought to consult this unfailing oracle. ARE WE ABOUT TO MARRY? Phrenology will tell us the Character and Disposition of those with whom our destinies are to be ever united in *this life*. HAVE WE CHILDREN? And do we wish to engage them in any Profession or Trade suitable to their probable capacities, to prevent cruel disappointments and to make them good and happy?... *Do we desire to know the true character of Clerks, Shopmen, or Domestic Servants?* We can be taught to read it by observing the unerring and wonderful Laws of Nature in the various shapes and developments of the Head.[35]

Although I can cite little concrete evidence that Phrenology had a direct influence on the actors of the time (Robert Elliston, manager of Covent Garden, rejected a play entitled *The Phrenologist* by one Dr Webb in 1825,[36] George Combe married Sarah Siddons's daughter Cecilia in 1833, and both Bulwer-Lytton and George Henry Lewes, intimates of Macready, wrote on the subject), its general influence, together with that of physiognomy and the study of physical gesture, gave further impetus to the reification of passions and mental states already seen in the 'point-making' of Edmund Kean. Both actors and audience wanted to know exactly what was happening in psychological terms; they had no time for hidden motives or suppressed emotion. In the disturbed society of the time, when people, uprooted from rural communities and thrown on to an urban labour market, became prey to unscrupulous strangers, landlords and employers; or, on the other side of the class divide, were dependant on unknown employees or unreliable servants, and frightened of the revolutionary tendencies of trade unions or 'Jacobin' Reform Clubs, then to be able to recognise exactly what was happening on the stage in terms, not only of the conflict of good and evil, but within the very minds of the characters, must have been a source of reassurance. Nineteenth-century society was much more fluid and unpredictable than that of the eighteenth, and so the subtle niceties of the comedy of manners were replaced by the obvious moral certainties of melodrama, and the ironical depiction of, say, Sheridan's Charles and Joseph Surface – behind the brash surface of one lay a heart of gold, behind the smooth surface of the other a vicious hypocrite – was replaced by the undisguised virtue and villainy of, say, Virginius and Appius Claudius in Sheridan Knowles's play *Virginius*, in which Macready made his first original triumph in 1820.

This play was an excellent stock theatre piece. It remained in Macready's repertoire throughout his career, and was performed regularly into the 1880s, with a successful revival by Wilson Barrett as late as 1893. It could be staged easily by any theatre with the sets and costumes for *Coriolanus* or *Julius Caesar*, and centred on one complex character surrounded by stock types. Knowles, an Irish schoolmaster, with no experience of the theatre, recognised its function as a star vehicle from the start, writing to the actor, 'Now my Dear Mr McCready, don't stand upon any formality with me – cut out what you like. I leave the management of the thing in your hands – if they will be so kind as not to decline the trouble.'[37] The story is of the Roman centurion who stabs his daughter rather than let her be ravished by the tyrant, Appius Claudius. Although there was doubtless political significance in a play about tyranny and rebellion, produced in the year of the Cato Street Conspiracy, and following that of the Peterloo Massacre, the whole emphasis of the piece was on the personal anguish of Virginius and was constructed precisely according to the principles of what Donahue describes as the 'affective drama of situation', in which scenes are primarily written, not to advance the plot or present an argument, but to give the actors an opportunity to indulge in emotional distress.

For instance, in Act IV, Virginius's return is unnecessarily delayed to heighten the suspense, giving Virginia a chance to express her fears, and allowing father and daughter to exaggerate their joy at the eventual reunion; Appius, in defeat, is given a speech in which he contemplates despair and suicide, his hopes are then revived for no good reason, except to be dashed again when confronted by the vengeful Virginius; even in the climactic moment, when the father stabs his daughter, an objective reading of the scene suggests that the murder might have been avoided, as the mob are already on the side of Virginius, and, after the deed, he has no difficulty in breaking single-handed through the ring of soldiers, who were supposedly threatening him and his daughter. The final act is taken up with Virginius's madness after the killing, but as he has suppressed all memory of what he has done, there can be no reflections, moral or philosophical, on the justice of his action, only the pathos of his imbecility and the terror of his manic attack on Appius. Nevertheless, these faults are not immediately apparent, and the 'affective scenes' are indeed well written to allow the actors to display their passion. Macready, aged twenty-eight, found that ageing himself into a middle-aged father helped focus and control a style that previously had been too wildly modelled on Edmund Kean. The *Daily News* reported that 'Faults hitherto attributed to his style were studiously avoided; his love of sudden transitions was controlled within the bounds of propriety, and his rich manly voice, which has too frequently tempted him to rant, was subdued and mellowed down to a tone of exquisite touchingness.'[38] When, in 1828, Macready performed the play in Paris, a French critic admitted that he was moved to tears and described the performance in terms that precisely define the ideals of the Romantic tragedian: 'Never have such terrible emotions so expressed themselves in the countenance of a man as to pass into the hearts of his audience; the illusion was complete, and almost painful.'[39]

No doubt the political virtues of the noble Virginius appealed to radical audiences, and to Macready himself, who held liberal and republican views, but it was the personal emotions of fatherhood, filial devotion and the protection of unspotted virginity that explain the emotional appeal of the play well into the Victorian age. For Macready it had a specially personal significance: he met his wife Kitty Atkins when she played Virginia with him in Aberdeen, and on 3 January 1851 he recorded how his mind turned to his daughters:

> Acted Virginius, one of the most brilliant and powerful performances of the character I have ever given. I did indeed 'gore my own thoughts' to do it, for my own Katie was in my mind, as in one part the tears streamed down my cheeks; and in another she who is among the Blest, beloved one! *[Nina, who had died the previous year]* Such is the player's mind and heart![40]

Of the final performance in January 1851 he wrote:

> Acted Virginius, for the last time, as I have scarcely ever – no, never – acted it before; with discrimination, energy, and pathos, exceeding any former effort... I was much affected during the evening, very much, something with a partial feeling of sorrow at parting with an old friend, for such this character has been to me, and, alas, no trace of it remains. The thought, the practice, the deep emotion conjured up, the pictures grouped so repeatedly throughout the work, live now only in the memory.[41]

Macready's phrase 'the pictures grouped so repeatedly throughout the work' indicates another crucial element in theatrical technique. Just as the play was made up of 'affective situations', each scene or speech could be broken up into specific moments of emotion, each of which was illustrated by the actor's passionate gesture. For the most part these gestures moved on from one to another like the static frames in a movie, or through the technical modulation of a 'transition', but they could at a particularly significant moment be frozen into an 'attitude', such as the 'statue representing horror' that Robert Elliston had recommended to his leading lady [see above p. 2]. If all the characters paused simultaneously a 'picture' or tableau was formed, which could be held while the scene closed, the curtain fell or the audience applauded. Edward Mayhew in his *Stage Effect* (1840) described such tableaux: 'To theatrical minds the word "situation" suggests some strong point in a play likely to command applause; where the action is wrought to a climax, where the actors strike attitudes, and form what they call a "picture"' during the exhibition of which a pause takes place.'[42] In *Virginius* several such situations are clearly supplied by the text, as when the crowd attack Appius's henchman Claudius in front of the tribunal where the tyrant is presiding: '*The Lictors and* CLAUDIUS *are driven back;* CLAUDIUS *takes refuge at* APPIUS'S *feet, who has descended, and throws up his arms as a signal to both parties to desist – whereupon the people retire a little.*' The pause here would be similar to that described by Mayhew of Othello interrupting the drunken brawl between Cassio and the guard.[43] Similarly the climax of Act IV would have been held as a dramatic picture:

VIRGINIUS: My dear child! My dear Virginia!   *[Kissing her.*
There is one only way to save thine honour –
'Tis this! –
 [Stabs her, and draws out the knife. ICILIUS *breaks from the soldiers that held him, and catches her.*
Lo! Appius! with this innocent blood,
I do devote thee to th'infernal gods!

In the final scene the effect was one often used on a stage where scenic shutters could be pulled aside at the end of one scene to reveal another. In Act V, iii, Virginius chases Appius out of the dungeon where he has been imprisoned, and a moment later the final scene is revealed: 'Another Dungeon. VIRGINIUS *discovered on one knee, with* APPIUS *lying dead before him.*' Finally, of course, the play closed with the picture of Virginius regaining his senses when confronted with the urn containing his daughter's ashes: '*He bursts into a passion of tears, and exclaims* "VIRGINIA!"– *Falls on* ICILIUS'S *neck. Curtain drops.*'

Such concluding or climactic effects had been used ever since the Restoration theatre had adopted the pictorial stage, and even before that in masques and dumb-shows, but the attitudes struck by actors within the action of the scene was a more recent technique, such as Virginia's interrupting her father's rage: 'Dear father, be advised – Will you not father?' Macready's anger immediately disappeared and he changed his tone: 'I never saw you look so like your mother/ In all my life!' The moment of domestic pathos was held, and greeted with applause. The signalling of a such a moment was not only an example of the reification of 'universal' emotions, as discussed above, but indicates an increasingly pictorial use of the proscenium stage. Martin Meisel in *Realizations* (1983) argues that in nineteenth-century art, not only did the stage create 'speaking pictures', but novelists concentrated on 'telling scenes', and painters produced series of genre-paintings to tell a story as if they were acts of a play. Indeed such pictures were often subsequently dramatised. For example, George Cruikshank's temperance tract of eight engravings, *The Bottle* (1847), and its sequel *The Drunkard's Children* (1848), were both swiftly brought to the stage as tableaux marking the opening or climax of separate scenes, and, although there were a number of versions, T. P. Taylor's *Bottle* and T. H. Reynoldson's *Drunkard's Children* both claimed 'The whole of the Tableaux under the personal superintendence of MR GEORGE CRUIKSHANK.'[44]

In the second half of the century with the introduction of 'box-sets' performers became fully integrated into the scenic picture, but in the Romantic period the effect was more like that of statues set against a painted ground. The most developed form of this statuesque acting was the *tableau vivant*, a fashionable salon entertainment in the early years of the century. The most renowned example was Lady Hamilton's 'Attitudes', which were mostly based on classical models, but also included original 'attitudes of passion'. The painter George Romney, for whom she had modelled, described her performances as 'simple, grand, terrible and pathetic'.[45] Eventually the 'art' of the attitude developed into the erotic display of the *Poses Plastiques* in which well developed models, clad in skin-tight 'fleshings', imitated nude statues for the titillation of their spectators. The *poses plastiques* arranged by 'Professor' Keller and Madame Warton, in various theatres, halls and art galleries in London between 1845 and 1848, provoked 'A Lover of Art' to protest 'against the wholesale display of female nudity to an indiscriminate mass of people... there is an evident preference in the choice of subjects... to attract the worst sort of audience'.[46] When 'Baron' Renton Nicholson introduced 'pictures' by 'Mme Pauline and her talented company of female artistes' to the infamous Coal Hole Tavern, a club-cum-brothel, he was anticipating the twentieth century's use of *tableaux vivants* – the nude spectaculars of the Folies Bergère and Caesar's Palace.[47]

Even more bizarre than these 'Living Statues' were the performances by Andrew Ducrow, the 'Celebrated Equestrian of Astley's Amphitheatre', of such characters as Rob Roy Macgregor, Vanderdecken the Flying Dutchman, The British Tar and The Dying Gladiator, for they were enacted in dumb-show as he balanced on the back of a galloping horse. These performances were not just feats of agility within a narrative framework, as are still presented in Russian circuses, but involved a representation of character and emotion of such quality that Ducrow's biographer, Leman Rede, claimed that 'No actor on the stage (not even Kean) could exceed his powerful expression... *His* pantomime, indeed, reminds us of that celebrated eulogy on the mimes of old. Their very nods speak – their hands talk, their fingers have voices.'[48] The Edinburgh *Evening Courant* described how the performances

> Consist in the display of character; of humour and pathos, and all the various emotions of the mind, in which Mr Ducrow shews himself a great master. The positions which he takes on horseback are truly amazing; at times they seem to go counter to the fixed laws of gravitation; yet they are only a subordinate part of the performance, the main purpose of which seems to be to display the character which Mr Ducrow is for the time representing. The basis of the whole is no doubt equestrian skill; on which, however, Ducrow has raised a superstructure of the most amusing representations; insomuch that the skilful rider is frequently lost in the fine performer; and we almost forget that we are witnessing feats of horsemanship, so deeply are we interested in the dramatic illusion.[49]

Figure 3. Andrew Ducrow performing 'The Roman Gladiator' on horseback, *c.* 1835

This extraordinary ability to create character and emotion while standing on a horse's back, suggests once again that the performer and his audience had a clear and shared vocabulary of physical expression that communicated itself despite the absurdly artificial context of its performance.

Ducrow also used his mimetic ability in several non-equestrian melodramas, most notably in Barnabas Rayner's *Dumb Man of Manchester* (1837) and his own play, *The Poor Idiot; or, The Souterain of Heidelberg Castle* (1838). Both dramatised how his mute characters triumphed over their disabilities. In *The Dumb Man of Manchester* Tom is unjustly condemned for murder and his encounter with his sister on the way to the scaffold had all the noble passion of Virginius and his daughter:

Solemn music, TOM *enters, conducted by four jailers.*
    JANE: My brother! *(she rushes to him and embraces him eagerly – both weep.* TOM *disengages himself, and with his handkerchief wipes away his sister's tears)* My brother! *(music, very pathetic –* TOM *expresses the thought they were leading him to execution; he adds 'Now that I have seen my sister I can die in peace – but Heaven knows my innocence')* You shall not die – the judge will pardon you. *(Music, bold –* TOM *rises proudly and intimates he has no need of pardon – he is innocent. Music, plaintive).*[50]

The Dumb Man, with its last-minute reprieve, was a fairly typical domestic melodrama, but *The Poor Idiot* was Gothic in the tradition of Monk Lewis's *The Captive* (1803), and its effect was disturbing, even tragic. The directions indicate some of the means that Ducrow used to communicate without words, and suggest how important music was in creating atmosphere and indicating the mental processes of thought and feeling – as does the use of the recently invented limelight:

Music. – The *IDIOT* is cramped up under straw on the matting, his eyes turned towards the window as if watching for someone's arrival – all his movements express anxiety and eagerness. – Music changes. – He places beside him a flower, the companion of his solitude – the flower has grown in the remains of a broken earthen vase – he seems to pity and caress the poor flower. – A glimpse of light is seen through the bars of the window, as if day were breaking – he shivers with cold – his teeth chatter in his head – his whole body trembles – the rays of the sun finally penetrate through the bars of the dungeon – he rises joyfully as the obscurity disappears – bounds about, making strange noises and inarticulate sounds of *'Ah – ah – ah!'* – He places himself in a gleam of sunshine, and by pantomime expresses that he feels its genial warmth – he takes the flower, and places it in the light of day – he regards it with affection, and seems to say that, like himself, the sun will give the plant fresh vigour. – In a reverie, he demands from whence come the light and day – then, by a movement of pious resignation, he points to the holy picture affixed to the pillar – he approaches it, kneels, and seems to indicate the revelation come from holy source. As he bends the music changes to an *'Ave Maria'*. – Music again changes. – Suddenly the Idiot starts as if he heard a sound – he places his ear to the earth, rises quickly, takes his flower, hides it behind pillar, and signifies his food is being brought. – A hand appears through the wicket of the door, *L*, and presents to the Idiot, who seizes it with avidity, a phial – the hand is then withdrawn, the wicket closed, and all again silence. – The Idiot regards the phial, then swallows the opium it contains, and falls by degrees asleep, first placing the flower by his side, as if serving for a companion in his slumbers. – A storm rises, the clouds become dark, the beams of light no longer penetrate the dungeon, where reigns obscurity the most profound.[51]

How this kind of emotional dumb-show developed into full-blown melodrama will be discussed in Chapter 9, but before that it is necessary to see how even an actor at the head of the profession concentrated on the expression of emotion. William Charles Macready was nothing if not seriously concerned for the aesthetic, moral and philosophical purpose of the theatre, and he had nothing but contempt for what he considered to be the vulgar attitudinising of the Minor Theatre actors, and yet he too gave priority to emotion over thought, and this seems, from a twentieth-century point of view, to have led to performances in which sentimentality replaced genuine moral and political argument.

4

Richelieu
by Edward Bulwer-Lytton

Covent Garden Theatre, 7 March 1839

LOUIS XIII	Mr Elton
COUNT BARADAS	Mr Ward
CARDINAL RICHELIEU	Mr Macready
The CHEVALIER DE MAUPRAT	Mr Anderson
The SIEUR DE BERINGHEN	Mr Vining
JOSEPH, a Capuchin,	Mr Phelps
FRANÇOIS, first page to Richelieu	Mr Howe
JULIE DE MORTEMAR, ward to Richelieu,	Miss Helen Faucit
MARION DE LORME, mistress to Orleans,	Miss Charles

The Action is set in France in the years 1641-42

Act I, First day

Scene 1. Count Baradas & the Duke of Orleans are plotting against Louis XIII. One of the party, the young Chevalier de Mauprat, is suddenly arrested by Richelieu's men.

Scene 2. Richelieu, Louis XIII's first minister, already knows of the plot, but he has arrested de Mauprat to test his loyalty before agreeing to his engagement to Richelieu's ward, Julie de Mortemar.

Act II, Second day

Scene 1. Baradas persuades de Mauprat that Richelieu let him marry Julie as part of a scheme to make Julie the King's mistress. De Mauprat vows revenge.

Scene 2. Richelieu arranges for his page François to intercept the traitor's plans for their *coup d'état*, while himself will withdraw to his castle.

Players and performances

Act III, Second day, midnight

Scene 1. Richelieu's castle: François reports the documents have been stolen from him. Julie arrives, fleeing to her guardian from the King's advances. De Mauprat comes to attack Richelieu, but the Cardinal explains the deception and reconciles the young couple. As Baradas's assassins arrive, de Mauprat pretends he has killed Richelieu.

Scene 2. The assassin, Huguet, reports the Cardinal's death to Baradas, who has him arrested. He intends to have him killed in prison.

Act IV, Third day

Scene 1. A reconciliation between Orleans and King Louis, who believes Richelieu is dead. De Mauprat challenges Baradas but is arrested. He manages to tell François that the incriminating documents are with Huguet. Richelieu returns, but Louis refuses to reinstate him. But at least he can protect Julie from the King, by evoking sanctuary in the name of Rome. He collapses exhausted.

Act IV, Fourth day

Scene 1. François seeks admission to the Bastille, and arrives in time to challenge Huguet's murderer for the documents.

Scene 2. In order to force Julie to become the King's mistress, Baradas makes her attend as de Mauprat is given his death warrant. Before he is taken to execution, Louis arrives, surrounded by treacherous courtiers, to be met by the sick Richelieu and his secretaries, who are to surrender their portfolios. It is clear Baradas and Orleans can not advise the King as wisely as his old minister. As Louis dithers, François arrives with the incriminating papers. The traitors are denounced, and de Mauprat freed. Richelieu regains his strength as Louis asks him to resume his power.

The production of Edward Bulwer-Lytton's Richelieu has been remarkably well documented. Not only did Macready record its genesis in his diaries, but he and Bulwer corresponded at length during its composition, and the performance itself was appreciatively analysed by the drama critic Westland Marston.[1] However, the play, the author and the star were all flawed by contradictions. Envisaged as a modern classic, the play's contemporary relevance was obscured by antiquarianism, and its theatrical effectiveness blurred by pedestrian blank verse; the author, Bulwer-Lytton, could not decide whether he was writing a tragedy, melodrama or political play, and thus produced a hybrid 'Historical Romance'; the star, Macready, though head of his profession, harboured an extraordinary hostility towards his fellow actors. All these factors help explain the low regard in which Richelieu, and similar serious drama of the mid-1800s, has been held, when compared with the poetry and novels of the period. Yet Dickens, Tennyson, Browning, Carlyle and Thackeray all considered the play's production an artistic triumph.

As other branches of culture were flourishing, it was hoped that with Victoria's succession a new Elizabethan age would dawn, and that soon a modern Shakespeare would emerge. No one was more anxious to find him than Macready, who in October 1837 took over the management of Covent Garden with the express policy of championing the legitimate drama. His social circle, based in the Garrick Club, included several important authors, one of whom, Edward Bulwer-Lytton, was particularly concerned with the state of English drama. Bulwer, ten years Macready's junior, had established his reputation with his 'silver fork' novel *Pelham* (1828). Indeed *Pelham* might be a portrait of Bulwer himself; a dandy dedicated to gambling, dressing and flirting, and yet: 'Beneath the carelessness of my exterior, my mind was close, keen and inquiring, and under all the affectation of foppery, and the levity of manner, I veiled an ambition the most extensive in its object, and a resolution.'[2] In 1830, inspired by the Revolution in Paris and by agitation in England, Bulwer entered Parliament and strongly supported the 1832 Reform Bill. In 1833, he campaigned for a Select Committee to look into the patent house monopoly and the protection of authors' rights. Although the Committee collected a vast amount of evidence, and playwrights were granted copyright protection, no change was made to the theatre monopoly.

In 1836 Bulwer submitted his first play, *Cromwell*, to Macready, who buried it under a welter of criticism. It was followed by *The Duchess de la Vallière*, which Macready produced at Covent Garden on 4 January 1837. Led by *The Times*, newspapers opposed to Bulwer's politics condemned it as 'in the worst taste of the worst school, the school of the modern French romance'.[3] Bulwer's next attempt, *The Lady of Lyons* (Covent Garden, 13 February 1838), was a great success, even though, set in the French Revolution, it was more overtly political than *La Vallière*. That it was presented anonymously may have helped. It was a particular triumph for the actress, Helen Faucit; Macready was not ideally suited to the role of Claude Melnotte. He wrote to Bulwer, 'I wish I were younger and that my chere amie and myself had put our heads out of the window, when it was raining beauty – but as Falstaff says "That's past praying for."'[4]

The hero of Bulwer's next play also seemed unsuitable for the actor-manager; Marillac (eventually de Mauprat) was a juvenile character like Pelham, superficially frivolous, 'celebrated for his extravagant valour & his enthusiasm for enjoyment – but in his most mirthful moments – a dark cloud comes over him at one name – the name of Richelieu!'[5] The cause of this melancholy was a suspended death sentence, which could be evoked at any time by the despotic Cardinal. Macready immediately recognised that Richelieu was the part for him, and that Bulwer would have to adopt a different hero. The author was immediately compliant:

> You are right about the Plot... But Richelieu would be a splendid fellow for the stage, if we could hit on a good plot to bring him out... He would be a new addition to the Historical portraits of the Stage; but then he must be connected with a plot in which he would have all the stage to himself, & in which some Home interest might link itself with the Historical.'[6]

In this sentence Bulwer encapsulated all the assumptions that makes Victorian plays so unacceptable today. The hero is a portrait rather than a protagonist; the plot is an intrigue to provide effective scenes, rather than a matrix for dramatic action; and the interest is domestic rather than political. These assumptions were not just catering to a popular audience, but an expression of the Romantic Liberalism of the 1830s. History was the story of Great Men, and politics the sphere of individual initiative. Post-1832 Liberalism was the *laisser-faire* policy of the newly enfranchised merchant classes. Individual Liberty and Free Trade had inspired Bulwer's campaign for theatre reform, just as Romantic self-expression had motivated Macready's lonely trek to the summit. Between them Bulwer and Macready created in *Richelieu* a play that was a genuine expression of Victorian ideology.

Bulwer intended Richelieu to be a Machiavellian politician, dedicated to the good order of the state and ruthless in his suppression of aristocratic conspiracies. However, the plot was dominated by the love interests of Richelieu's ward, the orphaned Julie de Mortemar, desired by the King but devoted to the young chevalier, de Mauprat, and this emphasised the Cardinal's role as paterfamilias rather than as statesman. Thus, as in *Virginius*, Macready had to express more domestic benevolence than political shrewdness. The lack of real political argument in a play written by a Member of Parliament about a great statesman might strike a post-Brechtian, even a post-Shavian, audience as irresponsible, but in the context of the 1830s it was inevitable, not because of the Lord Chamberlain's censorship, or a reactionary press, but because of the conventions of theatrical performance. The political meaning of nineteenth-century plays was conveyed by sentiments and imagery, rather than by overt argument.

The *image* of Richelieu as guardian of his innocent ward carried political as well as personal significance, and his senility in the last act symbolised his loss of power over the state, as was revealed by his instantaneous rejuvenation when the conspiracy was foiled. Bulwer explained the symbolism to Macready:

I do not mean it as a show illness. He is really ill, though he may exaggerate a little. When they are going to tear France from him, they do really tug at his heart-strings... and it is the mind invigorating the body – it is the might of France passing into him, which effects the cure.[7]

Similarly, his political responsibilities were symbolised by the procession of secretaries with bundles of documents. This image of a workaholic minister with a train of bureaucrats was contrasted with a procession of foppish courtiers led by a flirtatious King. Political dialectic was conveyed in a scenic tableau.

However, the most concrete symbol in the play was the one that most troubled the author, and remained the most 'melodramatic': the packet of papers that reveal the treachery. Whoever has the packet can settle the fate of France, of the lovers, and of the aged Richelieu. Much of their correspondence concerned the itinerary of this packet – from villain to henchman, from duped hero to innocent juvenile, from the dungeon of the Bastille to the royal chambers of the Louvre. Henry Smith, a 'green-room critic', lay awake after the first reading 'endeavouring to devise some means to make Julie the retriever of the packet', and even Bulwer was worried that 'the final triumph is not wrought by the pure intellect of Richelieu, but depends on the accidental success of François *[the page]* – a conception which wants grandeur'.[8] This seems a damning criticism of the play's contrivance, but we must remember Bulwer's assertion that 'it is the fate of France, of the heart of Europe, as embodied in the Packet... which makes the greater interest'.[9]

Nevertheless, despite symbolically suggesting that a cunning minister is better than either idealistic aristocrats or a decorative monarch, the play's potential republicanism got lost in Macready's domestication of Richelieu's portrait as Julie's guardian rather than as father of the state. Bulwer saw what the actor had done:

There they are before you, flesh and blood – the old man and the young Bride involved in the same fate & creating sympathy of a Domestic relation. More than all my dependence on the stage is in the acting of Richelieu – the embodiment of the portraiture, the work, the gesture, the personification which reading cannot give.[10]

It was a fine performance, but Macready's Richelieu was more a private than public figure. Actor and author also disagreed about his personality. Bulwer kept asking Macready to emphasise the humour, 'the high physical spirits that successful men nearly always have & which, as in Cromwell, can almost approach the buffoon, when most the Butcher'.[11] Macready, however, had consulted the French novelist Alfred de Vigny, whose *Cinq Mars* presented a different view of Richelieu, and recorded:

February 20, 1839. Gave my attention to the consideration of the character of Richelieu, which Bulwer has made particularly difficult by its inconsistency; he has made him resort to low jest, which outrages one's notion of the ideal of Cardinal Richelieu, with all his vanity, and suppleness, and craft.[12]

Guided by de Vigny and his own 'notion of the ideal', Macready suppressed all buffoonery and played the part as sardonic when being political, tender when dealing with Julie, and dignified when apostrophising France. Macready's solemn approach to his art, as well as his orthodox style of deliniating separate passions, led him to exaggerate the expected, rather than explore the eccentricities.

In 1856, five years after his retirement, Lady Pollock induced Macready to reflect upon his early training, and his account shows how he adopted and adapted traditional techniques. He had been taught the use of gestures, but

I soon had misgivings suggested by my own observations of actual life. These became confirmed by marking how sparingly, and therefore how effectively, Mrs Siddons had recourse to gesticulation... I adopted all the modes I could devise to acquire the power of exciting myself into the wildest emotion of passion, coercing my limbs to perfect stillness. I would lie down on the floor, or stand straight against a wall, or get my arms within a bandage, and so pinioned, or confined, repeat the most violent passages of Othello, Lear, Hamlet, Macbeth, or whatever would require most energy and emotion; I would speak the most passionate bursts of rage under the supposed restraint of whispering them in the ear of him or her to whom they were addressed, thus keeping both voice and gesture in subjection to the real impulse of feeling... I was obliged also to have frequent recourse to the looking-glass, and had two or three large ones in my room to reflect to myself each view of the posture I might have fallen into, besides being under the necessity of acting the passion close to a glass to restrain the tendency to exaggerate its expression – which was the most difficult of all – to repress the ready frown, and keep the features, perhaps I should say the muscles of the face, undisturbed, whilst intense passion would speak from the eye alone.[13]

But if he aimed to be more 'restrained' than Kean or Kemble, it was only in the expression, and not in the experience, of feelings; intense passion was essential in Macready's interpretation of character. As for the enforced physical stillness, according to fellow actor John Colman, 'He had never been able to eradicate his native awkwardness and angularity... if seen from the side, his head was thrown back till it was fully six inches out of plumb with his heels. As to fencing, he handled a foil like a pitchfork, but the glamour of his genius blinded his audience to these blemishes.'[14] (See Plate II.) In Richelieu even these physical defects could be used to advantage; his stance was hidden by the Cardinal's robes, and the

only business involving a sword was the highly effective moment when
the old man took up a two-handed weapon to impress his young page,
François:

> Ah, boy, with this
> I at Rochelle did hand to hand engage
> The stalwart Englisher – no mongrels, boy,
> Those island mastiffs – mark the notch, a deep one,
> His casque made here – I shore him to the waist!
> A toy – a feather – then! *[Tries to wield, and lets the blade fall.]*
> You see a child could slay Richelieu now.
> FRANÇOIS *[his hand on his hilt]*. But now, at your command
> Are other weapons, my good lord.
> RICHELIEU *[About to write, lifts the pen]*. True this!
> Beneath the rule of men entirely great
> The pen is mightier than the sword!

According to a 1861 New York prompt-copy in the Havard Theatre
Collection the sword 'Is caught by Jos[eph]. supported to chair L of R
table – François takes sword from Riche's hand as he drops point on
stage.'[15] It made a telling scene – a tableau of physical debility allied to
spiritual pride. Macready probably did not play the part quite as
decrepitly as this American actor, who even in the first scene had to be
helped out of his chair by Father Joseph, but he did use the technique of
'pictures', as illustrated in this prompt-copy: In Act I, ii, when de
Mauprat is restrained from striking Richelieu, the direction reads: 'Hold
picture till – "He can wait"', and in Act IV, i, after Richelieu has
described a circle round Julie placing her under the protection of the
Church: 'Characters kneel. Pages kneel & cross themselves. Guards present – (Pause) Richelieu is falling & Joseph catches him. Julie jumps up
on his R. Picture held till Richelieu staggers upstage.' Earlier in the
scene Macready may have followed Bulwer-Lytton's suggestion:

> When you say 'And sheltered by the wings of sacred Rome', I want you actu-
> ally to shelter her with the priestly robe, and to cower over her like an old
> eagle. When I wrote this I had in my mind a dim recollection of an action of
> yours, somewhere, I think, as Lear with Cordelia. I think it was Lear; but I
> remember that, wherever it was, it was thoroughly grand and tender in its
> protectiveness.[16]

Since he had already used the gesture, and it inspired only a 'dim recollection', I suspect Macready would have preferred some new business.
The climax of the play came in Act V, when the conspiracy is laid bare
and Richelieu throws off the illness, which Bulwer had argued was genuine and symbolic, but which to John Colman looked like a 'simulated
trance':

He leaped up, and, dilating to preternatural proportions, exclaimed, 'There at my feet!' he realised a picture, once seen, never forgotten. When in this situation he glided down to the stage, I protest he always suggested to me the Divine Image grown grey and ghastly through the efflux of the ages and once more floating over the Sea of Galilee.[17]

Not since Edmund Kean had a 'transition' been so effective. Macready prepared for it by stressing Richelieu's physical weakness. John Forster described a performance in 1850:

Nothing can be happier than the way in which the suffering and ailments of the great Cardinal help the better to throw out his humour, wit and spirit. His cough is part of his character. Even at the noble close of the 4th act, where the apparent ruin of worldly schemes throws him back upon spiritual pretensions, his age and feebleness give more awful character to the threats he launches against his foe.[18]

Westland Marston records how at this moment 'The vast pit seemed to rock with enthusiasm, as it volleyed its admiration in rounds of thunder.' He too praised the contrasts in the final act:

How touching was the proud humility of the weak old man as he relinquished, seemingly for ever, the splendid cares of State; how arresting the sight of him as, supported in his chair, his face now grew vacant, as through the feebleness of nature, now resumed a gleam of intelligence, which at times contracted into pain, as he gathered the policy of his rivals – a policy fatal to France! One noted the uneasy movements of the head, the restless play of the wan fingers, though the lips were silent... Then came the moment when, recovering the despatch which convicted his foes of treason, he caused it to be handed to the King, and sank supine with the effort. Slowly and intermittently consciousness returned, as Louis thrice implored him to resume his sway over France. So naturally marked were the fluctuations between life and death, so subtly graduated (though comprised within a few moments) were the signs of his recovery, that the house utterly forgot its almost incredible quickness when, in answer to the King's apprehensive cry as to the traitors – 'Where will they be next week?' Richelieu springs up resuscitated, and exclaims – 'There, at my feet!'[19]

Writing some fifty years after the event – though no doubt guided by contemporary notes – Marston realised that the effect was 'almost incredible', but in 1839 such sudden transitions were part of orthodox technique. Marston also saw that the rejuvenation was not just an actor's trick, but that it conveyed the symbolic significance that Bulwer had intended: 'He had from the beginning of the play so seized every opportunity of identifying his fortunes with the greatness of his country, that when the King besought him to live for France, it seemed quite in the order of nature such an adjuration should have magical force.' Indeed, Marston makes the whole play seem more political than a reading of the text might suggest, and more subtly political in Macready's performance than in other actors':

> Macready carefully avoided the error into which some of his successors have fallen – that of over-idealizing Richelieu, by delivering his patriotic speeches in such tones of exalted devotion as might have befitted Brutus. Macready's apostrophes to France, on the contrary, were given with a self-reference, sometimes fierce in its expression, that showed her triumphs to be part of his own. Her glory was the object of his ambition, for it made him great... Thus his haughty boast in the foregoing lines ['Who dares in Richelieu murder France!'] was no expression of abstract and ideal patriotism (of which the Cardinal was incapable), but of passionate and practical sympathy.

If *Richelieu* gave Macready unusual scope for physical expression, language was something he used in all performances. Hazlitt wrote at the start of his career that 'his voice is powerful in the highest degree and at the same time possesses great harmony and modulation', but it could lapse into 'mere melodious declamation, which he used to deal out sentence after sentence, like a machine turning ivory balls'.[20] Later Lewes described his voice as

> Powerful, extensive in compass, capable of delicate modulation in quiet passages (though with a tendency to scream in violent passages) and having tones that thrilled and tones that stirred tears. His declamation was mannered and unmusical; yet his intelligence always made him follow the winding meanings through the involutions of the verse, and never allowed you to feel... that he was speaking words which he did not thoroughly understand. The trick of a broken and spasmodic rhythm might destroy the music proper to the verse, but it did not perplex you with false emphasis or intonations wandering at hazard.[21]

Macready was very aware of how he manipulated both rhythm and tone; playing Macbeth in 1833 he 'acted with much energy, but could not (as I sometimes can, when holding the audience in wrapt attention) listen to my own voice, and feel the truth of its tones', and a week later he reflected that 'I find the good effect of that natural manly tone of dialogue, with which I must endeavour to improve the colloquial groundwork of my acting.'[22] This self-consciousness and concern for both meaning and feeling sometimes gave Marston the impression that,

> Reasoning carried it over intuition; all had been too obviously reasoned out. the thoughts did not sufficiently hurry upon and partly confuse each other, as they do in real tumults of the soul... here again various mental states seemed too sharply defined and separated. The emotions of shame, terror, remorse, momentary despair, and selfish fear, might, I fancied have more often flowed into each other.[23]

The most distinctive vocal trick that Macready used in defining these various mental states was the famous 'Macready Pause'. Acting each emotion distinctly he separated them with a swift or ponderous transition. A short pause in the midst of a sentence was what Garrick had defined as a 'suspension', in which emotion causes a break without 'closing the sense'.[24] A longer pause indicated that the character was thinking, and its effect was that of striking an attitude or creating a 'picture'. I have compared this technique to the frames of a cine-film, and Marston saw precisely this in Richelieu: 'His brilliant resume of *Richelieu...* was so given, flash after flash, that its various effects seemed simultaneous rather than successive.' It depended on 'his just perception of the right note of *feeling* even to a semi-tone.'[25]

The virtuosity of Romantic acting lay in the expression of feelings, and although my analysis of points, attitudes and tableaux may have made this seem mechanical and contrived, it was so much a part of the automatic thinking of the age, that there was no contradiction between Macready's use of such technical means and his emotional identification with the role. He knew his finest performances were given when he felt he was the character, though this identification depended on the equal involvement of the audience:

> *April 26, 1847.* Acted Hamlet, taking especial pains, and as I thought, really acting well; generally in the very spirit and feeling of the distracted, sensitive young man; but I did not feel that the audience responded to me; I did not on that account give way, but the inspiration is lost, the perfect abandon, under which one goes out of oneself, is impossible unless you enjoy the perfect sympathy of an audience; if they do not abandon themselves to the actor's powers, his magic becomes ineffectual.[26]

When considering this quality of identification, George Henry Lewes described Macready's technique in the same terms as he had Edmund Kean's use of theatrical 'symbols', but whereas Kean had never relied on the inspiration of the moment, he stressed the contrary quality in Macready:

> Whenever he had an emotion to depict, he depicted it sympathetically and not artificially; by which I mean that he felt himself to be the person, and having identified himself with the character, sought by means of the symbols of his art to express what that character felt; he did not stand outside the character and try to express its emotions by the symbols which had been employed for other characters by other actors... [When performing Shylock], Macready, it is said, used to spend some minutes behind the scenes, lashing himself into an imaginary rage by cursing sotto voce, and shaking violently a ladder fixed against the wall. To bystanders the effect must have been ludicrous, but to the audience the actor presented himself as one really agitated. He had worked himself up to the proper pitch of excitement which would enable him to express the rage of Shylock.[27]

Macready's rejection of other people's points made him impatient with the stereotypes of the stock-repertory system, and his desire not only to portray emotions, but to actually feel them, confirms he was a star of the Romantic Movement.

5

The comedian:
comic or actor?

Given the subjectivity of Romantic art, it is not surprising that the early nineteenth century produced no masterpieces of comic drama. Farce and the comedy of manners, the forms popular in the eighteenth century, had both depended on the objectivity of their audiences, who were prepared to laugh at the folly, affectations and even misfortune of the characters. From the 1760s there had been an increasing dichotomy between this traditional 'laughing comedy' and the new 'sentimental comedy', in which the audiences were expected to empathise with distressed lovers and admire their moral scruples. As these comedies provided little to laugh at in terms of character, they had to rely instead on absurdity of situation. For instance, in *She Stoops to Conquer*, perhaps the greatest English Sentimental Comedy, it is the misunderstandings that are amusing, while we sympathise with the characters, even those who in a true comedy of manners would have been ridiculed, as the country bumpkin, the tyrannical father and the snobbish old lady. In the event we laugh more *with* Tony Lumpkin than at him, we warm to Mr Hardcastle's basic good-nature, and Mrs Hardcastle, for all her snobbery, seems to be unjustly punished for being an over-fond mother. The general good-humour of the play may make us smile, but it is the farcical business that makes us laugh.

When Sheridan introduced elements of sentimentality into *The School for Scandal*, the impression is less satisfactory; we know we should laugh at the traditional affectations, but our responses become confused by the excessive scruples of the young lovers and the villainy of Joseph Surface. Perhaps, the balance between amused detachment and concerned involvement is so well poised as to create a masterpiece, but subsequent writers tended to swing towards either broad farce or distressful melodrama, or incongruously combined the two. One such play was *John*

Bull (1803) by George Colman, who, according to Michael Booth, enjoyed 'equal facility in comedy, melodrama, farce, spectacle, dramatic satire, and song writing'.[1] *John Bull* contained all these elements in the one text. Looking back from 1846, William Robson thought that the old Covent Garden company was the last one able to give the ensemble performance the play needed:

> So cast that every part was equally well played... Harris [the manager] was rich, and could afford to keep a company round him that could play anything. I care not a rush for all the volumes that have been written against the monopolizing patents; the real play-goer had never seen a piece perfectly filled in all its parts since respectability was taken from the profession, and talent that could make two theatres brilliant and efficient was diffused over twenty... Gods! only think of Cooke, Johnstone, Emery and Davenport in one scene![2]

Actors created an ensemble because they worked together for a lifetime. Since then the system of 'stars and supers' prevailed in both major and minor houses. The tragedy stars Macready, Phelps and Charles Kean developed into actor-managers, with responsibility for production as well as acting, and there was a similar development among the comedians, from the traditional stock ensemble, through the foregrounding of individual stars, towards, in the second half of the century, the recreation of an ensemble, but now dedicated to the long run. Even at the Haymarket, which tried to maintain an ensemble suitable for comedies of manners, individual stars emerged. Audiences wanted individuals with whom they could identify and whose feelings they might share, rather than sparkling wit or biting satire. So performers cultivated a close rapport with their audiences. It did not matter if the characters they played were stupid or affected, so long as there was direct communication between actor and spectators. At times this rapport acted as the theatrical equivalent to the author's commentary which undercut the sentimentality of many Victorian novels.

Just as Edmund Kean's performances in the 1810s and 1820s set both good and bad examples, so the influence of the two great comedians of the same period, Munden and Liston, was a mixed blessing. If Kean's particular technique had been 'starting', Munden's speciality was 'mugging', as Charles Lamb described:

> There is one face of Farley, one face of Knight, one (but what a one it is!) of Liston; but Munden has none that you can properly pin down and call his. When you think he has exhausted his battery of looks, in unaccountable warfare with your gravity, suddenly he sprouts out an entirely new set of features, like Hydra.

Munden's face-acting was used to signal the working of his mind, just as the attitudes of the tragedians communicated their emotional responses. The other skill that Lamb praised was Munden's use of props:

> Who like him can throw... a preternatural interest over the commonest daily life object? A table or a joint stool, in his conception, rises into a dignity equivalent to Cassiopeia's chair; it is invested with constellatory importance... His pots and his ladles are as grand and primal as the seething-pots and hooks seen in old prophetic vision. A tub of butter, contemplated by him, amounts to a Platonic idea. He understands a leg of mutton in its quiddity. He stands wondering, amid the commonplace materials of life, like primeval man with the sun and stars about him.[3]

This use of props reminds one of Chaplin eating his boot, Marceau plucking a flower, or Jacques Tati trapped in a revolving door. That he was also a master of bodily expression can be seen in the description of Old Dozy, the drunken sailor:

> It is truly tacking, not walking. He steers at a table, and the tide of grog now and then bears him off the point... There was something cumbersome, inde-cisive, and awful in his veering. Once afloat, it appeared impossible for him to come to his moorings; once at anchor, it did not seem an easy thing to get him under weigh.[4]

But if Munden was a virtuoso soloist with a wide range of techniques, John Liston seemed to transform all the characters he played into him-self. Off-stage he was a serious cultivated man, who originally wished to be a tragic actor, but his rotund figure and lugubrious features were incompatible with romantic heroism, so instead he specialised in 'drollery'. Being 'droll' was a quality much appreciated throughout the nineteenth century; it implied a self-awareness in the comedian, who consciously shared his own amusement with the audience. Drollery did not involve nudging or winking at the audience – that was being 'arch' – but was expressed by a chuckle and a steady gaze: 'The great peculiarity of Liston's manner, on and off the stage is its gravity. What he says is less remarkable than the way he says it.'[5] 'He is the best quiet comedian that we remember... His exclusive province is calm drollery – the laugh which he excites without exhibiting, and the easy pungency with which the sar-casm is shot, apparently without taking aim at any one.'[6] Hazlitt saw Liston as a personality detached from his character, a solo performer who related with the audience outside the context of the play. Like Munden, he invited them to laugh, not at the play, as if 'sending it up', but at his having to contend with complications specially created to con-fuse him. It is not that the situations are funny of themselves, but that Liston – whom we all know so well! – has to deal with them:

> We consider Mr Liston in the light of an author rather than an actor, and he makes the best parts out of his own head or face, in a sort of *brown study*, with

very little reference to the text... No one is *stultified*, no one is *mystified* like him – no one is so deep in absurdity, no one so full of vacancy; no one chuckles so over his own conceit, or is so dismayed at finding his mistake: the genius of folly spreads its shining gloss over his face, tickles his nose, laughs in his eyes, makes his teeth chatter in his head... Liston's humour bubbles up of itself, and runs over from the mere fullness of the conception. If he does not go out of himself, he looks into himself, and ruminates on the idea of the idle, the quaint, and the absurd, till it does his heart good within him, and makes 'the lungs of others crow like chanticleer'.[7]

Munden died in 1832, and Liston retired in 1837, having been for a while the highest paid actor in the profession, playing the minor houses as well as the patents, but first and foremost he had been a stalwart of the Haymarket where his most famous part, Paul Pry, had played, on and off, for years.

The role of leading low-comedian on the London stage was inherited by J. B. Buckstone, who as actor, and, from 1853 to 1879, as manager, maintained traditional comedy at the Haymarket. Like Munden and Liston, Buckstone played with rather than for his audience, and, although he undertook quite a range of characters, it was his own personality that attracted – or appalled – the critics:

Mr Buckstone has talents, Mr Buckstone has humour, Mr Buckstone has much waggishness, but Mr Buckstone has no refinement. A *double entendre* lurks in each eye; his smirk is a hint of an unclean presence... His voice is in perfect keeping with his person... it seems to lazily flow from a mind charged with fat thoughts and unctuous conceits. He has the true low-comedy air in his walk and gesture; his face looks dry and red with long roasting before footlights. He is the son of mirth and vulgarity. His mind is a machine which manufactures afresh the stuff it is fed on; what is wholesome and plain is reproduced in new form, with a different colouring and an original aroma... Mr Buckstone takes care to impart a meaning of his own, and makes plain speech a sort of intellectual perspective for the satyr who leers with dewy eyes upon the spectator, and whilst he forces him to laugh, compels him to despise the occasion of his merriment.[8]

Written in 1862, this suggests that Buckstone's crudely familiar style offended bourgeois respectability in the high Victorian period. In the 1840s, however, he was considered capable of 'sound legitimate acting', and by 1877 he had, according to Pascoe's *Dramatic List*, 'played almost all the principal low comedy parts of the English Drama presented on the London stage within living memory', which included parts in Shakespeare, Farquhar and Goldsmith.[9] Westland Marston records that

[Although] to carry drollery to its furthest point seemed the height of Buckstone's ambition, it would be untrue to say he cared little for the exhibition of character. His genial people were ultra-genial, his cowards thorough poltroons, his mischief-makers revelled in their sport; but it is quite true to say that characterisation with him was quite subordinate to mirth. The brainless, conceited, cowardly Sir Andrew Aguecheek, with his efforts at wit and his repugnance to cold steel, is, even when acted with moderation, a very laughable person; but with Buckstone's smirking self-complacency, with his variety of grimace and contortion, a height of absurdity was reached which delighted the public, if not always the critic.[10]

Although of a boisterous personality and capable of hacking a play to pieces to give himself more scope as an actor, Buckstone was not quite the soloist Munden and Liston had been. He was at his best when in a double act, as when acting with John Pritt Harley in Maddison Morton's *Box and Cox* (Haymarket, 1847). Harley, like Buckstone, was a physical, grimacing, actor who, according to Westland Marston, indulged 'his overdone effects of facial expression', but who, 'in his own airy chattering, mercurial way, overflowed with fun and self enjoyment'. The play (to be adapted in 1867 by F. C. Burnand and Arthur Sullivan into the comic opera *Cox and Box*) was popular throughout the century. The situation was of classic simplicity: a landlady has let the same room to two different tenants, Cox, a hat-maker, and Box, a newspaper compositor, who works nights. Each actor is given a solo passage to introduce his character and establish the essential rapport with the audience. Cox (Harley) complains that his excessively short haircut has made all his hats too large; Mrs Bounder, the landlady (Mrs Macnamara), takes us through the necessary exposition; Box (Buckstone) discusses his breakfast, and puts a rasher of bacon on the gridiron. Eventually this, as well as Cox's mutton chop, is thrown out of the window. The joke of destroying food was a common one, which reflected on the real hunger of London's poor – indeed, some of the galleryites may have cut a meal to buy a seat.

Also typical was the repetitive and symmetrical dialogue, as when the two men realise they share the same room:

BOX: *[Seats himself; COX does the same.]* I say, sir –
COX: Well, sir?
BOX: Although we are doomed to occupy the same room for a few hours longer, I don't see any necessity for our cutting each other's throat, sir.
COX: Not at all. It's an operation that I should decidedly object to.
BOX: And after all, I have no violent animosity against you, sir.
COX: Nor have I any rooted antipathy to you, sir.
BOX: Besides, it was all Mrs Bouncer's fault, sir.
COX: Entirely, sir.   *[Gradually approaching chairs.*
BOX: Very well, sir!
COX: Very well, sir!   *[Pause.*
BOX: Take a bit of roll, sir?
COX: Thank ye, sir.   *[Breaking a bit off, Pause.*

BOX: Do you sing, sir?
COX: I sometimes join in a chorus.
BOX: Then give us a chorus.   *[Pause.*

Soon they discover they are both engaged to the same lady – and both want to be rid of her. The symmetry of their bickering is rounded off when:

BOX: *[Seizes* COX's *hand, and looks eagerly in his face.]* You'll excuse the apparent insanity of the remark, but the more I gaze on your features, the more I'm convinced that you're my long-lost brother.
COX: The very observation I was going to make to you!
BOX: Ah, tell me – in mercy tell me – have you such a thing as a strawberry mark on you left arm?
COX: No!
BOX: Then it is he!   *[They rush into each other's arms.*

On the page such absurdity merely seems to conform to Bergson's mechanistic theory of comedy, but, in its own way, the farce contrived a series of 'affective scenes of emotion', and, as in serious drama, the portrayal of this emotion was more important than any rational motivation. Moreover, when we bear in mind the close relationship between the performers and their public, that Harley and Buckstone had a separate 'personal' existence over and above the absurd fiction of the play, seeming to be in a permanent state of antagonism, then we can appreciate how the actors could flesh out the skeleton of Morton's automaton with genuine humanity.

A far more subtle partner than Harley was Robert Keeley. Marston described how, in contrast to Buckstone's florid personality, Keeley seemed abashed and put-upon: 'Buckstone, in all his characters, was metaphorically the trombone-player, calling attention to his humour by salient and very effective appeals to his audience, demonstrative, various, gesticulatory. Keeley, on the contrary, was usually phlegmatic, impassive, and pathetically acquiescent in the droll inflictions which fate had in store for him.'[12] He was, in his own way, just as much a personality player as Buckstone, but, being less assertive, his effects seemed more restrained and artistically controlled. Critics either enthused or complained, like Thomas Marshall, that 'he is amusing enough... if the puerile ineffectiveness of his voice and the monotony of his manner could have been forgotten... To see him once was to see him always; he never changed face, voice, action; there it was, the same as ever.'[13] Henry Morley, on the other hand, thoroughly enjoyed Keeley's performances: 'He never grimaces, he never winks at the audience, he never takes anybody but himself into his confidence – yet what a never-tiring figure of fun he is, how unconscious he seems of the laughter he provokes, and what solidity he appears to give to the most trivial expressions.'[14]

In 1852 Buckstone and Keeley performed an even more 'personalised' double-act than *Box and Cox*. It was written by Mark Lemon, editor of *Punch*, and Ben Webster, manager of the Haymarket, and was called bluntly *Keeley Worried by Buckstone*. In *Box and Cox* the whole point lay in the similarity of the two performers, whose characters and circumstances were so identical as to anticipate Ionesco's *Bald Prima Donna*, but Keeley, according to Charles Dickens, was the antithesis of Harley:

> Harley was an excellent artist in his way; but he was always full of his own humour, and showed it, as much to say, 'See how funny I am!' His audiences were willing enough to admit that he was, indeed, who could help it? but Keeley's was the truer art... a master of pathos in his way and many of our most delightful memories of him are connected with characters into which, by a few words or a little touch, he threw a certain homely tenderness quite his own.[15]

Given this difference of style and personality, the comedy in *Keeley Worried by Buckstone* was one of contrast; Buckstone exaggerating his bumptiousness, and Keeley his long-suffering. The dramatic situation was that Keeley had decided to retire – he was fifty-nine at the time – and Buckstone determines to dissuade him.

> There was, of course, not much 'plot' in this farce, while the fun was of the fast and furious kind. The main purpose, however, was to bring forward the best-known mannerisms and characteristics of the two low-comedians... [Buckstone] invades Keeley's peaceful home at Pelham Crescent, and behaves so badly... by converting the neatly-arranged appartment into a perfect bear-garden – that altogether its owner is driven nearly distracted...[so] that he eventually determines to accept an engagement from Webster... With this the curtain falls, leaving Keeley alone on the outside.[16]

In many respects this farce reworks the situation of Maddison Morton's *A Most Unwarrentable Intrusion* performed by Paul Bedford and Edward Wright at the Adelphi in 1849. This too relied on the performers' known personalities, and was subtitled as *Committed by Mr Wright to the annoyance of Mr Paul Bedford*. As in the Buckstone/Keeley farce, the quiet, respectable home of a bourgeois householder was invaded by an absurd intruder, all proprieties were overthrown and 'status-symbol' property destroyed. On the surface it followed the same bizarre, mechanistic logic of *Box and Cox*, but subliminally it had all the sinister threat of an early Pinter play. The newly established security of the *petit-bourgeois* is demolished by someone, who appears to be of the same class and attitude as the victim, but who behaves like an anarchist or lunatic. Such has always been the nature of the clown, but in the mid-nineteenth century comical anarchy took on a specifically social aspect, and although there seems to be no conscious satirical intent in the aimiable familiarity of Buckstone, Harley or Wright, they always championed the gallery and pit against the boxes and orchestra stalls.

If the gallery delighted in the destructive vitality of broad comedians, who broke the conventions of the drama by overt appeals to the audience, it could also sympathise with the victims. Although Keeley or Bedford remained trapped in the nightmare world of the play, impersonating its emotions with consistency and precision, yet, by a subtle stylisation, they distanced themselves from the 'reality' of their persecution. George Henry Lewes tried hard to elucidate the mystery of this comic style:

> It matters little what the actor feels; what he can express gives him his distinctive value... The humorous predominated in Keeley... one took kindly to his vices; he was a glutton, a liar, a coward, was kicked and bullied, and bemoaned his lot without ever forfeiting our good-will. He never made a pretense of virtue... [but] he was never despicable; even in the moments of abject terror (and no one could represent comic terror better than he did) somehow or other he contrived to make you feel that courage ought not to be expected of him, for cowardice was simply the natural trembling of that human jelly. He lied with a grace which made it a sort of truth – a personal and private truth. He chuckled over his sensuality in such an unsuspiciousness of moral candor, and with such an intensity of relish, that you almost envied his gulosity. He was, in fact, a great idealist.[17]

Although Lewes's main point is about the audience's moral attitude towards Keeley's characters – a major factor in all Victorian appreciation of art – he seems to be suggesting a performance technique in which, even though Keeley did not share his enjoyment directly with the audience like Buckstone, Harley or Wright, he relished it to himself, and that even the 'comic terror', that he represented so well, was observed rather than felt by the actor. Thus the objectivity needed for a comic response was encouraged by the actor, even when he was portraying emotions that in a tragedy or melodrama would have appealed to the empathising sensibilities of the open-hearted audience.

It was precisely because audiences of the Romantic period identified so readily with the emotions on the stage, that comedians needed to signal their own detachment and amusement so blatantly. In traditional five-act comedies this sometimes led to performers failing to act with each other, and competing for the audiences' attention and sympathy. In 1898, when playing in *The School for Scandal*, Mrs Patrick Campbell, an actress of the 'new' school, was disconcerted by this old-fashioned approach: 'Mr William Farren – over eighty years of age – played Sir Peter with the traditions of his father and grandfather in the part in his bones. Never once did Sir Peter address himself to me. The audience was his friend, his companion, and to them he confided his emotions.'[18] In fact the elder Farren had not been quite as self-absorbed as his son, for when he was upstaged:

> He was so provoked by an actor, in the course of the dialogue in a comedy, stepping back so as to get his full face to the front, that he paused – and said to the audience, 'When this gentleman returns to his proper place (pointing to it), and speaks to me face to face, I will proceed.'[19]

Unlike Mrs Pat, however, who felt that the traditional method hindered her involvement in the scene, Farren felt his 'opponent' thwarted his involvement with the audience. As Macready put it when rebuking an actor for up-staging: 'Sir, by doing this you deprive the audience of what I am able to do for them, and you deprive me of their applause, which I should gain thereby. Stand thus, sir! ... Now turn, and be – !'[20] If a leading tragedian, who lost himself in the emotions of his role, was conscious of projecting his performance over the footlights, how much more con-cerned were comedians with 'putting themselves across'! Indeed 'acting out' was such an essential convention that an 1872 handbook instructed:

> Take care to retire, apparently without studied object, a step or two up the stage, when within three or four paces of the wing, and a few lines before the last so as to make you exit diagonally with the wing, by which your face and figure are almost full front to the audience as you make your exit.[21]

Playing out to the audience was not restricted to low comedy. The two outstanding light comedians of the 1830s, Mme Vestris and her husband Charles James Mathews, both created a personal rapport with their audi-ences. However, as they acted for the more fashionable, it had none of the anarchic quality of the aggressive low-comedians. Westland Marston wrote of Vestris:

> It was, I fancy, her practice of taking the house into her confidence, com-bined with her coquetry and personal attractions, that rendered Vestris so bewitching to the public. When she sang, she looked with a questioning archness at her audience, as if to ask, 'Do you enjoy that as I do? Did I give it with tolerable effect?' And though in the delivery of dialogue she could hardly be called keen or brilliant, she knew what mischief and retort meant. When she had given a sting to the latter, she would glance round, as to ask for approval, with a smile that seemed to say, 'I was a little severe there. He felt that I suppose?'[22]

Mathews too, although capable of considerable versatility as a mimic, relied on his personal charm, elegance and vocal dexterity to enchant the Olympic audiences:

Charles Mathews was eminently vivacious: a nimble spirit of mirth sparkled in his eye, and gave airiness to every gesture. He was in incessant movement without ever becoming obtrusive or fidgety. A certain grace tempered his vivacity... But... I now see, in retrospect, that it was the charm of the man rather than any peculiar talent in the actor which carried him so successfully through those little Olympic pieces... No good actor I have ever seen was so utterly powerless in the manifestation of all the powerful emotions: rage, scorn, pathos, dignity, vindictiveness, tenderness, and wild mirth are all beyond his means. He cannot even laugh with animal heartiness. He sparkles, he never explodes.[23]

Like the Haymarket farces, the 'little Olympic pieces' were specially tailored to the talents of the starring couple. J. R. Planché's rhyming and punning burlesques gave Vestris scope to flirt with her audience – and show off her elegant wardrobe – while his farces allowed Mathews to flirt with her – and show off his. Mathews also wrote plays to exploit his own talents, as in *Patter versus Clatter* (1838).

In this short piece Mathews revealed a skill of mimicry which inherited from his father, who had performed his *At Homes* as one-man-shows in which he played several parts. Charles James's *Patter versus Clatter* was a more regular farce in which Captain Patter confuses everybody by continually switching characters. According to the stage directions, Mathews accomplished these transformations by adjusting his cravat and 'turning his wig' (see Plate III). The virtuoso performance depended as much on Mathews sharing the joke with the audience, as on his mimicry:

Though he successively changes himself into a Jew moneylender, a man with a cold, and a barber, he preserves his eternal chattering throughout, and talks every one of the other characters into literal silence. Not satisfied with interrupting them through the piece, and allowing them to speak only broken sentences, he sings for them their respective solos in the finale, and when, after the fall of the curtain, Wyman comes forward to announce the piece for repetition, he rushes forth, stops him, and delivers the announcement himself.[24]

As well as speaking continuously and swiftly, Mathews included patter songs as tongue-twisting as Gilbert and as nonsensical as Edward Lear. G. H. Lewes thought this clarity of expression and subtlety of inflection distinguished Mathews from the broad comedians. In 1845 Planché's burlesque Greek tragedy, *The Golden Fleece*, featured Vestris as Medea and Mathews as the Chorus:

Another actor in such a part as Chorus would have 'gagged' or made grimaces, would have been extravagant and sought to startle the public into laughter at broad incongruities. Charles Mathews is as quiet, easy, elegant, as free from points and as delightfully humourous as if the part he played and the words he uttered belonged to high comedy; he allows the incongruity of the character and the language to work their own laughable way, and he presents them with the gravity of one who believed them. Notice also the singular unobtrusiveness of his manner, even when the situation is most broadly sketched. For example, when the King interrupts his song by an appeal to Chorus, Charles Mathews steps forward, and, bending over the footlights with that quiet gravity which has hitherto marked his familiar explanations of what is going on, begins to sing *fol de riddle lol*. There is not one actor in a score who would not have spoiled the humour of this by a wink or a grimace at the audience, as much as to say, 'Now I'm going to make you laugh.' The imperturbable gravity and familiar ease of Mathews give a drollery to this 'fol de riddle lol' which is indescribable. Probably few who saw Charles Mathews play the Chorus consider there was any art required to play it; they can understand that to sing patter songs as he sings them may not be easy, but to be quiet and graceful and humourous, to make every line tell, and yet never show the stress of effort, will not seem wonderful. If they could see another actor in the part it would open their eyes.[25]

Lewes was never impressed by broad characterisation, and in his own play *A Game of Speculation* (Lyceum, 1851) he wrote the part of a society sponger, Mr Affable Hawk, to utilise Mathews's charm in a more serious way. Marston agreed:

Here, as in the various other characters of this actor, moderation was a large element in success... the desire to keep close to truth, to adhere strictly to the sentiments and habits of a typical man of the day...the careless air...the bland superiority...the look of conviction...the curt, business-like manner... was a triumph of unscrupulous ingenuity... Hypocrisy has seldom indeed been so skilfully masked. The colloquial ease and absence of strain in the various stratagems made them to the last degree plausible, while his changes of expression, and certain familiarity, everyday actions, gave life and point to the dialogue. A finger inserted in a waistcoat-pocket, the deprecatory movement of an arm, or the flourish of a handkerchief, gave with him as much emphasis in comedy as the heroic gesture of serious actors have given in tragedy.[26]

The 'telling details' of this performance indicate how in the 1850s comic technique was approaching the 'gentlemanly' style of *The Corsican Brothers*. This precise social observation was to be developed by comedy companies at the Prince of Wales, the Court and St James's Theatres.

But before pursuing the further development of legitimate comedy acting, we need to examine another, very different, burlesque actor, Frederick Robson. The burlesques that Planché wrote for Vestris and Mathews are best described by the alternative title of 'extravaganza'. They were charming fantasies set in a fairyland of beautiful scenery and costumes, containing little genuine parody or satire. The humour lay in the fantastical use of language in patter songs and, particularly, in puns. Although it is possible for a clever pun to make a satirical point – by superimposing two apparently contradictory meanings to subverting the original concept – most Victorian puns were just nonsense, relying on a coincidence of sounds rather than meaning. The radical potential of burlesque, as exercised by Henry Fielding in the eighteenth century, was ignored by Planché in *Olympic Revels*, with which the Vestris managment was launched:

> The extraordinary success of this experiment – for it may justly so be termed – was due not only to the admirable singing and piquant performance of that gifted lady, but also to the charm and novelty imparted to it by the elegance and accuracy of the costumes; it having been previously the practice to dress a burlesque in the most outré and rediculous fashion. My suggestion to try the effect of persons picturesquely attired speaking absurd doggrel fortunately took the fancy of the fair lessee, and the alteration was highly appreciated by the public; but many old actors could never get over their early impressions. Liston thought to the last that Prometheus, instead of the Phrygian cap, tunic, and trousers, should have been dressed like a great lubberly boy in a red jacket and nankeens, with a pinafore all besmeared with lollipop![27]

Liston's idea had a genuinely satirical intent, subverting the grandeur of the classical hero, but Planché's method was to divorce the content of his extravaganza as far as possible from real life.

The older, subversive type of burlesque did survive in less fashionable minor houses, and aggressive parody was to re-emerge in music-halls later in the century. Fantasy had been used to confront life, rather than escape from it, by Joey Grimaldi, the famous pantomime clown. He retired in 1828, but his influence on all forms of fantastic comedy lasted for many years, though no one could recapture his precise genius. Grimaldi, in his bizarre costume and make-up, indulged a freedom which was denied the lower-class members of his audience by cocking a snook at his merchant master, Pantaloon, by parodying the fashionable costume of the dandies, or – favourite trick of all – by stealing a string of sausages from a butcher's basket.[28] A Grimaldi pantomime was a subversive fantasy in an increasingly entrepreneurial society, while an Olympic extravaganza was the self-indulgent fantasy of the leisured class, in which elegance replaced satire. It was Robson who reintroduced a cutting edge to burlesque, and he did it, not through his scripts, but by his acting.

Frederick Robson was born in 1821 in Margate, and at fifteen he was apprenticed to a printer in Vauxhall. Mollie Sands suggests that, 'like Dickens, he was an adopted not a born Londoner, and perhaps this gave them both an especially keen relish for the special characteristics of the people among whom they came to live'.[29] An awkward little boy, he remained five feet tall with a large head, so that on stage he could appear either dwarf-like and grotesque, or childlike and pathetic. Although Robson had always wanted to be a legitimate actor, this unprepossessing appearance, allied to his undoubted comic talents, led to engagements as

Figure 4. Frederick Robson as Jem Baggs in *The Wandering Minstrel*,
Olympic Theatre, 1853

a singer–comedian in music-halls. The distinction between the halls and
the 'proper' theatre had been exacerbated by the 1843 Theatre Act, and
music-hall success was no passport to the legitimate theatre. When
William Davidge recommended Robson to the Dublin Theatre Royal,
he was asked '"Where did you see him?" "At the Grecian Saloon," I
replied. "Ugh! wouldn't have him if he'd come for nothing!" '[30] However
Robson was determined to join a legitimate theatre in Dublin, and was
employed at the Queen's before, despite the manager's prejudice,
moving to the Theatre Royal in 1853. He performed much of the standard repertoire while in Dublin, but his success as Jem Baggs in Henry
Mayhew's *The Wandering Minstrel*, with its comic song, 'Vilikens and his
Dinah', won him a London contract from William Farren at the
Olympic.

Robson's *Wandering Minstrel* was described as being of almost shocking realism: 'So vivid a picture of an outcast street musician, ragged,

[74]

miry miserable, his limbs racked and distorted with rheumatism, his voice hoarse and broken with constant exposure to rough weather, had not been seen before on the stage.'[31] Yet this depiction of distress and poverty inspired the audience to uncontrollable laughter:

> What a roar of merriment greeted the appearance of the woe-begone little figure of Robson, who, in smashed hat, shambling on in muddy shoes that could hardly be held together by bits of string finished on the flageolet the last notes of no air in particular, as after looking up beseechingly at the windows of the street, disappointed of coppers, he wandered down to the 'flote' [*float: footlights*] where with an intensely comic look of abject misery, he silently surveyed the already convulsed audience.[32]

There was an astonished tension between emotional identification with the beggar's distress and amused recognition of his musical incompetence. When laughter greeted his ditty 'Vilikins and his Dinah', Robson would appeal plaintively, 'This is not a comic song!'[33]

The second surprise Robson produced was in Thomas Talfourd's burlesque *Macbeth*, following Chales Kean's Princess production of 1853. Talfourd originally thought that Paul Bedford would be an ideal Lady Macbeth.[34] At the Olympic, however, Mrs Alfred Phillips played the Lady, and this 'straight' casting helped Robson to create his impression of intense reality in a part made up of nonsensical doggerel and puns: 'Mr Robson does not caricature any existing actor, but simply exaggerates the part, painting the terror and horror of the part and the deed in ludicrous colours without altering the outline or feeling.'[35] 'He really seems to be aware of the tragic foundation which lies at the bottom of the grotesque superstructure; and hence, however extravagant his gestures and articulation, they are odd expressions of a feeling intrinsically serious.'[36] Robson was not guying Shakespeare's hero, but playing – with great sincerity – an equivalent character drawn from 'low-life', 'a red-headed Scottish sergeant of militia in a modern uniform, much addicted to whiskey',[37] a little hen-pecked husband dominated by the statuesque wife of Mrs Phillips.

Macbeth was followed by Shylock, and again Robson acted a well-known London type. Of course to the Victorians, who idealised and idolised Shakespeare, this bringing of the character down to earth seemed the height of incongruity, but for Robson the passions of a local Jewish tailor were just as powerful as those of the Venetian money-lender: 'His Shylock simply reduces the Jew to a Holywell Street type, and then trusts the rest to the natural development of the passions... Many of his bursts are truely tragic, and might have done justice to Edmund Kean in his best days.'[38] The image may have been stereotypical, but the emotional intensity made Henry Morley reflect: 'The only regret in observing his execution of Mr Telfourd's Shylock is that he had not made trial of Shakespeare's in preference.'[39] But this was to miss the point of Robson's art, which gave tragic status to those the audience expected to laugh at because of their low social status.

Alfred Wigan, who took over the Olympic from Farren in 1854, also felt that Robson ought to attempt a serious role, and cast him as a henchman of Napoleon's ruthless police chief Fouché, in Tom Taylor's *Plot and Passion*. Like *The Corsican Brothers*, the play was historically precise in its setting, and gave Wigan another French aristocrat to play. Apparently Robson was reluctant to take the part, but Wigan, like his mentor Charles Kean, wanted to cast according to personality and physical appearance, rather than stock 'lines of business': 'I flatter myself I have discrimination in the casting of my people for the characters. I am positive you are the very man for the part... Don't get ventilating your supposed grievances to everybody in the theatre!'[40] In the event, Henry Morley too felt vindicated in having identified a remarkable talent:

> But one hardly expected it so soon. The part he plays... is that of a mean, double-faced, fawning, cunning, treacherous tool, in which the sordid passions have nevertheless not wholly extinguished others that place him finally at the mercy of his victims. Here the actor's opportunity is that of a constant and quick transition within the limited range of the emotions expressed; and from meanness to malice, from cringing humility to the most malignant hate, from a cat-like watchfulness to occasional bouts of passion that seemed to defy control, Mr Robson passed with a keen power... Mr Robson's great quality is the downright earnestness by which he makes others feel what he very evidently· feels himself... General interest fixed itself on that ill-dressed, meagre, dwarfish figure, and, whoever else might occupy the scene, the eye still sought him out.[41]

For all his comic effect, Robson was a master of the Theatre of Feeling, displaying, like Kean or Macready, great passions and the startling shifts between them.

Robson's seriousness in burlesques had caused Planché himself to reconsider the genre: 'The rage for mere absurdity which my extravaganzas so unintentionally and unhappily gave rise to, has lasted longer than I anticipated, but there are unmistakable signs, I think, of its subsidence.' Writing in 1872, Planché associated this change with W. S. Gilbert, but it can be seen in his own contributions to the Olympic during Robson's reign, including *The Yellow Dwarf* of 1854. In his introduction to the published script Planché praised Robson's performance as 'so powerful was his personation of the cunning, the malignity, the passion and despair of the monster, that he elevated Extravaganza into Tragedy'.[42] G. A. Sala described him as the

> jaundiced embodiment of the spirit of Oriental evil: crafty, malevolent,

greedy, insatiate. How that monstrous orange-tawny head grinned and wagged! How those flaps of ears were projected forward like unto those of a dog! How balefully those atrabilious eyes glistened! You laughed and yet you shuddered. He spoke in mere doggrel and slang, he sang trumpery songs to negro melodies, he danced the Lancashire clog hornpipe, he rattled out puns and conundrums, yet did he manage to infuse... an unmistakable tragic element. The mountebank becomes inspired.[43]

In another parody-burlesque, *Medea* (1856) Robson took off the Italian star Adelaide Ristori, and once again the effect was overwhelming. Dickens wrote to Macready that Robson was not so much a parody of tragic acting, but a model for it:

The scene with Jason is perfectly terrific; and the manner in which the comic rage and jealousy does not pitch itself over the floor of the stalls is in striking contrast to the manner in which the tragic rage and jealousy does. He has a frantic song and dagger dance, about 10 minutes long altogether, which has more passion in it than – could express in 50 years.[44]

Robson's performances may well have inspired some of Dickens's own creations, specifically that of the dwarfish Quilp in *Little Dorrit*, which was written during Robson's reign. Like many of Robson's characters, Quilp is comic in style and expression, but frightening and sinister in the intensity of his passions of both love and hate. Robson certainly inspired a Dickensian play from Palgrave Simpson, *Daddy Hardcastle*, based on Balzac's *Eugénie Grandet*. With its portrayal of a 'low-life' character, enobled by the sheer depth of his none too reputable passion, Robson at last had a script that he could work with rather than against. The play comes as close to a critique of capitalism, or at least cupidity, as any in the Victorian repertoire:

The old man loves his daughter and his gold, handles and hugs them with so equal an affection, that to subdue either of the two loves... is impossible. To save an uncle's life the miser's daughter robs him of five thousand pounds that he has stubbornly refused to lend. When he is frantic with his loss, the daughter owns herself to be the thief. He will fell her to the earth; he will fondle her; he will starve her into more confession. He has sent her to her room, and sits before the stairs that lead down to his money and the stairs that lead up to his daughter. He sees her weeping and praying. 'Shut the door,' he cries to the old servant, 'I'll never forgive — I didn't tell you to shut it close, you stupid fool!' The knot is untied at last without violence to either of the miser's ruling passions.[45]

This performance marks the transition from the broad comical style, which appealed overtly to the audience's sympathy, to the more elaborate character acting of later years, when the playing was between the characters within the scene, and the emphasis was on 'telling details'. Robson's heightened passion used traditions of both tragic gesture and comic mugging, while his uniquely devised business anticipated both the comic style of Irving, as in Mr Jingle, and his melodramatic style, as in *The Bells*.

The use of points and attitudes had presented the different aspects of a characterisation separately, each aspect being performed with maximum effect but little sense of unity. Robson's *Daddy Hardcastle* used such contrasts, but Marston thought it also had integrity of conception:

> The sordid aspect of the half peasant, half farmer, with his strange pronunciation, was, indeed, so thoroughly and minutely represented as to be generally comic, but without in the least detracting from its reality or from the emotional interest... What a true and laughable touch was that of venting rage on a minor character, who has, unbidden, helped himself to roll and butter, by a scowl and an aside, which seemed to relieve his exasperation – 'How ugly yon chap looks wi' his mouth full!'... His disappointment because Esther, his daughter, received so calmly the guinea he offered her. 'Thank you, father.' Was that all she had to say for a gift dear to him 'as a drop of his heart's blood'? 'Hey, hey, lass!' he cries, withdrawing the coin for a time; 'Does it rejoice thee no more than that to look on a guinea – to know it is thine own, all alone – to hear it chink, chink?' What depths of rapture did his tones convey – tones crooning and gloating... The scene [when he learnt of the robbery] was appalling... His changed, almost choked voice, startled you with a sense of catastrophe before he entered. 'Whose voice' you asked – 'surely not Robson's?' At length he tottered in, gasping 'Mary – Mary!' to the servant. His face drawn and convulsed, his reeling gait, his stifled tones gave the notion of one who had been struck and shrivelled by lightening... his limbs fail, and he staggers to his chair. Reviving a little, he bids them bring the thief. He will search him himself, and then he'll have him 'hanged – hanged – hanged!' – this in a voice which, by its very exhaustion – a last effort of speech – showed a depth of hatred from which the listeners recoiled.

Marston thought Robson had departed from the 'idealising' style of the stock actor, and moved closer to the 'particularising' technique of the naturalistic school: His 'acting had no touch of strain... He was colloquial even in passion; his voice had the rise and fall of all the natural changes which, in real life and in real men, denote mental impulses in their varying excitement and calm.'[46] Sadly, however, the little man was burning himself out. Like many of his profession he drank too much, and his memory began to go. His last performance at the Olympic was 4 April 1863, and he died the following year, aged forty-three. Marston's last word on Robson repeats the highest praise you could give to any nineteenth-century actor: 'Robson made the listener feel, because he felt himself.'[47]

Later in the century J. L. Toole combined something of Robson's seriousness with the drollery of the low comedian. His acting in the 1880s demonstrates the remarkably longevity of Victorian comic acting styles. Toole developed a large and varied stock of characters, some in new plays, but many from the repertoire of Buckstone, Bedford and Wright. One of his favourites was Paul Pry, which Toole performed, using the same style and costume as Liston, into the 1890s. The 'Paul Pry' character, as an inquisitive intruder into serious situations, was particularly suitable for injecting comic relief into melodrama. As late as 1903 the same characterisation appeared in an American film of *Uncle Tom's Cabin* (see Plate IV).[48] The New Jersey company filmed a stage production of the play, probably dating from the 1880s, and the comic character of Marks was dressed, like Paul Pry, in a Regency style quite out of keeping with the other character's costumes. His outfit of tight trousers, cut-away tails and a hugely wide top-hat was completed by a 'Paul Pry' umbrella. The actor's posture and movement were also quite unlike the rest of the cast's – his bottom thrust out and his knees slightly bent. It was the same comic stance used by Liston, Buckstone, Bedford and Toole.

A review of Toole as Joe Bright in *Through Fire and Water*, at the Adelphi in 1865, suggested that 'although the majority of characters to which Mr J. L. Toole devotes his talents belong to the region of broad farce', occasionally, as in this instance, he made 'an impression of more than ordinary strength, as if convinced that his proper vocation was to follow the late Mr F. Robson in semi-pathetic illustrations of plebeian life'.[49] However, Joseph Knight's assessment of 1880 confirmed that Toole's real talent lay in traditional drollery:

> There is no gift of the low actor which Mr Toole does not possess in a high degree. His individuality is as comic as that of the best of his predecessors; his vitality is as unflagging as theirs; his methods as irregular and as effective... Mr Toole is unequalled in the expression of comic bewilderment. Unlike some of the best remembered of his predecessors who assumed, in the face of difficulty, a stolidity against which fate itself seemed powerless, he contrives to add to his comic perplexities by his own apparent quickness of invention. He is always ready with an explanation which is invariably wrong... His vulgarity upon the stage is like his perplexity in the total absence of stupidity.

Knight concluded with the comment that 'he is not free from the faults of his craft; and the means he adopts to force a laugh are not always artistic'.[50] But then a lack of 'artistry' – an ability to break the dramatic proprieties with the force of an irrepressible personality – has always been the hallmark of great comedians. Although such 'drollery' has usually been associated with low comedy, from Bully Bottom to Alfred Dolittle, E. A. Sothern proved that familiarity with an audience could be just as effective when playing the part of a peer of the realm.

6

Our American Cousin by Tom Taylor
adapted by E. A. Sothern

Laura Keene's Theatre, New York, 15 October 1858.

LORD DUNDREARY	Mr E. A. Sothern
ASA TRENCHARD	Mr Joseph Jefferson
Sir EDWARD TRENCHARD	Mr E. Varrey
ABEL MURCOTT	Mr C. W. Couldoon
Mr COYLE	Mr J. G. Burnett
Mr BUDDICOMBE	Mr McDouvall
FLORENCE TRENCHARD	Miss Laura Keene
MARY MEREDITH	Miss Sara Steven
Mrs MOUNTCHESSINGTON	Miss Mary Wells
Her daughter, GEORGINA	Mrs Sothern

Haymarket Theatre, London, 11 November 1861.

LORD DUNDREARY	Mr E. A. Sothern
ASA TRENCHARD	Mr J. B. Buckstone
GEORGINA	Mrs Sothern

The Action takes place in the present, and is set in Trenchard Manor.

Act I

Guests at Trenchard Manor, including Lord Dundreary, greet the arrival of Asa Trenchard from America to claim an inheritance, which they had hoped would have gone to poor Mary Meredith. Asa proves to be the brash opposite of the ineffectual Dundreary. Meanwhile Sir Edward Trenchard is confronted by a demand for the hand of his daughter, Florence, from his crooked agent Coyle, who holds a mortgage on the manor.

Act II

Preparations are made for an archery competition, during which Asa watches Dundreary's inept proposal to Georgina Mountchessington, and then learns of Coyle's dastardly plans. In the park he meets Mary Meredith, who is having to work as a milkmaid. Asa begins to fall in love with her. He recruits Dundreary to help advance the navel career of Florence Trenchard's sweetheart. There are general celebrations when Asa wins at archery.

Act III

Learning that Mary ought to have inherited the fortune that he came to England for, Asa uses the will to light a cigar. But before he can propose to her, he has to fight off the advances of other fortune-hunting guests, and, by making Coyle drunk, regain Sir Edward's mortgage. Dundreary has a solo scene in which he reads a letter from his brother Sam. Finally Asa denounces Coyle and saves the manor. Everyone pairs off happily.

If in the early Victorian theatre comedians used their roles to display their own personalities, in direct rapport with audiences, then E. A. Sothern's success as Lord Dundreary in *Our American Cousin* was remarkable in that he subsumed his personality within an eccentric creation, the popularity of which threatened to overwhelm his own acting career. Dundreary, like Chaplin's tramp or Larry Hagman's J.R., so caught the imagination of the public that he developed an existence outside the original dramatic script. Cartoons and anecdotes in the press, together with fashions in clothes and hairstyles, all testify to the character's appeal. Significantly, it was the actor himself who constructed the character from the flimsiest of material provided in Tom Taylor's script, and, surprisingly, he created this quintessentially English eccentric in America.

Our American Cousin was originally written for Joshua Silsbee, an American comedian engaged at the Adelphi in 1850, in the expectation of an influx of American tourists to the Great Exhibition, but the Adelphi manager, Webster, rejected the play. It was eight years later, after Silbee's death in America, that the script was submitted, at Taylor's suggestion, to Lester Wallack, who recognised

> it wanted a great Yankee character actor; that Mr Joseph Jefferson, then a stock-actor in Miss Laura Keene's company, was the very man for it, and advised its presentation to her... She did not see any great elements of popularity in it, but she thought that it might do to fill a gap some time, and she pigeon-holed it.[1]

Eventually on 15 October 1858, after a production of *A Midsummer Night's Dream* had to be postponed, she presented it with Joe Jefferson cast as Asa Trenchard, the Vermont backwoodsman, who turns up in

England to claim an inheritance. E. A. Sothern was offered the minor role of Lord Dundreary, a visitor to Trenchard Manor (see Plate V). The comedy centred on the good-natured but brash American being thrown into a genteel English house-party. There was some melodramatic intrigue about a dishonest estate manager, whom Asa unmasks, and a love intrigue with the girl who was to have inherited the Manor had he not turned up. The plot was slight and the comedy fairly predictable. However, Jefferson saw 'the chance of making a strong character of the leading part, and so I was quite selfish enough to recommend the play for production... [During the preliminary reading] poor Sothern sat in a corner, looking quite disconsolate, fearing there was nothing in the play for him; and as the dismal lines of Dundreary were read he glanced over at me with a forlorn expression, as much to say "I am cast for that dreadful part."'[2]

In the original script Dundreary, with some fifty lines, was a fussy old aristocrat who danced attendance on the hypochondriac Miss Georgina – 'I am so delicate!' – with a very minor function within the main plot.

> [Sothern] went to Miss Keene, laid it upon her desk, and told her that he absolutely declined to play it... At last, she appealed to his generosity and asked him to do this as a mere matter of loyalty to her. At last he said, 'Well, Miss Keene, I have read the part carefully, and if you will let me "gag" it and do what I please with it, I will undertake it, though it is pretty bad.' Miss Keene said, 'Do anything you like with it, only play it.'[3]

Many actors must have made such a request – or even gagged without their manager's permission – but few can have so completely transformed a play as Sothern was to do on this occasion.

Edward Askew Sothern did not come from a theatrical family: his father was a Liverpool businessman, and it was intended he should take up medicine, but, overcome with nausea in the dissecting theatre, he changed to theological studies with a view to entering the Church. However, success as an amateur actor eventually led to a professional engagement under the stage name of Douglas Stuart. Thin, elegant and well-educated, he was employed as a light comedian in the Charles Mathews line, appearing in roles that made no demand for high passion. As his career was slow to progress, and his family still disapproved of the stage,[4] he went to America and performed in Boston and New York. Gaining some success under Lester Wallack, he reassumed his real name before joining Laura Keene's company in 1858. Sothern therefore knew the English society of which Dundreary was a caricature, and he made the aristocrat as much a laughing-stock in America, as the backwoodsman was to have been in London.

He began by adopting the latest London fashions, and, although those who saw Dundreary later in his career describe Sothern's costume as absurd, the mid-1850s fashions were remarkable, having been influenced by the Crimean War. The names of Generals Cardigan and Raglan have passed into the language, as a knitted jacket and a design of sleeve, and so did Dundreary's when applied to the extravagant side-whiskers as worn by officers at the front. His ankle-length overcoat originated in the cavalry, and even his monocle was a recent invention.[5]

It is unclear how Sothern went about expanding his role. There may have been some spontaneous gagging on stage, but most of the lines and business were worked out beforehand. According to E. H. Sothern, his father was going to give up acting altogether when cast as Dundreary and 'enter his father's office in Liverpool, to devote himself to mercantile pursuits', but Jefferson 'worked hard to help [him], and, day by day, Dundreary was, as it were, superimposed upon the play'.[6] Jefferson himself, however, suggests it was not until the play had been running two weeks that Sothern started to elaborate the part:

> In despair he began to introduce extravagant business into his character, skipping about the stage, stammering and sneezing, and, in short, doing all he could to attract and distract the attention of the audience. To the surprize of everyone, himself included, these antics, intended by him to injure the character, were received by the audience with delight. He was a shrewd man as well as an effective actor, and he saw at a glance that accident had revealed to him a golden opportunity.[7]

According to Sothern himself:

> There is not a single look, word or act in *Lord Dundreary* that have not been suggested to me by people whom I had known since I was five years of age. . . one of the pastimes which I occasionally enjoy is that of studying idiosyncrasies of characters. Sometimes I have spent days and weeks in following and observing men whose eccentricities of dress or manners struck me as unique and suggestive.

He also attributed his success to:

> Earnestness – doing everything as well as I know how – never acting on the impulse of the moment, and thoroughly understanding what I have to do... Wallack showed me the necessity of conveying at rehearsal what you intend to do at night, and the importance of paying strict attention to the minutest detail.[8]

Clearly the creation of Lord Dundreary was not an accident of improvisation, whatever the first impulse may have been, but the product of thorough and continual invention. Eventually Sothern usurped all the functions of the author and reshaped the whole play around his own part. His son described how:

> The printed play as sold by French & Son represents the result of the first two seasons or so of performances. Every season that my father played the piece it was altered and added to; his work on it was constant and unremit-

ting... My father each year copied out his own prompt-books, or had them copied, and then wrote in his most recent additions.[9]

Sothern himself, however, argued that he had treated the script with respect, doing no more than any manager might have done with a script that had been left on his shelf for eight years.

> I have reconstituted it, retaining nearly the whole of the original dialogue, save that of *Dundreary*. Each character is longer than it was on its production at Laura Keene's, with the exception of *Abel Murcott*. His part is three times shorter than it used to be. I have cut one scene entirely out. It was the cellar scene, a bad melodramatic drunken scene where Coyle is made drunk by Asa and Abel Murcott, and finally hit on the head by a tea tray. By my alteration I have a piece now in four acts, with only one scene in each. I acknowledge that Asa's practising with a revolver in the library is farce, instead of comedy, but surely it is better than his going into a shower bath and pulling a string under the impression that it is a bell rope.[10]

Actually Sothern had made Tom Taylor's mid-century comedy conform to the pattern of a Robertsonian drawing-room drama, with box-sets to replace alternating front-scenes. Laura Keene's Theatre was a long-run rather than a stock company, and it was only the period of continuous performance that made it possible for Sothern to develop the role. However, after the initial runs in New York and London, he toured stock theatres as a solo artist, and an undated cast list, sent to Augustin Daly, indicates how Sothern would cast the play according to type:

> Dundreary – (written and created by) Sothern
> Asa – 1st low com. – Fawcett 40
> Murcott – leading man – Davidge 50
> Binney – 2nd low com. – Daly 35
> Buddicombe – Daly – most important part for me E. A. S.
> Coyle – 1st heavy – Jennings 30
> Sir Edward Trenchard – 1st old – Moore 30
> Vernon – light com. = Ringgold 30
> De Boots – 4 or 5 lines – Willard 25
> Georgina – 1st walking (most particular) Miss Deitz 50 [30?]
> Mary – 1st chambermaid = Gilman 40
> Augusta – 2nd walking
> Mrs Mountchessington – 1st old woman – Mrs Emhirst 50
> Florence – 1st light com = Miss Jeffreys Lewes.
> NB – Georgina & Buddicombe are most particular with me.[11]

On another occasion he wrote: 'Warn Buddicombe to play well down the stage, to speak very clearly, and wait till every laugh is followed by a dead silence.'[12]

The original production played for several months in New York, and then Sothern negociated an engagement at the Haymarket, with Buckstone playing Asa Trenchard. Worried that an American reputation might not ensure a London success, Sothern sent ahead the following announcement to the press:

> Report says there is a hitch from somewhere as regards Lord Dundreary visiting London, and that Tom Taylor has been prejudiced against Mr S's creation. Sothern on the other hand says *Aut Dundreary aut nullus*. All we can say is – that if he do not play that character in London, the cockneys will miss the funniest satirical sketch ever impersonated and the Haymarket a huge and prosperous gem of a piece, the extraordinary success of which was caused by Southern's creative genius.[13]

Not for nothing had Sothern acted with Phineas T. Barnum's in New York! He wanted all the publicity he could muster, fearing that the English might think that the play 'had become popular in New York because the American theatre-goers of those days revelled in a gross and insulting charicature of an English nobleman; in London the performance would, no doubt, be condemned as entirely wanting in humour, taste and judgement'.[14]

In the event, the play was slow to catch on, despite a warm review in *The Atheneum* (11 November 1861):

> In the hands of Mr Southern... it is certainly the *funniest* thing in the world. The part is abstractedly a vile caricature of an inane nobleman, intensely ignorant and extremely indolent. The notion once accepted that such an absurd animal could be the type of any class whatever, the author was free to exaggerate to any extent the representation of the ridiculous.[15]

This suggestion that 'the funniest satirical sketch ever impersonated' was absurd fantasy rather than social criticism perhaps helped free the inhibitions of those upper-class theatre-goers, who felt the portrait was in questionable taste:

> At first 'Our American Cousin' was a disastrous failure, and was acted night after night to empty benches. Buckstone was disheartened, and had resolved upon its speedy withdrawal – when, fortunately, Mathews came to see it. When the play was over, he went round to have a few words with Bucky, who avowed his intention to withdraw the piece immediately. Mathews urged him not to dream of doing so, but to hold on both to the play and the player.[16]

Mathews recognised a light comedian as skilful as himself, and whose eccentric aristocrat, like many of his own, transcended the traditonal stage-fop, which Tom Robertson had described as:

> A boisterous, blatant fellow in a green coat and brass buttons, buckskin breeches and boots, or in a blue frock, white waistcoat, and straw-coloured continuations, always talking at the top of his voice, slapping you heavily on the back, laughing for five minutes consecutively, jumping over the chairs and tables, haranguing a mob from your drawing-room window, going down on his knees to your daughter or your wife, or both, kissing your servant-

maid, borrowing your loose cash, and introducing a sheriff's officer to your family as an old college friend.[17]

Dundreary's appearance and behaviour was just as outrageous, but Sothern relied on what G. H. Lewes had described as 'his own artistic symbols' and not the traditional clichés of the stock type. Rather than the traditional costume, his was a parody of modern fashions; rather than slapping people on the back, he myopically bumped into them or sat in their laps; if he was continually laughing it was at his own childish puns: 'Let me ask you a widdle – why does a duck go under the water? for divers reasons. Now I'll give you another – why does a duck come out of the water? for sun-dry reasons'; rather than haranguing characters he interrupted them with his fatuous riddles or uncontrollable sneezing; and when he rebuked his servant, it was with urbane insolence: 'Go away. You're a nice person, but I've had enough of you.' As for his love-making, Dundreary's proposal to Georgina was just as patronising as the flirting of a dandy, but on the surface it seemed as aimiable as it was aimless:

Oh, talking of mud reminds me I want to say something. It's rather awkward for one fellow to say to another fellow, – the fact is, I've made up my mind to propose to some fellow or other, and it struck me I might as well propose to you as anyone else. (GEORGINA *turns slightly away from him.*) I mean sooner, of course. I only said that because I was nervous, – any fellow naturally does feel nervous when he knows he's going to make an ass of himself. Talking about asses, I've been a bachelor ever since I've been so high, and I've got rather tired of that sort of thing, and it struck me if you'll be kind enough to marry me I shall be very much obliged to you. Of course, if you don't see the matter in the same light, and fancy you'd rather not, – why, I don't care a rap about it! *(She turns aside, looking amazed)* I've got it all mixed up somehow or other. You see, the fact is, – hem – hem! *(Pause)* It makes a fellow feel awkward when he's talking to the back of a person's head. *(She faces him)* Thank you, that's better: you'll find me a very nice fellow, – at least, I think so, – that is, what I mean is, that most fellows think me a nice fellow, – two fellows out of three would think me a nice fellow, – and the other fellow – the third fellow, – well, that fellow would be an ass. I'm very good-tempered, too; that's a great point, isn't it? You look as if you'd got a good temper; but then, of course, we know that many a girl looks as if she'd got a good temper before she's married, – but after she's married sometimes a fellow finds out her temper's not exactly what he fancied. *(he laughs suddenly)* I'm making a devil of a mess of it! I really think we should be very happy. I'm a very domesticated fellow, – fond of tea, – smoking in bed, – and all that sort of thing. I merely name that because it gives you an insight into a fellow's character. You'll find me a very easy fellow to get along with, and after we've been married two or three weeks, if you don't like me you can go back again to your mother.[18]

Sothern's Dundreary was a parody of unthinking class arrogance, as the American critic 'Nym Crinkle' recognised; 'He represented the possiblity of a state of society in which nothing is preserved to the individual but personal vanity in appearance. The satire is doubtless overdrawn, but it anticipates the fashionable man whose artificial tastes have eaten up his natural faculties.'[19] Yet the impression given in performance was generally sympathetic. Dundreary's stupidity was basically honest and throughout the performance Sothern managed to convey, like all the best Victorian actors, the workings of the mind: 'Mr Sothern conceived the idea of an elegant ass, perfect in all his imperfections, rich in the absence of brains, coherent in his incoherency, and polished in the proof of his stupidity. More than this, he undertook to show us the internal character of it; the very workings of the addled intellect; and it was possible to put our finger with accuracy on the weak spots in his head whenever we got through laughing'.[20] One affectionate weak spot that Henry Morley identified was that Dundreary could no more understand other people, than we can understand him, and as he tolerates their inanity, so we are tempted to tolerate his: 'He is polite and good-natured, although inane, and very indulgent to an outside world that puzzles him sorely, by consisting chiefly of people whom he takes to be lunatics.'[21]

John Oxenford, in trying to define this inanity more precisely, reveals a similarity between the mental processes of the eccentric aristocrat and the disturbing dream-worlds of Lewis Carroll and Edward Lear:

> His sense of the ludicrous is most keen, his perceptive faculties are even over-developed. He grasps blindly at most original notions and these slip away from him for a want of tenacity of brain and continuity of thought... He has, as it were, no back to his head, and consequently no back bone to his character... He might have been as logical as the best of us; shone forth as a mathematician, a politician, an orator, what you will, had he not been subjected to a perpetual counter action. He has impediments of all kinds – in speech, in gait, in eyesight, and, worst of all, in judgement. Moral respect he always commands, and none of the many laughs that are raised at his expense involve contempt... utterly incapable of intentional rudeness, or ill-nature... he is a man that sees everything askew.[22]

Fred Lyster made the same point when he likened 'the mind of Dundreary to a shattered mirror, which reflected the images of things about it, but deflected them at the same time'.[23] Thus in a distracted, elliptical way the folly and the fantasy of Lord Dundreary reflected the state of society around him. He was a true clown, subverting accepted standards, not from the viewpoint of the traditional clown-tramp, but from the equally alienated viewpoint of the clown-aristocrat.

Following the inglorious victories of the Crimean War, which ended in 1856, the balance of power had changed significantly in both Europe and English society. The 1860s saw the expansion of British Imperialism, while, at home, triumphant middle-class professionals dominated the political and social scene. Lord Derby's first Conservative government of 1859 lasted only long enough for Disraeli to introduce a reform bill, thus giving notice that old aristocratic Toryism was dead, and the rest of the period was dominated by the Liberals led by Palmerston, champion of the Empire, and Gladstone, champion of Free Trade and low taxation. Earlier fears of working-class rebellion had been channelled into 'responsible' trade-unionism, and much overt suffering had been alleviated by social reforms and widespread philanthropy. The City was flourishing, and, although the American Civil War hurt the cotton trade, industrial expansion in engineering, railways and ship-building confirmed Britain's status as 'workshop of the world'. It was generally felt, however, that Britain's emergence as 'top nation' owed little to the traditional virtues of the aristocracy. The economic scene was dominated by industry rather than agriculture, and the centre of political power was now clearly the House of Commons, rather than the Lords. As an Irish peer, even Palmerston remained in the Lower House, where debates were dominated by two obvious 'outsiders', the fashionable Jewish novelist, Disraeli, and the Scottish Liverpudlian economist, W. E. Gladstone. Their very appearances, as caricatured in the press, showed them representing the two strands of the triumphant bourgeoisie: the fashionable man-about-town and the puritanical businessman. In fact, both were, in their different ways, thoroughgoing professionals.

Throughout society, professionals were replacing aristocratic amateurs. The heroes of the Crimean War had not been the noble Lords Raglan, Cardigan and Lucan, who had let the cavelry be massacred at Balaclava, nor the Tory ministers, Lords Aberdeen and Derby, who had started the war, but the journalist, W. H. Russell, the nurse, Florence Nightingale, and the artillery engineers, who eventually brought victory. No wonder the emergent professional classes tended to patronise the aristocracy as an amusing anachronism, and a no more patronising portrait of an aristocrat can be imagined than Lord Dundreary. Aimiable, stupid, decorative and dim, physically and mentally unco-ordinated, he even lacks any real dramatic function within the action of the play, on to whose stage he has aimlessly wandered.

It is this feeling of bewilderment, linked with an unshakable sense of his own superiority, that gives Dundreary the childlike quality of his near contemporary, Alice in Wonderland. The world as viewed through the broken mirror of Dundreary's mind, has a logical naivety that expresses both the confidence and the confusion of the second half of Victoria's reign, when, although Britain dominated the world politically, the old intellectual certainties of social order and religious belief were being undermined by developments in science, technology and philosophy. Something of this moral confusion can be seen in Dundreary's casual and callous story of the shipwrecked mariner:

Well, one day he went a stroll with his mother-in-law – a woman he hated like poison – and he got shipwrecked – had a very jolly time of it – lived on a raft for about a fortnight – lived on anything they could pick up – oysters, sardines – I don't exactly know what – until at last they had to eat each other. They used to toss up who they should eat first – and he was a very lucky fellow; and when he was left alone with his mother-in-law, he tied her to the raft – legs dangling in the water, and everything pleasant like that. Then he stuck his pen-knife in his mother-in-law, and cut her up in slices, and ate her. He told me he enjoyed the old woman very much.[24]

Of course Sothern and his audiences claimed that this was just 'whimsical balderdash',[25] but, however unconscious it may have been, Dundreary was someone for whom all substance and standards had disappeared and for whom only the surface remained, he 'did not suffer so much from lack of intelligence as from chronic misdirection of it. Wherever there was a possibility of a double meaning he was bound to adopt the wrong one.'[26] The climax of this cosmic confusion came with the letter from his brother Sam.

Sothern had introduced this into his first American performances, and a short version appears in the script published by French's but over the years it developed into a virtuoso cadenza with more and more postscripts being added to satisfy the audience's cries of 'encore'. The manuscript version in the Folger Shakespeare Library must have lasted several minutes. The speech always started with the letter, but it could wander off in all directions:

> (*Reading*) 'I am afraid you did not receive my last letter.' Why this is his last letter! He's mad! Oh, I suppose he means his other last letter. 'For in my hurry I forgot to put any direction on the envelope.' Then that's the reason I didn't get it! Somebody must have got it! Some man's got that letter that's got no name – yet the postman couldn't go about asking any fellow he met if he didn't have a name. Oh Sam's mad, he's a lunatic. 'I have just been interrupted by two fellows, who want me to toss for drinks, so I have been tossing with them and I've got stuck.' Sam's dead – Sam's got stuck – I've got a dead lunatic for a brother – No he can't be dead, for here's some more on the other side – 'and got stuck for drinks'. Oh! why the devil couldn't he get stuck all on one side. He's mad.

Later he introduced one of his most famous gags, the childish riddle of proving he had eleven fingers:

> I have to be in London by the 10th. How many days is it from the 10th to the first? (*counts his fingers 1,2,3,4,5 – 6,7,8,9,10 – then counts back beginning with the little finger of the right hand*) 10,9,8,7,6 and 5 is 11. Eh stop. I'll try them the other way – Eh, I've only got 10 in that way (*counting again backwards*) 6 and 5 is 11. Ah, I've got some other fellow's finger. Now that's one of those things no one can understand.[27]

These silly Dundrearyisms became the rage of the early 1860s. They were like the meaningless catch phrases developed by popular comedians in the halls, and later on radio and television, and yet, like the Goon Show in the 1950s and Monty Python in the 1970s, there was a philosophical dimension to Dundreary's dislocated logic which caught the imagination of his age.

The Haymarket Theatre was one of the last bastions of the stock theatre system, and initially *Our American Cousin* was expected to play for no more than a few weeks, but there were new incentives to play as long as possible, and it eventually ran for over four hundred performances. Macready, in his retirement, was appalled: 'What would actors like Lewis, Elliston, Henderson, or Garrick think of a Lord Dundreary running four hundred consecutive nights!'[28] The play was always demanded of Sothern by the provincial companies he acted with, and he wrote sequels to the play: *Dundreary Married and Settled*, with the aid of H. J. Byron, and *Dundreary a Father*, with Maddison Morton. He even got John Oxenford to help write *Brother Sam* so that Dundreary's equally eccentric brother could appear. Dundreary fashions were taken up, with the weeping sideburns, the tartan trousers and the ankle-length coat. 'His dressing-room at the Haymarket was crowded with parcels sent by energetic haberdashers, who knew that if by wearing it upon the stage he would set the fashion for a certain make of necktie, or a particular pattern of shirt-cuff, or collar, their fortunes would be half made.'[29]

Unlike Buckstone or Mathews, however, Sothern's popularity was not really for himself, but for Dundreary. He was one of the first actors to get trapped in the typecasting of a specific character, rather than in a 'line of business', like T. P. Cooke, who had specialised in sailors, or William Farren, who had played old men from his youngest days. Sothern's characterisation, with its hoppety gait and lisping wouble-woos, was unique and unadaptable to other roles. Indeed, the character ran for the rest of his life, and although he had successes with *David Garrick* by Tom Robertson, and *The Crushed Tragedian* by H. J. Byron, Sothern could never shake off Dundreary for long. He was still performing him in the year of his death, 1881. No other actor could make anything of the role, although his son played it several times. This was partly because Sothern kept a strict control over the text, continually changing his own part, but provided follow actors with no more than 'sides'.

It was a great solo performance, originally created by an actor using an actor's means, but eventually it hardened into a predictable formula, and, with Sothern in the cast, *Our American Cousin* could never be an ensemble piece. By the 1870s it seemed contrived:

Sothern was obviously an artist, but he acted mechanically for all that; one could see his Dundreary nine hundred and ninety-nine times, or only once; so far as novelty was concerned, it made no difference. Precisely the same features attended it at every presentation. That means art, not nature. His wig and costume were not more unvarying than his gestures, expressions and inflections. I enjoyed every moment of him, but, for all that, he was like machine-made chairs or theorem painted walls, always and everlastingly the same. Some men would prefer a rounded play in which all the parts are good. Southern preferred a tad-pole play – all head and very thin tail, Preceded by cunningly prepared anecdotes, accompanied by claquers, and welcomed uproariously by friends, he hopped, skipped and jumped upon the stage, and went on with his monologue in a characteristic style, while his company, some of the best talent in the country, at times stood idly grouped as his background, and ingloriously earned their salaries by vigorously looking on. It was rubbish, no doubt, but most enjoyable rubbish for all that.[30]

The way in which Sothern's undoubted talents as an actor became restricted to this one role, and the way in which the part itself became petrified into a tradition, indicates the danger of what had originally been a triumph. By throwing over the text, and relying on his own creation, the actor had made a monster – an enjoyable monster, no doubt, but a monster for all that.

7

French naturalism
and English ensemble

Tom Taylor, who had provided Sothern with Dundreary and Robson with his first serious role in *Plot and Passion*, became 'resident' playwright for the Olympic over the next twelve years. Most of his pieces, like *Plot and Passion* (1854), *Still Waters Run Deep* (1855), *Retribution* (1856), *Payment on Demand* (1859) and the highly successful *The Ticket of Leave Man* (1863), were adapted from the French, and this was no coincidence, as the manager of the Olympic was Alfred Wigan, who had made his name playing Chateau-Renaud in *The Corsican Brothers*, and not only looked French but was well acquainted with the Paris stage. *The Corsican Brothers* was originally described as 'unEnglish', and this chapter starts by considering why the 'naturalistic' style of acting was generally attributed to the influence of France.

John Mitchell, manager of the St James's Theatre from 1842, had a policy of presenting international entertainments. He introduced German conjurors, American minstrels, Tyrolean singers, Fanny Kemble's Dramatic Readings (she was an American citizen) and P. T. Barnum's infant prodigies, Kate and Ellen Bateman, aged eight and six, in scenes from Shakespeare. More significantly, Mitchell established a French-speaking company and imported stars from Paris, like Frédérick Lemaître (1845, 1847 and 1852), and Rachel (1850, 1853 and 1855), and in 1845 he arranged an engagement in Paris for Macready and Helen Faucit. The influence of Frédérick and Rachel on performance style was, on the whole, inspirational rather than innovatory, as both were exponents of a 'passionate' acting style, like that of Kean or Macready. The fragile looking Rachel astonished her audiences by her vehement tirades in Racine, and the extravagant Frédérick delighted them with his subversive Robert Macaire and Ruy Blas, but their basic technique of physical gesture and vocal pyrotechnics was nothing new to English actors.

French naturalism and English ensemble

The French at the St James's did, however, present at least two modern plays which, after adaptation, influenced English acting in the 1850s. *La Fille de l'Avare* (after Balzac), performed in 1842 with Bouffé, was the original of Robson's *Daddy Hardacre*, and Frédérick's *La Dame de St Tropez* (1845) provided Alfred Wigan, in 1861, with a vehicle of 'nauseating naturalism', in which the hero gradually succumbed to arsenic poisoning. The Illustrated London News described Lemaître's performance as 'one of the most frightfully vivid pictures of gradual death resulting from poison that was ever witnessed – so terrible, yet so faithful in every detail... that the revolting nature of the drama was entirely lost sight of'.[1] Henry Morley's comment on Wigan's 1861 performance suggests that his acting too eclipsed the play – and quite rightly!: 'Mr Wigan, as an English actor, meets the French on their own strongest ground, and reproduces life and suffering, disease and death, in French dramatic form with a delicacy and fidelity that no living actor could surpass. Such art surely is worthy better material.'[2] This squeamish response to the 'pathological' text was repeated in 1879 when Charles Reade and Charles Warner created *Drink* from Zola's *L'Assommoir* with its minute deliniation of delirium tremens. Yet even before Zola, the English found French 'naturalistic' drama distasteful, disturbing and very very fascinating.

But if individual performances by the francophile Wigan owed much to the French, Charles Fechter's performances in English during the early 1860s had a greater influence on theatrical taste. After a comparatively successful career in Paris – creating the dei Franchi twins in *The Corsican Brothers* and Armand in Dumas's *La Dame aux Camélias* (1853) – Fechter came to London in 1860 and performed Ruy Blas in English at the Princess Theatre. The Times noted 'the *small delicate touches* by which he indicated his uneasiness under a master's control. . . the fire of passion *tempered* by the feelings of respectful devotion. . . the *concentration* of passionate rage',[3] which suggests the restraint of the new style of 'telling details' rather than the old rhetorical gestures. In 1861, Fechter performed Hamlet, which, by applying French techniques to an English classic, was one of the most influential performances of the century. The most obvious 'telling detail', which signalled Fechter's originality from the start, was his blond Danish wig, but the subtlety of his interpretation went beyond mere make-up:

> To him the meditative element in Hamlet's nature has seemed most essential. The manner in which he throws out his answers, like one unwillingly awakening from a continued abstraction, into which he presently relapses, is admirably thoughtful... The stronger passions intrench as little as possible upon his solitude, and he is chiefly occupied with a play of intellect. The birth of his thoughts is more visible than the influence of his emotions.[4]

George Henry Lewes, who was not entirely sympathetic to the new naturalism, welcomed Fechter's interpretation:

> His Hamlet was 'natural'; but this was not owing to the simple fact of its being more conversational and less stilted than usual... the reason was that he formed a tolerably true conception of Hamlet's nature, and could represent that conception... Naturalism truly means the reproduction of those details which *characterize the nature of the thing represented.* Realism means *truth*, not vulgarity.[5]

Lewes argued that Fechter succeeded in representing Hamlet because his personality and appearance coincided with his conception, but that when the actor attempted Othello, the following year, the 'naturalistic' style failed as his personality did not fit: 'He vulgarizes the part in the attempt to make it natural. Instead of the heroic, grave, impassioned Moor, he represents an excitable creole of our own day'(p. 119). Perhaps 'trivializing' would have been a better word than 'vulgarizing', in that Fechter wished to make the part recognisable to a contemporary audience, and therefore, more sympathetic and even, to use a twentieth-century term, more 'relevant'. Lewes pointed out the error:

> Othello tells us he is 'declining into the vale of years'; Fechter makes him young. Othello is black – the very tragedy lies there... Fechter makes him a half-cast, whose mere appearance would excite no repulsion in any woman out of America. Othello is grave, dignified, a man accustomed the the weight of great responsibilities, and the the command of armies; Fechter is unpleasantly familiar, paws Iago about like an overdemonstrative school-boy; shakes his hands on the slightest provocation; and bears himself like the hero of French *drame*, but not like a hero of tragedy (p. 128).

Lewes was intelligent enough to recognise that what upset him was not just the misinterpretation of a single role, but the whole shift of aesthetic concern implicit in Fechter's approach:

> [He] wished to make 'Othello' a *drame* such as would suit the Porte St Martin. The principle has doubtless been the same as that which, in a less degree, and under happier inspiration, made the success of 'Hamlet': the desire to be natural – the aim at realism. But here the confusion between realism and vulgarism works like poison. It is not consistent with the nature of tragedy to obtrude the details of daily life (p. 129).

It was the same use of telling details, in both production and performance, that Lewes had found unacceptable in Charles Kean's Shakespeare. Fechter too 'has allowed the acting manager to gain the upper hand. In his desire to be effective by means of small details of 'business', he has entirely frittered away the great effects of the drama... tragedy acts through the emotions, and not through the eye; whatever distracts attention from the passion of the scene is fatal' (p. 130).

Although this kind of naturalism was generally attributed to the French, Lewes, in his conservative criticism, appealed to a phrase of the great French actor, Talma: '*l'optique du théâtre*', to guard against both over- and under-playing:

> Everyone initiated into the secrets of the art of acting will seize at once the meaning of this luminous phrase *l'optique du théâtre*; and the uninitiated will understand how entirely opposed to all the purposes of art and all the secrets of effect would be the representation of passion in its *real* rather than in its *symbolic* expression: the red, swollen, and distorted features of grief, the harsh and screaming intonation of anger, are unsuited to art... The poet may tell us what is signified by the withdrawal of all life and movement from the face and limbs, describing the internal agitations or the deadly calm which disturb or paralyze the sufferer; but the painter, the sculptor, or actor must tell us what the sufferer undergoes, and tell us through the symbols of outward expression; the internal workings must be legible in the external symbols; and these external symbols must also have a certain grace and proportion to affect us aesthetically. All art is symbolical. If it presented emotion in its real expression it would cease to move us as art; sometimes cease to move us at all, or move us only to laughter (p. 91).

This was the danger of the 'nauseating naturalism' of *La Dame de St Tropez* and *L'Assommoir*, but, on the other hand, in a less sensational French-style domestic drama, like Tom Taylor's *The Settling Day*, produced by Alfred's brother Horace Wigan at the Olympic, 4 March 1865, the danger was insipid underplaying:

> In art it is as easy to be untrue by falling below as by rising above naturalness. The acting of Mr Horace Wigan, as the pious banker in 'The Settling Day', which suggested these remarks, is quite as much below the truth of nature in its tameness and absence of individuality, as it would have been above the truth had he represented the conventional stage hypocrite. He did not by exaggeration shock our common sense; but neither did he delight our artistic sense by his art. If his performance was without offence, it was also without charm (pp. 103-4).

Lewes was not alone in regretting the loss of high passion. Westland Marston was 'greatly pleased' by Fechter's Hamlet 'but not carried away. It was, perhaps, something to see a Hamlet who might have trodden Pall Mall or the Boulevards in our own day. Yet it was to lose much that this impression should have been more vivid than that of the Hamlet who encounters the ghost at midnight.' His verdict on Alfred Wigan, 'the most French of English actors', was that he was 'a versatile actor, large in his range of character, though minute in his treatment of it. He could not claim...breadth or robustness of style. As regards finish, quietude, finesse, and a power to seize the subtler traits of sentiment or humour, he was admirable.'[6] Mrs Wigan displayed a similar restrained quality and Charles Pascoe claimed she 'inaugurated, under Mr Alfred Wigan's auspices, that more finished school of acting which of recent years has happily become the guiding principle of the London theatre'.[7] Henry Morley was less happy with their influence. He described Tom Taylor's *Up at the Hills*, with which the Wigans began the 1860 season at the St James's, as having 'a half-serious domestic plot of the French school of intrigue and encounter, because it is in such drama that those excellent artists have achieved their best successes. The actors are displayed and the audience is interested. No more is desired.'[8]

Indeed, for a new generation of audiences no more was desired than to see elegant, urbane, and preferably witty middle-class characters dealing with domestic crises with moral rectitude and social propriety, as this reflected their own lives and concerns. There was a new generation of actors, who knew from first-hand experience such lives and such concerns. If Hamlet could be conceived of as treading Pall Mall, then why should not the pedestrians of Pall Mall attempt to tread the boards? For centuries actors had either been born into the profession or been driven into it by necessity; now the sons – though not yet the daughters – of merchants and professionals were beginning to take up acting. In this too the Wigan brothers were pioneers: their father had been a schoolmaster and they had received public school educations. E. A. Sothern had changed his name when he became an actor in 1847, and this practice was followed by most non-theatrical debutants in the 1850s and 1860s: Henry Irving, Squire Bancroft, William Kendal, Charles Wyndham, John Hare, Charles Kelly, William Terriss and Arthur Cecil were all stage-names.[9] If this indicates there was still social stigma attached to their choice of career, then it also explains the increasing preoccupation in plays of the second half of the century with questions of social respectability and class. Further, this influx of 'amateurs' dispelled some of the 'craft-mystery' of acting; in increasingly naturalistic plays normal behaviour, rather than artistic symbolism, was all that was required. This was the development that George Henry Lewes was afraid of, though a new generation of critics welcomed the change.

Clement Scott is remembered today as a reactionary, because of his hysterical rejection of Ibsen in the 1890s, but, when he began writing criticism for *The Sunday Times* in 1863, he cast Lewes as the reactionary. Scott saw the French style as a radical challenge to the conservative self-interest of managers such as Webster, Buckstone and Chatterton. He described it as a clash between protectionism and free trade:

> I had attached myself to a theatrical journal...whose principles were violently and obstinately Conservative... [My proprietor] held that to mention a French play or a foreign actor in any shape or form was to insult our artists, and 'to take the bread out of their mouths'. Chauvinism in dramatic art was rampant... I had to feel my way very gingerly indeed to the free-trade

doctrine that I was determined to preach one day or other from the house tops... I knew this was to be the great fight, to give free trade to the theatre and the music hall, which were both degraded by the policy of protection. In this good work such bold and determined fighters as John Hollingshead and Edmund Yates had preceded me; and when the time came for the battle royal which ended in that memorable breakfast at the Crystal Palace [10 July 1871] to the full company of the Comédie Français, with speeches by Lord Granville, Lord Dufferin, and Alfred Wigan, I fought side by side with such champions for free trade as Joseph Knight, Herman Merivale, Lewis Wingfield, W. S. Gilbert, W. R. McConnell, and many more. *Finis coronat opus.*[10]

From this list of journalists and literary gentlemen it is clear that a new section of society was concerning itself with the development of the theatre, and on a wider scale than Macready's friends, Dickens, Forster and Bulwer Lytton, who had tried to revive Shakespearian traditions in the 1840s. Scott wrote that one of the 'strongest influences' on his becoming a critic was 'being elected a member of the Arundel Club... where I met the flower of Bohemia Land in those days, Bohemian authors, Bohemian actors, Bohemian barristers, artists, men of science, solicitors – all the very "pick of the basket"' (p. 405). At literary and social clubs, like the Arundel, the Savage and the Garrick, leading actors and theatre managers could meet on equal terms with the more 'respectable professions', and it was here that theatrical fashion was to be determined, and, via such crusading journalists as the young Clement Scott, the public was to be manipulated. John Colman was horrified at the gall of these amateurs:

> Young gentlemen, with the down not yet fledged on their lips, who knew as much of art as the present writer does of Sanscrit, maintained that French art was the beau-ideal of perfection, and that English actors, with rare exceptions, and those principally amateur friends of the writers, were not artists at all. The self-constituted mission of these airy youths was to deride, to ridicule, and to hold up to contempt everything noble and manly – everything which generations of educated men and women had been taught to esteem and admire.[12]

Out of this self-congratulatory atmosphere of Bohemia came Tom Robertson's play *Society*. Its production at the Prince of Wales's theatre in 1865 was acclaimed by Scott, in rose-coloured retrospect, as 'The Dawn of the Renaissance'.[12] Moreover, the French critic Augustin Filon also wrote that 'From that evening dates not only the success of the Princes of Wales's Theatre, but a new era for English Comedy – the era of Robertson.'[13] Indeed the play did mark a change, but it would be wrong to overestimate its originality, or to underestimate the influence of traditional English comedy acting on its cast, the influence of Mathews, Vestris, E. A. Sothern, H. J. Byron and even the Wigans.[14]

Squire Bancroft, who was in part responsible for this 'Renaissance' at the Prince of Wales's, was seventeen in 1858 when he saw Sothern's first ever performance of Lord Dundreary in New York. He was so impressed that he kept the play-bill, and gave it to Sothern six years later, when, having become an actor himself, he supported him at the Dublin Theatre Royal. Before that, he had delighted an audience in Plymouth with his own performance of Dundreary, 'as much like the original as it possibly could be, and has shown not only a wonderful amount of imitative talent, but an appreciation of character without which imitation would be mere mimicry, and which stamps him as an able actor'.[15] Bancroft's father had been a oil merchant who died young, thus denying his son the university education he had been brought up to expect. After failing to make his fortune in America, Bancroft returned to London and used the example of Sothern, another merchant's son, to persuade his family to accept his becoming an actor.

> Often as I went to the play, dearly as I loved the theatre, until I tried to become an actor I had never known one, and very rarely seen one off the stage. And so it has been with many of my comrades, Henry Irving, John Hare, Charles Wyndham, W. H. Kendal, Charles Coghlan, John Clayton, Arthur Cecil, Johnston Forbes-Robertson, William Terriss, and E. S. Willard, as also with some of a later generation, a few of whose names pass at once through my mind, Herbert Beerbohm Tree, George Alexander, Cyril Maude, Arthur Bourchier, Lewis Waller, and Charles Hawtrey – all of whom, I believe were unconnected with the theatre as I was (p. 33).

Virtually all these actors, apart from Irving, were to be associated with modern drama of the 'well-made' variety – drawing-room comedy, gentlemanly melodrama, socially realistic drame – the new repetoire of Robertson, Grundy, Sardou, Pinero, H. A. Jones and Oscar Wilde. It was with the first of these, Robertson, that Bancroft was to be intimately concerned.

Although the new generation of actors had not been reared from their cradles in the traditions of the theatre, most did serve an appenticeship with provincial stock companies – Bancroft played 346 parts in four years. Many of them also married actresses with the professional experience they lacked. Mrs Wigan, Mrs Kendal, Mrs Boucicault, Mrs Herman Vezin and Mrs Bancroft all greatly advanced their husbands' careers. John Colman suggested that Mrs Wigan was 'a very pushing, sagacious, active, indefatigable woman', who manipulated her husband's career: 'he thought he was acting of his own volition, when in point of fact he was carrying out her wishes'.[16] In Bancroft's case too his wife was for several years the dominant partner in their professional relationship. He met Marie Wilton in 1864, while acting in Liverpool. She was two years older than him and had many more years' professional experience.

As a child she had played Fleance for Macready's Macbeth, had impressed Charles Kemble with her Prince Arthur, and had established her reputation at sixteen by playing the mountebank's boy, Henri, in Charles Dillon's celebrated melodrama *Belphegor* (1856). By 1865 she was the star of H. J. Byron's Strand Theatre burlesques, which parodied hit plays in rhyming couplets and with absurd puns. Marie Wilton performed her soubrette or breeches parts in a style that was as conventionally 'arch' as Buckstone's was 'droll'

During 1865 she approached several London managers for work in legitimate comedy rather than in burlesque, but without success. She decided therefore, with the aid of a thousand pounds from her brother-in-law, to buy her own theatre. Engaging H. J. Byron as business partner and resident author, she took over the dilapidated Queen's Theatre off Tottenham Court Road. They renamed it the Prince of Wales's, and engaged a troop of straight actors, which included Squire Bancroft and another young 'non-theatrical' from the Liverpool Theatre Royal, John Hare. Liverpool had been Hare's first engagement, and this early London contract meant he had less 'stock' experience than his friend Bancroft. He was, however, a clever mimic and quickly developed into a remarkable 'modern-style' character actor.

It was in Liverpool that the company first opened Robertson's *Society* before bringing it to London on 11 November 1865. In Pinero's thinly disguised dramatisation of the founding of the Prince of Wales's Theatre, *Trelawny of the 'Wells'* (1898), Robertson, in the guise of Tom Wrench, is attributed with the crusading zeal of Clement Scott. However the playwright stumbled on his successful formula accidentally and developed it especially to suit the young company. Robertson, eldest son of the manager of the Lincoln circuit, had been employed as prompter by Vestris and Mathews at the Lyceum in 1854, and he obviously appreciated the scenic realism and ensemble playing that they had pioneered in the thirties. In many ways the development of the Prince of Wales's under Wilton and Bancroft, seemed to follow the earlier pattern: Wilton, like Vestris, had specialised in burlesque; Bancroft, like Mathews, was as much at home in society as on the stage. But, whereas Vestris and Mathews failed to develop the vein of legitimate comedy opened to them by *London Assurance*, the Bancrofts were to exploit the Robertsonian comedy so as to change the whole complexion of drama in the late Victorian period. Their success must be largely attributed to their finding an audience ready for the new style.

Society had originally been rejected by Buckstone as 'rubbish' before its try-out in Liverpool. In fact the play made use of many 'Haymarket types', such as the eccentric aristocrat and the pretentious bourgeois, the scheming hypocrite and the sentimental moralist, but there was a topicality in its setting – a Fleet Street public house, the Owl's Roost, filled, like the Arundel Club or Savages, with a crowd of Bohemian journalists, critics and would-be men-of-letters. The *Daily Telegraph* described it as 'a clever, sketchy picture of modern men and manners, dashed off in a spirited style, and giving perhaps a new view of some of the graduations in the social scale'.[18] If the production was not 'got up' with all the naturalistic details that were to become a speciality of the Prince of Wales's, at least the vivacious young actors seemed as much at home in the upper-class drawing-room of Lord Ptarmigan, as Robertson was amongst the Bohemians of the Owl's Roost. It was this sense of easy familiarity which particularly appealed to the new socially confident audiences. *Society* was followed by *Ours*, set in the Crimean War (1866); *Caste*, his most famous play (1867); *Play* (1868); *School*, which ran for 381 performances (1869); and *MP* (1870). A revival of *Ours* ran for 230 performances in 1870, and in 1871, six months after the author's death, *Caste* received 195 performances.

The special quality brought to these plays was not just a naturalistic restraint, like that of the Wigans, but an *ensemble* style that grew out of the general policy of the theatre. When Horace Wigan took over the management of the Olympic in 1864 he had promised a menu of great variety: 'I shall not exclude any dish from the Olympic 'spread'... from the whipped cream of burlesque... to the *pièce de résistance* in the shape of drama, with removes of comedy, vaudeville, farce and comedietta.'[19] The Bancrofts rejected such variety in favour of specialisation, and thus developed a consistent 'house-style'.

Many aspects of society at this time were marked by specialisation. Across London, as it continued its sprawling growth, different localities took on a particular class complexion; in trade, retailers and manufacturers developed sophisticated specialities; in the professions restrictive associations were introduced with formal qualifications; and in the theatre different companies developed special house-styles and repertoires, while variety acts were banished to the music-halls. Marie Wilton had always wanted to appeal to the professional family audience of Bloomsbury, Mayfair, Regent's Park, Belgravia and Kensington. And although the immediate locality of the old Queens Theatre on Tottenham Court Road was hardly fashionable, it was convenient for West End residential areas. She also decorated her auditorium appropriately:

> The house looked very pretty, and, although everything was done inexpensively, had a bright and bonnie appearance, and I felt proud of it. The curtains and carpets were of a cheap kind, but in good taste. The stalls were light blue, with lace antimacassars over them; this was the first time such things had ever been seen in a theatre. The pampered audiences of the present day [1909], accustomed to the modern luxurious playhouses, little know of how

much my modest undertaking was the pioneer, and would hardly credit that a carpet in the stalls was, until then, unknown.[20]

The success of the Robertson plays led to a policy of presenting only one attraction a night, so patrons could dine before, or supper after, the performance. The size of the company was restricted to that of a single cast for as long as a particular play ran, and – with a policy of high seat prices (6s stalls eventually rising to 10s in 1874) and the introduction of matinee performances from 1878 – all this meant high profits. The Bancrofts were so financially successful that they could retire in 1885, when Squire Bancroft was only forty-four. When he died in 1926 he left over £174,000.[21]

This prosperity was shared with the company, and salaries rose several-fold during their management. For instance, George Honey received £18 a week when he first played Eccles in *Caste* in 1867, but was paid £60 for the revival in 1871. A further indication of the increasingly professional status of the Prince of Wales's actors was the abolition of benefit performances, and the 'humiliation' of the weekly treasury-call when 'every one had to assemble on Saturday mornings outside the treasury at a certain hour – carpenters, ballet girls, cleaners, players, dressers, musicians, mixed up together'; from now on the treasurer was to wait on the performers, rather than their waiting upon him.[22] Michael Baker has summed up these changes, initiated by the Bancrofts and followed over the next ten or twenty years in similar fashionable theatres, such as the Royal Court, St James's, the Lyceum and Her Majesty's:

> This group [of regular London actors], swelled by the ranks of middle-class recruits entering the theatre after 1860 in growing numbers, accounted for an increasing proportion of the total profession by 1890. Their real earnings were unquestionably higher than they had been in 1830, their hours were visibly shorter owing to the reduction in regular rehearsal time and in the length of the nightly bill, and their status within their companies and in society now rested upon a more assured foundation. These improvements had important implications for the growing respectability of acting as a profession, for it was just this group which could be identified with the increasingly middle-class image of the theatre. In almost all respects, pensions apart, their conditions of work now associated them with the salaried professional man as opposed to the wage-earner.[23]

The increased respectability of the profession also helped undermine the star-plus-supers method of production. From the relatively small company of the Prince of Wales's, several actors eventually set up as managers: they had all been equally well educated, and they came from a class that expected men to take on organisational responsibility. John Hare, Charles Cochlan, Frank Archer, Arthur Cecil, Forbes-Robertson, W. H. Kendal, William Terriss and Arthur Pinero all had experience at the Prince of Wales's. Neither Marie Wilton nor Squire Bancroft had extraordinary star quality themselves, and did not wish to dominate the stage with passionate displays, like Irving or Bernhardt, or monopolise their audience, like the comedians Buckstone or J. L. Toole. Augustin Filon noted that:

> It has been curious to observe at the Prince of Wales's how performers, who elsewhere had made but little mark, have acquired good habits in that whole-some atmosphere of dramatic art. No theatre had more often sustained the inevitable losses which must follow the secession of actors; yet, when the changes which necessarily came about deprived the management one by one of their services, the loss, which threatened to be severe, was so ably met as to be scarcely perceptible. [24]

The Bancrofts' example was followed most notably by John Hare, who left them in 1874 to manage the Royal Court. He also practised the 'self-abnegation' which 'had, throughout their management, been a strong point with the Bancrofts. How frequently they strengthen their admirable productions by appearing themselves in small parts.'[25] Ellen Terry, who acted at both the Prince of Wales's and the Royal Court, praised Hare particularly for his concern for *ensemble* playing:

> Mr Hare was one of the best stage managers that I have met during the whole of my long experience in the theatre. He was snappy in manner, extremely irritable if anything went wrong, but he knew what he wanted and got it. No one has ever surpassed him in the securing of a perfect *ensemble*... The members of his company were his, body and soul, while they were rehearsing. He gave them fifteen minutes for lunch, and any actor or actress who was foolish or unlucky enough to be a minute late, was sorry after-wards. [26]

Ensemble playing was not just a matter of respectful interaction between intelligent actors, it depended on the instruction of a director; not just a *metteur en scène* like Charles Kean or Saxe-Meiningen, who set the moves and drilled the supers, but a sensitive director who could advise about interpretation, style and scale. John Hare was such director, but at the Prince of Wales's it had been Tom Robertson. According to Hare, Robertson

> had a gift peculiar to himself... of conveying by some rapid almost electric suggestion to the actor an insight into the character assigned to him. As nature was the basis of his own work, so he sought to make actors understand it should be theirs.[27]

When he was too ill to visit the theatre during the preparation of *MP* the actors took extra pains; 'We rehearsed it persistently and patiently for six weeks, a thing then quite unknown, and a longer time than we had yet given to any play. Towards the end we used to meet at his house and show poor Robertson, act by act, the results of our labours.'[28]

Although in content the new drama was hardly the 'Dawn of a Renaissance' that Scott had proclaimed, the new dramatists were to have a very different relationship with their casts than the hacks who had serviced Macready or Buckstone. Then the actors and the stage manager had shared the responsibility for production, but now the playwrights began to insist on personally directing the cast, or, at least, inserting prescriptive stage-directions into the text. Henry Arthur Jones always insisted that his plays were to be 'played absolutely without deletion or addition':

> Threats and entreaties will not move him. He is adamant. At rehearsals he insists that, as the author, he is the person who alone knows the exact intention of each scene, and freely criticises the movements, gestures, and intonations of even the leading performers.[29]

W. S. Gilbert, whose early farce, *Allow Me To Explain* (1867), and Robertsonian comedy, *Sweethearts* (1874), were both produced at the Prince of Wales's, has often been described as an autocratic director-playwright, and he acknowledged Robertson as his model:

> I frequently attended his rehearsals and learnt a great deal from his method of stage management, which in those days was quite a novelty, although most pieces are now stage-managed on the principles he introduced. I look upon stage management as now understood, as having been invented by him.[30]

In fact Gilbert had more reason to instruct his actors than Robertson, in that his style was not 'naturalistic' but ironical, and his roles had to be performed with a certain detachment if the comedy was not to seem cynical or tasteless. Augustin Filon contrasted the two dramatists as 'conformist' and 'radical':

> Robertson is a craftsman brought up in the theatre, amenable to outside influences; he collaborates with his actors and the public – one may say, with his entire generation. The ideas of his time, good, bad and indifferent, exude from him at every pore. He becomes, therefore, unconsciously, a representative man and the leader of a school. Where Robertson is a natural product, a symptom, Gilbert is a freak, an accident... As to the bent of his mind, its originality was evident from the first... So cruel a farce [as *Engaged*] had never been seen. The public was accustomed in farce to two or three comic characters, to satire at the expense of two or three ridiculous types. Here was a caricature of all mankind. The spectators laughed, but the jest was too bitter for their palate. It was at once too unreal and too true.[31]

In other words, unless Gilbert's comic vision was cast in the absurd mould of burlesques, such as *Pygmalion and Galatea* (Haymarket, 1871) and *Thespis; or, the Gods Grown Old* (Gaiety, 1871), or of the famous Savoy operas, it seemed subversive and uncomfortable – 'too true', unless perceived as being 'unreal'. Robertson, on the other hand, as a 'natural product, a symptom', was reassuringly recognisable. Thus as his actors – and their audiences – were in general sympathy with his 'naturalistic' vision, it was not difficult for them to find a 'naturalistic' style of performance. Gilbert, in order to communicate his jaundiced viewpoint, had to coach his casts to the correct level of satirical exaggeration. George Bernard Shaw, too, found that he had to instruct his actors, in order to achieve the ironical detatchment needed for Shavian satire.

Perhaps the most dictatorial director-playwright of the late nineteenth century was Arthur Pinero. After acting in Irving's company at the Lyceum, he joined the Bancrofts at the Haymarket in 1881 and from both managements he learnt to appreciate the power of the single directorial imagination. In the eighties and nineties his plays were produced either by John Hare at the Court Theatre, or by George Alexander at the St James's; at both theatres Pinero insisted on a rigid control over the interpretation:

> All that we call 'business' is in the printed matter that I carry into the theatre. Why should it be altered when it has all been carefully and even laboriously thought out, every detail of it, during the process of construction? The movements of a man and what he has to say are inseperable. Expression is multiform and simultaneous; to alter one phrase is to weaken all. I try to think of these things beforehand. Rehearsal is not – or certainly should not be – a time for experiment. It is to prepare for the acting together of the players, not for the making of the play.[32]

Nor did Pinero rely solely on the precision of his stage-directions to determine the interpretation. Irene Vanburgh described how in rehearsals for *His House In Order* (St James's, 1906), 'taking it sentence by sentence, I may almost say word by word, he guided us through that scene like a true master knowing ever word of the play by heart. Not one syllable could you alter without his immediate correction'.[33] If one reason for this authorial direction was to achieve a particular style of playing or an attitude, as in the comedies of Gilbert or Shaw, a second was to assist in the correct *ensemble* balance between performers – Pinero's 'acting together of the players' – particularly if some were newcomers to the profession, without the traditional skills of the professional stock actor.

This increase in the dramatists' authority also arose from a general shift in cultural attitudes. Walter Houghton, in *The Victorian Frame of Mind* (1957), argues that during the 1860s and 1870s there was an increase in 'cultural dogmatism' in reaction to the disturbing theories of Darwinism and Revolutionary Socialism. Neither ideology directly threatened the material prosperity of Victorian capitalism, but they gnawed away at the intellectual certainties of the age. Though revolution was now unthinkable in England, anarchists were exploding bombs all over Europe, and though science had created the technology which had made Britain the most wealthy and powerful nation in the world, scientists were now questioning the very doctrine of creation. There was little political or economic action the Victorians could, or needed to, take to protect their physical supremacy, but they did want the intellectual and spiritual reassurance provided by the authority of a cultural leader or expert. The individualism of the late Victorian period was not that of the rebellious visionaries of the Romantic era, but of dogmatists who propagated their own opinions with all the authority of absolute laws. Houghton claims the Victorians found such assertiveness natural, even attractive: 'They liked it. One might even say they asked for it. The prophets who put on the mantle of infallibility did so as much from public demand as from a personal sense of fitness.'[34]

Macaulay expounded the inevitable laws of history that had evolved the British constitution; Ruskin proclaimed the infallibility of his critical judgement of the visual arts; Carlyle pontificated on every subject under the sun. Laws of behaviour, moral and social, were inculcated by philanthropic autocrats like Charles Kingsley, Arnold of Rugby, and Samuel Smiles. Those who expressed ambiguous ideas, courted controversy, or seemed to hold double standards, were distrusted and even castigated as free-thinkers. Certain names were banned in the more orthodox homes – Darwin, Mill, Zola, Bradlaugh the atheist, Parnell the adulterer, Rosetti the Pre-Raphaelite (until Ruskin proclaimed him safe), and Whistler the Impressionist (who won only a farthing's damages from Ruskin's libels). Thus it was with the radical playwrights Ibsen and Shaw, castigated by Clement Scott, who saw himself as the Ruskin of theatre criticism, while within the theatrical profession itself little tolerance was extended to such 'cranks' as William Poel and Gordon Craig.

Returning to the main theme of this chapter – the *ensemble* of cup-and-saucer drama – we can see a similar pattern of traditional standards and techniques being challenged and replaced, not by a genuinely free, anarchic, or radical style, but by the autocratic vision of the dogmatic playwright-director. The *ensemble* of the old stock companies, such as the Haymarket, Phelps's Sadler's Wells, and the best provincial Theatres Royal, had been created by shared methods and purposes. The new *ensemble* companies, however, considered the old emotional acting crude, but they could only achieve a harmonious style themselves by submitting their individual creativity to the guidance of the single authoritative director, whether he were a playwright, like Robertson, Gilbert or Pinero, or an actor-manager, like Hare, Irving or Tree. John Colman, a diehard stock actor, was with great reluctance persuaded by the playwright Charles Reade to go to Drury Lane 'to see the Meiningen people, who appeared to interest him'; such an autocratically directed company held little interest for Colman.[35]

In 1880 the death of stock theatre in London was symbolically confirmed when the Bancrofts took over that bastion of the old comedy, the Haymarket Theatre. Buckstone had retired in 1877, passing the lease on to the American comedian John S. Clarke. He was a comedian of the old school, who even attempted to revive Liston's farcial characters, like Paul Pry, but he did not have the affectionate following of Buckstone, his repertoire seemed hopelessly outdated, and none of the new plays he introduced as manager were successful. After the 1879 season he was prepared to sell out. Meanwhile, the Prince of Wales's Theatre was running into trouble with fire and safety regulations – to an extent the Bancrofts' improvements had never been more than cosmetic – and suffering from competition from new West End theatres offering similar 'society' plays. The Bancrofts considered moving to the St James's, but John Hare and the Kendals – all ex-Prince of Wales's actors – beat him to it, so Squire Bancroft took over the lease of the Haymarket from Clarke on the understanding that he would refurbish it.

The redesigning of the Haymarket, which opened on 31 January 1880 with a revival of Bulwer Lytton's comedy *Money*, was remarkable in several ways, all of which indicated a profound change of policy. The first was controversial, in that stalls completely replaced the pit. Expensive, upholstered, reservable individual seats with arms replaced the democratic benches that dated back to the Restoration theatre. In 1809, when Kemble had altered the traditional seating and prices at Covent Garden, the 'OP Riots' had lasted some two months, but in 1880, although Squire Bancroft faced a noisy demonstration with cries of 'Where's the pit?', after fifteen minutes the protesters wore themselves out. When Mrs Bancroft made her entrance 'it was to a roar of affectionate welcome, hearty and prolonged – as was my own, I may add, when I appeared as actor, not as manager'.[36] Thus the old stock theatre capitulated to the new middle-class audience.

The size of the Haymarket, however, was not ideal for the intimate comedies the Bancrofts brought with them from the Prince of Wales's. Reviewing *MP*, on 25 April 1870, *The Times* had written: 'In a more spacious theatre, and by an audience more largely leavened with the usual pit and gallery public, these light and sparkling pieces would probably be voted slow in movement, slight in texture, and weak in interest.'[37] Now that they had moved into a much larger building, Henry James was 'not sure this humorous couple have bettered themselves with the public by leaving the diminutive play-house'; nevertheless, he warmly approved of their refurbishments:

Mr Bancroft has transformed the Haymarket – which was an antiquated and uncomfortable house with honourable traditions, which had latterly declined – into the perfection of a place of entertainment. Brilliant, luxuriant, softly cushioned and perfectly aired, it is almost entertainment enough to sit there and admire the excellent device by which the old-fashioned and awkward proscenium has been suppressed and the stage set all around in an immense gilded frame, like that of some magnificent picture. Within this frame the stage, with everything that is upon it, glows with a radiance that seems the very atmosphere of comedy.[38]

This innovation in the design of the proscenium arch marked a crucial change in the actor/audience relationship. From now on the world of the stage was separated from that of the auditorium, spectators could sit back in comfortable anonymity watching a different world through a 'fourth wall', safe from the winking, leering, button-holing humour of a Buckstone and Keeley, or a Bedford and Wright. The fastidious Henry James may have felt that the stage glowed with an atmosphere of comedy, but it was a very different atmosphere from that of the early Victorian theatre, which from the 1880s was banished from theatres presenting legitimate drama to the stages of the music-hall.

8

Caste
by T. W. Robertson

Prince of Wales's Theatre, 6 April 1867

THE HON. GEORGE D'ALROY	Mr Frederick Younge
CAPTAIN HAWTREE	Mr Squire Bancroft
ECCLES	Mr George Honey
SAM GERRIDGE	Mr John Hare
THE MARQUISE DE ST MAUR	Miss Sophie Larkin
ESTHER ECCLES	Miss Lydia Foote
POLLY ECCLES	Miss Marie Wilton
	[Mrs Bancroft]

Act I

George D'Alroy and his friend Captain Hawtree wait for Esther Eccles, a chorus-line dancer, whom George wants to marry. The arrival of Esther's drunkard father prompts Hawtree to warn against the danger of marrying beneath one's class. Esther's sister Polly and her 'intended', Sam make Hawtree even more embarrassed when he stays for tea. The scene ends with George proposing to Esther, as father Eccles staggers in from the pub.

Act II

George and Esther are married, but he has not told his mother, the Marquise of the marriage; nor told Esther he has been posted to India with his regiment. The Marquise arrives to see him off, and is horrified to meet his new wife, and especially her relatives. When urged to buckle on George's sword, Esther faints.

Act III

George has been killed in India, and Esther is bringing up their child alone with help from Polly, who is soon to marry Sam, and no help from Eccles. The Marquise arrives and offers to take her grandson, Esther refuses. Hawtree announces that George has in fact survived, and he now returns. Polly breaks the news to Esther, and the couple are reunited. The Marquise is reconciled with Esther, but not with Eccles, whom Hawtree suggests should be packed off to Jersey, where spirits are cheap, to drink himself to death.

Caste is a sentimental exploration of class sensibilities. Squire Bancroft described its appeal to the new middle-class audience:

> Robertson succeeded in concentrating an accumulation of incident and satire more interesting and more poignant that might have been found in all the sensation dramas of the last half century. The play had that hearty human interest that springs from the vigorous portraiture of character and the truthful representation of life and manners as they really are. The characters looked and talked so like beings of everyday life that they were mistaken for such, and the audience had a curiosity to know how they were getting on after the fall of the curtain.[1]

This belief in the play's 'after-life' is similar to the reality fans attribute to characters in television soap-operas, and, indeed, the dramatic formula was much the same: comical business alternates with emotional situations, in settings that seem realistically detailed but which actually exclude many intractable contradictions of real life. A close reading of the text reveals that much of Robertson's apparent originality is superficial; his characters are variations on traditional types, and his 'poignant incidents' are as contrived as in any of 'the sensation dramas of the last half century'. It was neither psychological complexity nor social analysis that made the play seem 'modern', but the look of the sets and the style of the acting.

The Eccles's living-room looked astonishingly 'real' to an audience used to furniture painted on to canvas backcloths. The 'telling details', given emphasis in these stage-directions, were original in both practicality and appropriateness:

> *A plain set chamber, paper soiled. A window centre with* practicable *blind; street backing and iron railings. Door practicable up right, when opened showing street door (practicable). Fireplace centre of left-hand piece;* two hinged gas-burners *on each side of mantelpiece. Sideboard cupboard, cupboards in recess left,* tea-things, teapot, tea-caddy, tea-tray, etc. *on it. Long table before fire; old piece of carpet and rug down; plain chairs; bookshelf back left, a small table under it with* ballet-shoe and skirt *on it;* bunch of benefit bills *hanging under bookshelf. Theatrical printed portraits framed, hanging about; chimney glass clock; box of lucifers and ornaments on mantelshelf;* kettle on hob, and fire laid; *doormats on the outside* of the door. *Bureau centre of right-hand piece. Rapping is heard at door,* the handle *is then shaken as curtain rises. The door* is unlocked.[2]

During the first act realistic use was made of all these props, from George's unlocking the door and lighting the fire, to Polly's making the tea, when Captain Hawtree had some comic business deciding whether to put the kettle on the floor, on the mantelpiece, or on top of a plate of ham.

There had been fooling with food in *Box and Cox*, but *Caste*'s teatime comedy arose from characterful interaction, not simple slapstick, as Robertson explained: 'It seems a simple thing for a young lady to hand a young gentleman a cup of tea, but all depends on the manner.'[3] Augustin Filon described the interplay: 'When circumstances – quite simple and natural – lead to Hawtree's taking tea in humble East End lodgings... nearly all the fun of the scene comes from his mute expression of continual astonishment.'[4] Stage-directions show the scene was played broadly, but its use of real props was rather more subtle than the 'biz' of the Haymarket comedians, and Bancroft's use of facial expressions was not quite 'mugging':

> SAM *cuts enormous slice of bread, and hands it on point of knife to* HAWTREE. *Cuts small lump of butter, and hands it on point of knife to* HAWTREE, *who looks at it through eye-glass, then takes it.* SAM *then helps himself.* POLLY *meantime has poured out tea in two cups, and one saucer for SAM, sugars them, and then hands cup and saucer to* HAWTREE, *who has both hands full. He takes it awkwardly, and places it on table.* POLLY, *having only one spoon, tastes SAM's tea, then stirs* HAWTREE's, *attracting his attention by so doing. He looks into his teacup.* POLLY *stirs her own tea, and drops spoon into* HAWTREE's *cup, causing it to spurt in his eye. He drops eye-glass and wipes his eyes.*[5]

This may read like E. A. Sothern as Dundreary, and the signalling of the character's reactions seems heavy-handed, but Bancroft had taken particular care to avoid the 'silly-ass' stereotype that his role might have suggested in favour of real-life behaviour as he observed it:

> During the early rehearsals, I was dining on a Sunday evening with Sothern... I found myself seated next to a soldier whose appearance faintly lent itself to a make-up for Hawtree. With some diplomacy I afterwards went to Younge [playing D'Alroy] and suggested... that he should be the fair man. He asked how on earth he could do such a thing, being the sentimental hero, he of course was intended to be dark; while I was equally compelled to be fair, and wear long flaxen whiskers in what he called the dandy or fop, a conventional stage outrage of those days, for whose death I think I must hold myself responsible... I was by more than one actor thought to be mad for venturing to clothe what was supposed to be, more or less, a comic part, in the quietest of fashionable clothes, and to appear as a pale-faced man with short, straight black hair. The innovation proved to be as successful as it was daring.[6]

Bancroft's restraint arose partly from a lack of histrionic range; like many of the new generation, his style merely exploited his own personality. According to Archer:

> Mr Bancroft is an actor of limited range, but, within that range, of remarkable intelligence, refinement and power. His face is not very mobile and his features are so marked that the most elaborate make up is powerless to dis-

guise them, while his voice, though strong and resonant, is of a somewhat harsh and croaking quality. These peculiarities, combined with his tall and spare figure, were of the greatest service to him in embodying the languid, cynico-sentimental, military heroes of Robertson.[7]

The Saturday Review of 19 January 1878, writing of his performance in Sardou's *Dora*, suggested that Bancroft, like Alfred Wigan, had 'an unusual capacity for *indicating* rather than expressing a passionate emotion'.[8] Hawtree demanded no more, but Frederick Younge's role of D'Alroy was more emotional.

Younge, a long acquaintance of Tom Robertson, was really too old for the part, but he succeeded by taking the following line as his key: 'I know I'm a fool, and my having a thick tongue, and lisping makes me seem more foolish than I am.' Clement Scott praised his nerve in adopting the lisp, and for refusing to underplay potentially embarrassing scenes:

> Fred Younge was the only D'Alroy I have ever seen who dared to play the part with a lisp. It gave the exact manner of the man. And the scene with the baby... was the most touchingly natural, and pathetic thing, I have ever seen on the modern stage. Picture it! A great, hulking, handsome, well-bred officer, who becomes a 'great big baby' again, lisping inarticulate sentences over the infant that he could have crushed to death in his great, strong, manly arms. The modern generation will doubtless say, 'What rot!' But I said then, and repeat now, 'How true!'... [other actors] for the most part, thought the scene childish and feared the laugh. There never was a question of laugh with Fred Younge. There were many tears instead, I can assure you.[9]

Alfred Darbyshire, describing a provincial production, also drew attention to the emotional impact of physical business, without cliché dialogue to signal its significance:

> Robertson had a peculiar way occasionally of relying upon action only, accompanied by no vocal efforts... Those who saw Ada Dyas try to buckle on [her husband's] sword and belt will never forget the force of expression conveyed by action and facial working... On D'Alroy's return he finds...that various household comforts have been provided. On asking how this happened all heads turned to the man who believed in caste... D'Alroy walked up to his friend, Captain Hawtrey [*sic*.], and in dead silence grasped him by the hand. If any words were spoken they were drowned in applause. From that moment the audience loved the man on whom they had looked as a conceited nincompoop.[10]

Henry James was one of the 'modern generation' who, even at the time, found this rather banal, when he compared the 'natualistic' acting of England with that of France:

> A clever French lady narrated to us her impressions of a representation of *Caste*... One of the principal incidents in this piece is the leavetaking of a

young officer and his newly wedded wife... The pangs of parting, as the scene is played, are so protracted and insisted upon that our friend at last was scandalized; and when the young couple were indulging in their twentieth embrace – 'Mais, baissez donc le rideau!' she found herself crying – 'Put down the curtain! Such things are not done in public!' – while the company about her applauded so great a stroke of art, or rather, we ought to say, of nature, – a distinction too often lost sight of in England.[11]

James concluded that, although English naturalism may have owed much to French models, it over-indulged displays of emotion. London audiences were more sentimental, they lacked the refined irony – or cynicism – of the Parisians:

> The amount of kissing and hugging that goes on in London in the interest of drama is quite incalculable... Of such demonstrations French comedians are singularly sparing... The English would be greatly – and naturally – surprised if one should undertake to suggest to them that they have a shallower sense of decency than the French, and yet they view with complacency... a redundancy of physical endearment which the taste of their neighbours across the channel would never accept. It is wholly a matter of taste, and taste is not the great English quality. English spectators delight in broad effects... [but] when the embrace is strictly conjugal it is especially serviceable.[12]

In matters of passion the English were more concerned with moral propriety than aesthetic taste. As another American, Ralph Waldo Emerson, observed in his *English Traits* (1856) in public 'every one of these islanders is an island himself, safe, tranquil, incommunicable. In a company of strangers you would think him deaf... never betrayed into any curiosity or unbecoming emotion', in private, however, the sanctity of family relationships moved his passions deeply: 'Domesticity is the taproot which enables the nation to branch wide and high. The motive and end of their trade and empire is to guard the independence and privacy of their homes.'[13] This described exactly both D'Alroy, the imperial soldier, and Gerridge, the tradesman. It may also reflect the attitude of Squire Bancroft, who had 'married beneath him', and his wife, who continued to work 'in support' of her husband. There is no direct evidence that either of them saw a parallel between the play and their own lives, but Fred Younge apparently 'really grew to believe himself to be George D'Alroy, so earnestly did he seem to live the part and breath its joys and sorrows'.[14]

Stanislavski defined stage-truth as being 'that in which the actors themselves believe'; the intensity of the actor's involvement compels the spectators to believe them. Thus the young Bancroft company relied on emotional identification rather than technique. Henry James found it all rather naive and described Robertson's plays as 'infantile... addressed to the comprehension of infants', and the actors as 'essentially amateurish'.[15]

The Robertson revolution did not appeal to everyone. Productions might seem intimate and real, but the acting lacked the skill and variety of traditional comedians. Frank Benson, himself an 'amateur' at the end of the century, looked back at the reforms of the 1870s, and in agreement with Henry James and G. H. Lewes, saw that acting technique had been usurped by directing:

> What the cuff-and-collar brigade... gained in formal accuracy they lost in spontaneity, versatility, simplicity and dignity, which were some of the distinguishing marks of the older school. Granted that the style of some of its exponents had deteriorated into mere ranting... the older school at its best had a breadth of treatment, a directness and simplicity, that enabled them satisfactorily to portray the great ones of humanity, and the tense moments of their life, by methods unattainable by the average teacup-and-saucer actors... Because of the lack of the actor's technique, the producers at the St James's, the Haymarket [under the Bancrofts], the Criterion and the Court... had to fall back on the more mechanical method of count fifteen and stand at a certain instant on a certain particular mark.[16]

However, although such strictures might have been true of the cup-and-saucer style in general, *Caste* seemed ideally cast, not just because of Robertson's stage-management – which was not of the 'count fifteen' variety – but because he had specially written the parts to suit the actors. Lydia Foote as Esther, and Sophie Larkin as the Marquise repeated, like Bancroft himself, the performances they had given in *Society* and *Ours*. They were excellent, though unremarkable, members of the tight-knit ensemble. But three performances were original and outstanding: Honey as Eccles, Hare as Gerridge and Marie Bancroft as Polly.

The excellence of George Honey owed much to the part as written. He played the old boozer for laughs, but with variety and range: 'The make-up, the voice, the manner, the savagery in one part, the hypocritical maudlin grief in another, the toadying to wealth in another, the disgust and abuse when wealth refuses to deposit even a sovereign, the exits and entrances of this character are things to be gratefully remembered.'[17] Bancroft tells the sad story of Honey's final entrance during the revival of 1879. During Act I Honey suffered a stroke and collapsed behind the scenes. As the tableau at the end of the act was centred on his drunken return, Bancroft had to rattle the door and curse in Eccles's voice, then support the stricken actor in the doorway as the act-drop fell to the applause and laughter of the audience.

Although these end-of-act tableaux were hardly naturalistic, they were given greater dramatic significance by 'ingeniously changing' the poses for the curtain-call. Thus the Act II drop fell on Esther fainting into D'Alroy's arms, but for the curtain-call he and Hawtree had left and Polly, Sam and Eccles were seen comforting Esther. The importance of this minor novelty was that the audience were being asked to applaud the play rather than the performers.[18]

Marie Bancroft was a far more experienced performer than her husband, having been a star of that most technical of genres, the burlesque, in which she not only had to sing and dance, but portray, in a comically exaggerated form, characters and passions drawn from all sorts of successful plays, including classics. Dickens described her *travestie* performance in H. J. Byron's *The Maid and the Magpie*:

> While it is astonishingly impudent (must be, or it couldn't be done at all), it is so stupendously like a boy, and unlike a woman, that it is perfectly free from offence. I have never seen such a thing. She does an imitation of the dancing of the Christy Minstrels – wonderfully clever – which, in the audacity of its thorough-going, is surprising... I call her the cleverest girl I have ever seen on the stage in my time, and the most singularly original.[19]

Although she grew tired of playing burlesque, it was the most thorough training she could have received, and as Polly Eccles in *Caste* she had an opportunity to display her theatrical skills. Robertson always provided her with appropriate parts:

> [His] formula included two heroines in each comedy: one ideal, the other practical; one sentimental, the other humourous. the practical-humourous heroine – *Mary Netley, Polly Eccles, Naomi Tighe* – always fell to the lot of Mrs Bancroft, whose alert and expressive face, humid-sparkling eye, and small compact figure seemed to have been expressly designed for these characters.[20]

Robertson's description of 'The Burlesque Actress' in his sketches of 'Theatrical Types' in *The Illustrated Times* (1860), probably used Marie Wilton as his model:

> She is generally handsome, and when her features are irregular she more than makes up for them by expression – expression that combines good humour, malice, intensity of feeling, Bacchante-like enjoyment, and devotion. She can sing the most difficult of Donizetti's languid, loving melodies as well as the inimitable Mackney's 'Oh, Rosa, how I lub you! Coodle cum!' She can warble a drawing-room ballad of the 'Daylight of the Soul' or 'Eyes melting in the Gloom' school, or whistle 'When I was a-walking in Wiggleton Wale' with the shrillness and correctness of a Whitechapel bird-catcher. She is as faultless on the piano as on the bones. She can waltz, polk, dance a *pas seul* or a sailor's hornpipe, La Sylphide, or Genu-wine Transatlantic Cape Cod Skedaddle, with equal grace and spirit; and as for acting, she can declaim à la Phelps or Fechter; is serious, droll; and must play farce, tragedy, opera, comedy, melodrama, pantomime, ballet, change her costume, fight a combat, make love, poison herself, die, and take one encore for a song and another for a dance, in the short space of ten minutes.

Off-stage she blends the homely qualities of Esther Eccles with the entrepreneurial hard-headedness of Marie Wilton:

> She is a power in London, and theatrical managers drive up to her door and bid against each other for her services. Fortunate folk who see her in the day-time complain 'that she dresses plainly' – 'almost shabbily'; but, then, they are not aware that she has to keep half a dozen fatherless brothers and sisters and an invalid mother out of her salary – which intelligence, when known to the two or three men who really care for her, sends them sleepless with admiration. Here is a household fairy who can polk, paint, make puddings, sing, sew on buttons, turn heads and old bonnets, wear cleaned gloves, whistle, weep, laugh, and perhaps love.[21]

The part of Polly, as a dancer in a Minor Theatre, demanded all these burlesque talents. In Act II, when Hawtree calls for D'Alroy wearing his uniform, Polly marches about brandishing her parasol and singing:

> With a sabre on his brow,
>   And a helmet by his side,
> The soldier sweethearts serving-maids,
>   And cuts cold meat beside.

On D'Alroy's entrance she claps her hands and cries:

> Oh! Here's a beautiful brother-in-law. Why didn't you come in on horseback, as they do at Astley's? – gallop and say (*imitating soldiers on horseback and prancing up and down stage during the piece*) 'Soldiers of France! The eyes of Europe are a-looking at you! The Empire has confidence in you, and France expects that every man this day will do his – little utmost! The foe is before you – more's the pity – and you are before them – worse luck for you! Forward! Go and get killed; and to those who escape the Emperor will give a little bit of ribbon! Nineteens, about! Forward! Gallop! Charge! (*galloping to right, imitating bugle and giving point with parasol. She nearly spears* HAWTREE's *nose.* HAWTREE *claps his hand upon his sword-hilt. She throws herself into chair, laughing and clapping* HAWTREE's *cap (from table) upon her head. All laugh and applaud.*

No doubt the whole audience joined the applause for such a set-piece, the 'reality' of which was hardly justified by the dramatic situation. Even less naturalistic was the contrivance by which Polly breaks the news to Esther of her husband's return:

> POLLY: Do you recollect the ballet that old Herr Griffenhaagen arranged? – Jeanne le Folle, or, the Return of the Soldier?... How well I remember the scene! – The cottage was on that side, the bridge at the back – then ballet of villagers, and entrance of Delphine as Jeanne, the bride – tra-lal-lala-lala-la-la. (*Sings and pantomimes.* SAM *imitating her*) Then the entrance of Claude, the bridegroom – (*to* SAM, *imitating swell*) How-de-do, how-de-do?... arrest of Claude, who is drawn for the conscription (*Business;* ESTHER *looks dreamily*), and is torn from the arms of his bride, at the church porch. *Omnes* broken-hearted. This is Omnes broken-hearted. (*Pantomime*)
> ESTHER: Polly, I don't like this; it brings back memories.

The whole sequence, like many of Robertson's scenes, counterpointed comedy and pathos. As Esther realised the significance of Polly's play-acting, Sam slipped away to bring in D'Alroy, and during the emotional reunion, Polly played softly '*the same air played by* ESTHER act II, *on the treble only*'. As the passion of the lovers increased, so Polly enlivened the music: '*At last strikes piano wildly, and goes off into a fit of hysterical laughter*'. Thus, by exploiting the character's theatrical instincts, the production achieved the effect of musical accompaniment, without adopting the full-bloodied conventions of melodrama. The effectiveness of this scene, and of Marie Bancroft's whole performance, was achieved by a manipulation of contrasts between realistic and theatrical styles. By providing cake both to eat and to keep *Caste* became Robertson's most popular play, and Mrs Bancroft the company's favourite performer.

The performance of John Hare was of a different kind. Like Bancroft he had a non-theatrical background, but he did not just put across his own personality. He had been trained in the 'French naturalistic' school by Leigh Murray, rather than in the hurly-burly of provincial stock. An unlikely *jeune première*, being small and thin, he was from the start a character actor, mimicking physical traits and eccentricities, rather than expressing emotion. Like William Farren, earlier in the century, he made a speciality of old men, but was more self-contained than Farren, who always acted out to the audience in the tradition of the Haymarket. Augustin Filon had recognised Hare's remarkable talent at his London debut as Lord Ptarmigan in *Society*, with his eccentric 'habit of dragging about a chair with him wherever he went, and of falling asleep in it the moment he sat down':

> Hare had realised that an actor does not make his name by giving out a witticism or telling phrase with effect, but by putting before us a live human figure, if only a silent figure, in all its eccentricity of brain. His facial expression was wonderful, and his mimicry excellent; – he had in him the genius of metamorphosis.[22]

Many of Hare's performances combined extravagant eccentricity with the 'quiet natural' style, as James described it, and the 'propriety and good taste with which he acquits himself of those ordinary phrases and modulations which the usual English actor finds it impossible to utter with any degree of verisimilitude'.[23] It would seem that, unlike most mimics, Hare was content to live within his creation, allowing audiences to find him funny, rather than drawing attention to the comedy. Above all, despite the singularity of his roles, he was an ideal ensemble actor.

The part of Sam Gerridge does not seem particularly eccentric, but there had been few such detailed characterisations of working-class characters on the Victorian stage. Many of the heroes of domestic melo-

dramas were drawn from the lower classes, but they tended to be gener-
alised 'peasants', and, even when Tom Taylor and Boucicault introduced
more accurate depictions of city life, as in *The Ticket of Leave Man* and
The Streets of London, their working-men tended to be either mawkishly
heroic, or broadly comical. Sam could easily have been overplayed as a
stereotype cockney, particularly as Robertson had used the highly artificial convention of larding Sam's dialogue with the jargon of his trade,
such as: 'Polly, my pet, my brightest batswing and most brilliant
burner... Come and be Mrs Sam Gerridge, Polly, my patent-safety-day-
and-night-light. You'll furnish me completely.' Hare, however,
impressed the *Daily News* with the accuracy of his portrayal:

> The real working man, a mechanic whose flow of speech is not great, but
> who makes his presence felt by judicious 'business'... Mr Hare is so refined
> and perfect an actor, so true an observer of life, that we were not surprised to
> find him made up a sharp, wiry, veritible working man who might have
> stepped out of any carpenter's shop in England... The scene in which he
> reads to his 'intended' the trade circular he has just composed is the most
> exquisite and unforced bit of comedy we have seen in years.[24]

Yet there was always something artificial in Hare's meticulous imper-
sonations. He was not a showy actor, but inevitably audiences were
aware of the skill with which he transformed himself, and though not a
satirist, there was always a certain detatchment in his acting. Bernard
Shaw makes the point well:

> [Hare's] fame rests largely upon that most unreal of all stage pretences; a
> young man pretending to be a very old one. Mr Hare, in these parts, used to
> make himself up cleverly... but that any playgoer who had seen Chippendale
> could have mistaken Mr Hare's business for the real thing is beyond my
> belief. As a matter of fact we did not make any such mistake: the fun of Mr
> Hare's old men was the cleverness of the imitation, which was amusing even
> when his part was utterly uninteresting in itself.[25]

The appeal of his Sam Gerridge came from Hare's being known as a
'gent' giving an affectionate impersonation, rather than a realistic portrayal, of a working-man.

In fact the whole play used the issue of class-division to create, in typically Victorian fashion, situations of pathos and humour. *Caste* was no
more an example of social realism than the old farces and melodramas
had been. Like them, though its tone and style was different, the play
was still concerned with creating 'affective scenes of feeling', rather than
dissecting society, which is what Zola – and indeed Henry James, in his
own way – claimed to be the artistic purpose of the Naturalistic
Movement. Actually it was in the less 'realistic' theatre of melodrama
that genuine political awareness was to be found; most of the 'society'

drama of the West End theatres was conformist and reassuring. They were to be very slow in accepting the truely radical plays of Ibsen and Shaw into their repertoire, even though their style of production, as created by the Bancrofts, was eminently suitable for those naturalistic master-pieces.

9

The conventions
of melodrama

All the performances considered so far reveal a certain contradiction between intention and effect. The Robertsonian style aimed at naturalism, but was most successful when flirting with theatrical stereotypes; E. A. Sothern's own personal qualities of intelligence and wit shone through the opaque stupidity of Lord Dundreary; Macready's Richelieu was an ambiguous compound of strength and weakness, ruthless cunning and sentimentality; and Charles Kean's portrayal of Fabien dei Franchi made the Corsican vendetta seem almost respectable. One might attribute these contradictions to long-derided Victorian hypocrisy, but much ambiguity was the unintentional product of the theatrical conventions of the genre, and, as J. L. Styan explains, such an ambivalent response is often no bad thing:

> In non-illusory performance, dramatic perception can be more intense because it is self-aware; its tensions arising not just from the interaction between the characters of an illusion, but from the impact of the actuality of the stage upon the reality of the spectator. In non-illusory drama perception can create a double response, one to the fiction of the inner play, another to the sense of oneself in the role of spectator – in a word, ambivalence.[1]

He explains how effective this is in great plays from Shakespeare to Beckett, and in such conventionalised genres as Japanese *kabuki* theatre, but when discussing melodrama he suggests the ambiguity was 'an untrustworthy mixture of moral indignation and vicarious pleasure'. The intensity of the villainy and the excitement of the action are quite 'unreal', but they stir a childlike desire to participate in the pretence: 'Indeed, it is hard to separate reality from make-believe at critical moments':

> In the simple moral patterns of these plays, Victorian evangelism preached a system of rewards and punishments which had little to do with the real world outside... Characterization was uncomplicated, with never a sense of development, and marked by the clearest signals... No wonder [there are] so many

tableaux or 'pictures'... suggesting the clichés of the penny novels of the time transformed into living action. Yet they also indicate a vigorous, lusty and almost acrobatic display designed for immediate meaning within a convention familiar to author, actor and audience (pp. 133-6).

This is a fair description, as far as it goes, of many popular melodramas, but fails to take account of Styan's own concept of ambivalence as a 'self-aware' process – the suspension of disbelief must be *willed*. At least he did not make the common error of describing melodrama as 'escapist'.

J. L. Smith, concentrating on melodrama texts, identifies affective scenes of passion in which 'emotions are savoured singly and in isolation', but suggests they are savoured uncritically: 'We enjoy triumph without considering its cost to others, despair without seeking for alternative courses, and protest without questioning the bases of our own superior moral integrity.'[2] By underrating the ambivalence of an audience's response in the theatre, his argument tends to become patronising: 'They want to forget the drudgery and drabness of everyday life and escape into a more colourful, less complex and plainly perfect world' (p. 17). As Bernard Sharratt asks, in his challenging essay 'The politics of the popular?', what is so perfect about this melodramatic world which is typified by 'fear, terror, violence, disaster and agony'?[3] The fact that all turns out well in the end does not necessarily negate the problems nor tranquillise anxiety. Rather than being a perfect, or, as Michael Booth describes it, a 'dream world',[4] Sharratt suggests melodrama is more like a nightmare, in which the intensity of the experience provides the cathasis, rather than any 'poetic justice'.

The behaviour of melodrama heroes was often morally suspect, as in the case of *The Corsican Brothers*, and all commentators note how audiences particularly enjoyed the villains. Sharratt argues that this does not mean that audiences were blind to the moral content of the plays, or incapable of making sophisticated judgements on the social or political issues raised, but that the *performance of the actors* created Styan's ambivalence – even a Brechtian alienation – and this encouraged a certain objectivity of response. The blatant artificiality of the genre gave its performance some of the quality of a spectator sport, in which

> the man on the terraces is his own expert... he often claims a curious kind of knowledge of the players as persons, almost acquaintanceship or friendship... But both the expertise and the intimacy seem to be, to a large extent, forms of self-pretence or semi-fantasy. Yet they both seem, in various ways, constitutive of the pleasure of much popular entertainment. The stand-up comedian in a working men's club, for example, is treated by the audience precisely as a kind of old acquaintance and the success of his act often depends upon his establishing a knowing intimacy with that audience (thereby enabling him, often, to get laughs from fears and insecurities he knows they know he

knows about). The same is true of the pantomime dame and perhaps was true of the melodrama villain. What is involved in all these cases is a complex interplay between the player and the role: the panto dame, or villain, makes no sense unless we simultaneously see through the character to the actor and react 'exaggeratedly' to the personality of both character and performer – we are allowed to subvert the role and asked to make it live, in quite explicit ways (boos, hisses, 'Watch out behind you' etc.).[5]

Booing, applause, laughter and tears may well have been prompted by the emotions of the fictitious situation, but the ambivalent 'subversion' to which Sharratt refers enabled audiences to enjoy the conflict between black and white without necessarily losing their own moral and political sense of reality; the excitement of the game was more important than the morality of the outcome.

As the result of the game was always a foregone conclusion, the skill of the dramatist lay in contriving extraordinary situations of conflict or distress, while the skill of the protagonists was to confront the situations with a complete mastery of the rules of the game. The rules, or conventions, of melodrama dictated a highly formalised style of acting. In the 'higher' forms of melodrama, which the Victorians described as 'dramas' or even 'tragedies', such as *Virginius* or *Richelieu*, actors developed a serious virtuosity, but in popular melodramas there was always an element of playfulness as the actors displayed their mastery of the semiotics of gesture and attitude. Points and transitions were common to the acting of both melodramas and classics, and, though actors working under pressure in minor houses, penny-gaffs or booths might lack the skill and sensitivity of Siddons or Macready, and repeated gestures mechanically or crudely, in principle the technique for expressing passion was the same for all.

Peter Brooks, whose analysis is based principally on the work of the French dramatist Pixerécourt,[6] argues that the usual climax of melodrama was the public recognition of virtue after it has been forced into exile or disguise by the menace of evil. However, this recognition is not sprung on the audience by surprise as in a detective story, its existence is apparent from the start. The audience shares the relief of the ritualistic climax, when the characters on stage are forced to acknowledge what the audience has known all along. The theme of the 'guilty secret' was a common one, from *The Iron Chest* of 1796 to *The Bells* of 1871, but it was seldom kept a secret from the audience, and even when the precise nature of a crime or relationship was withheld, there was never any doubt as to whose secret would turn out to be criminal, or who would turn out to be a long-lost relative. The criticism 'You could see it coming a mile off' was irrelevant to the popular melodrama; the motives, emotions and the trustworthiness of characters were signalled from the actor's earliest entrance.

This need for semiological clarity explains the stereotyped 'stock characters' of the genre. The very appearance of villain or hero, comic servant or evil henchman was enough to identify them, and although types of melodrama might range from the Gothic to the Modern Domestic, and from the Oriental to the Nautical, the colour code of black villain, scarlet woman, spotless maiden and motley fool was immediately recognised in their costumes. In his satirical description of the stock types, *Quizzology of the British Drama* (1846), Gilbert à Beckett deplores how changes in dressing the villain, recently introduced into the 'gentlemanly' French melodramas, had undermined the legitimate expectations of the theatre audience:

> The old Stage Assassin is fast fading away and is almost entirely surplanted in the dramatic world by a smooth-faced sort of villain... We confess we have a preference for the 'fine old Stage Assassin all of the olden time' – the regular minor melodramatic murderer, with a voice hoarse from an accumulation of colds supposed to have been caught in a long course of crime carried on at midnight, among cut woods and canvas caverns. We prefer his ample crop of black worsted, falling in raven ringlets half-way down his back, to the hair of the modern Stage Assassin, whose locks are gracefully curled... the latter's well mascaraed hair confounds the distinction between innocence and guilt.[7]

If the mere appearance of a character was not enough to establish his credentials, then the dramatist introduced asides and soliloquies, and the actors cast expressive glances at the audience, to indicate their supposedly hidden motives. Mugging was a regular feature of the droll comedian, but in melodrama it was the villain who most regularly indulged in acting out. This was partly because villains had more to hide than bluff straightforward heroes, who blurted out their thoughts for all to hear. This ability to manipulate the theatrical situation by his direct address to the audience reinforced the villain's control over the dramatic situation, and his manipulative power over the more virtuous, but gullible, characters. It is a distinction found in *Othello*, Shakespeare's nearest approach to domestic melodrama, where the Moor's soliloquies are personal outpourings against the cruelty of fate, whereas Iago, adopting the roles of both villain and clown, takes the audience into his confidence. The effect is to emphasise Iago's power and Othello's noble bewilderment. In melodrama too it was villains and clowns who could manipulate situations, while virtuous victims were left complaining to heaven. In the naturalistic well-made plays of the 1870s and 1880s this formal communication with the audience was discarded. Gordon Craig, who learnt explicit theatricality when working under Irving, suggested that these performers were betraying their first duty as actors, which was to *reveal* emotions, not hide them:

> I have seen such actors recently in London. The villain of the play comes on to the stage smiling: he is quite alone; and though he remains alone for five minutes, he does not tell us that he is 'the villain' – has not dared to let any tell-tale look escape him; he has failed to explain anything to us. It is called realism – it is no such thing: it is mere incompetence – an incapacity to understand that *everything* has to be clearly explained to the spectators, and little or no thought paid to whether the other characters on the stage overhear or see. If they overhear, if they see, they, too, have failed in the simplest rudiments of their craft.[8]

But the conventionality of melodrama was not just 'over-acting' or 'acting out'. The very feature that defined the genre – the music – was artificial. Melodrama grew out of burletta and always maintained certain operatic elements, as in scenes of wordless action accompanied by atmospheric music. In Edward Fitzball's *Flying Dutchman* (Adelphi, 1827) Vanderdecken's immortality is assured only as long as he remains silent. In the final scene the ghostly Dutchman's seduction of the heroine in the Devil's Cave is interrupted by the romantic hero:

> *[MUSIC. – LESTELLE discovered, supporting herself against the rock, L.S.E., in an attitude of distress. – VANDERDECKEN comes down with a torch in his hand – he gazes at Lestelle, puts down the torch, and points to the magic book.*
> LESTELLE: Thine, earthly or unearthly! Never! Terrible being, thou mayst indeed trample on my mortal frame, but the soul of Lestelle is far above thy malice.
> *[MUSIC. – He is angry – takes her hand, and, approaching the book, it flies open and displays hieroglyphics – Lestelle screams, and sinks at the base of the rock – footsteps heard without – Vanderdecken listens.*
> *Enter MOWDREY, from the rock, L.S.E.*
> MOWDREY: *[Calling]* Lestelle! I am here – you are safe! Lestelle! *[He descends, and sees Vanderdecken.]* Ah, wretch, is it you? Tremble!
> *[MUSIC. – Vanderdecken laughs, then draws a sword – a terrific fight – Mowdrey, after repeatedly stabbing his opponent in vain, is taken by Vanderdecken, and furiously thrown down.*
> VANDERDECKEN: Mortal die! *[Thunder.]* Ah, what have I done! *[He displays bodily agony.]* I have spoken! *[MUSIC.]* The spell which admits my stay on earth is distroyed with my silence. I must begone to my phantom ship again, to the deep and howling waters!

However, before disappearing, he conjures up a flood to drown his victims:

> VANDERDECKEN: Tremble! The rushing waters which rise to welcome the return of Vanderdecken, shall bury ye deep, deep in their unfathomed darkness. Burst, stormy clouds and overwhelm them; rise, ye many waters of ocean, cover them up for ever! *[Thunder.]* Rockalda! I come.

[MUSIC. – Vanderdecken goes behind the rock-table, whereon the magic-book was placed, and sinks with the altar, amidst thunder and flames of red fire...

Luckily the comic sailor, Toby Varnish, is at hand to loose their ropes and they all climb up onto the rock as the floods rise:

MOWDREY: Alas, there is no hope! – Hark, hark! the torrent is rushing down upon us. See! see! Assistance is at hand – help! help! help!
[Waves handkerchief. MUSIC. – Varnish continues waving his torch, and the agitated waters rush furiously into the cave, entirely covering the stage to the orchestra – the sound of the gong, and loud peals of thunder heard – Peter Von Bummell, with a torch, Captain Pepperpot, &c., appear in a sloop from the very back – they come under the rock, R.U.E., and receive Lestelle, Mowdrey and Varnish aboard – sails are hoisted, with British flag, and as the cutter turns round to return, shout, 'Huzza!' –incessant noise, as on board a vessel, with crash, gong, and thunder, until the Curtain falls.]

This was hardly the great romantic opera that Wagner was to make of the same legend in 1843, but, like many melodramas, its structure owed as much to musical logic as to dramatic plot. Though melodramas were not through-composed, individual characters had personal tunes, like Wagnerian *leitmotifs*, to introduce their entrances; scenes of pathos and comedy alternated like the fast and slow movements of a divertimento; the final scene of spectacle created an audial and visual climax; and even the unrealistic happy ending provided the sensual satisfaction of a symphonic finale returning to its dominant key. Peter Brooks argues that:

The emotional drama needs the desemanticized language of music, its evocation of the 'ineffable', its tones and registers. Style, thematic structuring, modulation of tone and rhythm and voice – musical patterning in a metaphorical sense – are called upon to invest the plot with some of the inexorability and necessity that in pre-modern literature derived from the substratum of myth.'[9]

This combination of emotional excess and performance virtuosity was similar to that of Romantic Opera, and it is not surprising that the only melodrama scripts still regularly performed today are the libretti of Rossini, Verdi and Puccini.

Music was such an integral part of performance that by the 1850s few critics mentioned it, and few scripts indicate its inclusion. In *The Corsican Brothers* the specially composed Ghost Music was specified, but most melodramas were accompanied from the orchestra's stock of 'agits', 'hurrys' and 'melos'. The stage-directions of the first English play to be billed as a 'Melodrama', Thomas Holcroft's *Tale of Mystery* (Covent Garden, 1802), indicate more clearly than in later scripts the effects for which music was employed. The entrance of huntsmen is accompanied by '*Hunting music*' and archers by a '*Quick march*'. Seperate cues are introduced each time the dumb Francisco writes or gesticulates, one being described as *'Music to express disorder'*. At a moment of confrontation: *'Music plays alarmingly, but piano when [MONTANO] enters and while he stays... Loud and discordant at the moment the eye of MONTANO catches the figure of ROMALDI; at which MONTANO starts with terror and indignation. He then assumes the eye and attitude of menace; which ROMALDI returns. The music ceases.'* These directions clearly indicate how music was used to accompany the starts, attitudes and tableaux of passionate acting. In Monk Lewis's monodrama *The Captive* (Covent Garden, 1803), an abused wife is locked in a lunatic asylum, and here the music was required to enhance the lighting effects: *'Music expressing the light growing fainter, as the Gaoler retires through the gallery'*, as well as illustrating mental processes: *'She remains fixed in this attitude (her hands pressed forcibly against her forehead), with a look of fear, till the music, changing, expresses that some tender, melancholy reflection has passed her mind.'*[10] A manager even instructed his musical director: 'The delights of country life want to be brought before the minds of the audience, and I think you had better give me a little *music expressive of clothes drying in the wind.*'[11]

The published scripts of Charles Reade's 1854 melodramas, *The Courier of Lyons* and *Plot and Passion*, contain no musical directions, as by that time accompaniment had become an unremarked convention. However, in an appreciation of the musical director, Edwin Ellis, who died in 1880, Reade suggested that few spectators recognised the contribution of the musical director,

> who used to compose, or set, good music to orchestral instruments, and play it in the Theatre with spirit and taste, and to watch the stage with one eye and the orchestra with another, and so accompany with vigilant delicacy a mixed scene of action and dialogue; to do which the music must be full when the actor works in silence, but subdued promptly as often as the actor speaks. Thus it enhances the action without drowning a spoken word... Mr Ellis has lifted scenes and situations for me and other writers scores of times, and his share of the effect never been publicly noticed. When he had a powerful action or impassioned dialogue to illustrate he did not habitually run to the poor resource of a 'hurry' or a nonsense 'tremolo', but loved to find an appropriate melody, or a rational sequence of chords, or a motived strain, that raised the scene or enforced the dialogue.[12]

Speaking over music had a crucial effect on acting in melodrama. It inevitably led to a heightened, deliberate and passionate mode of delivery, particularly as not all musical directors were as sensitive as Edwin Ellis.

Just as we need to consult the earliest melodrama scripts for details of musical convention, so the conventions of speaking over music were not analysed until after melodrama was giving place to unaccompanied plays. Frederick Corder, who composed for the solo recitation of poetry in the 1890s, considered that 'stage melodrama has a faint, unheeded background of music', unlike his own specially composed accompaniment. Yet most actors would have agreed with his observation:

> In speaking through music the higher tones of the voice require to be constantly employed, especially in the case of a male reciter; the lower inflections grating too harshly against the musical notes. Yet there must be no suggestion of 'chanting' or 'sing-song', but only great clearness and purity of utterance – never any colloquial or ordinary quality except where the music ceases.[13]

The necessity of speaking clearly and adapting vocal tone and pace to that of the accompaniment must have been a major influence in creating the 'theatrical voice', like that of the stage-fathers who pronounced 'my child' as 'm' cheeald'.

Even with the aid of modern mechanical recording it is difficult to appreciate the extent to which pronunciation changes over the years. In the 1980s the clipped delivery of the 1940s seems highly self-conscious, but, as newsreel commentaries and radio interviews reveal, it was not an affectation restricted to actors and actresses. In the nineteenth century however, Macready was accused of distorting his natural voice to conform to theatrical fashion: 'He acquired some of the peculiarly expressive traits of certain distinguished performers... In consequence of this change of base, his acting became more theatrical or stagey... his voice lost its clear ring and other attractive qualities of tone, and became harsh, and was at times repulsive.'[14] On the other hand, Helen Faucit wrote: 'What a splendid voice he has! How much nature has favoured him there. You hear with distinctness his lowest whisper. But Mr P. Farren [her acting teacher] tells me it is not only the voice that causes this, but the clear and open articulation... How I wish I could aquire this rare qualification.'[15] A transliteration of Macready's pronunciation suggested that he tended to add 'a' to the end of his words: 'Be innocenttta of the knowledge, dearesttta chuck, Till thou applauddda the deed.'[16] Such a practice would certainly give his delivery clarity as well as portentousness. Years later John Colman, who had scoffed at the theatricality of Macready's vocal mannerisms, was himself described by Chance Newton as an 'actorrr-managerrr and Shakespearrrean trrragedi-an'.[17]

When Sidney Dark looked back on melodrama in 1904 he concluded:

> Elocution is practically a lost art... The 'mouthing' actor is found no longer. He had his faults; he would always tear a passion to tatters, and he ranted and he raved. But he had this one virtue: he was always distinct, his words could always be heard, and his training gave him the power of expressing the beauties

of blank verse... Your modern actor mumbles under his breath, his inflections are wrong, his use of his voice ignorant and careless.[18]

The 'amateurs' who started entering the profession in the 1870s preferred the languid drawl of the drawing-room, and their well-bred conversational tones made the declamatory style of early melodrama seem even more artificial by comparison.

In the 1870s, encouraged by the physiological enquiries of Charles Darwin, whose *Expression of the Emotions in Man and Animals* was published in 1872, studies of vocal technique began to appear. If physiognomy and phrenology had been the scientific fads of the 1830s, elocution was to be the fashion of the eighties. Typical of many elocutionists was Charles Pumptre, who published an exhaustive set of lectures on *Elocution; or, the Physiology and Culture of Voice and Speech, and the Expression of the Emotions by Language, Countenance, and Gesture.* (3rd ed. 1880). Much of his book is taken up with anatomical diagrams and explanations of voice production, but from his instructions on public speaking we can gain some idea of Victorian vocal delivery. Actors were not Dr Plumptre's favourite models he preferred preachers, barristers and, above all, W. E. Gladstone. For him elocution did 'not mean anything pompous, stilted, bombastic or stagey', rather 'the perfectly audible, distinct, pure and effective pronunciation... either in the shape of prose or poetry' (p. 2). His attitude towards the stage was patronising, like many high-minded Victorians. He referred to the work of Thomas Sheridan and to Joshua Steele's attempt in 1772 to notate Garrick's delivery, but, although he mentioned Macready with respect, he describes the elocutionary 'secrets' of most actors with scholarly condescension. He attributed to George Frederick Cooke the 'trick' of breathing in through the nose, rather than the mouth (pp. 72-3), and to Talma the 'trick' of taking an extra breath with his diaphragm before his lungs were empty (p. 68). Many actors and singers tended to breath with their stomach muscles, rather than their diaphragms, which may explain the barrel-like corpulence of some of the more energetic performers.[19]

Plumptre's own notation of speeches suggests extreme deliberation. In Hamlet's advice to the players, he indicates both emphasis and pauses: 'I think their effect after any chief word, be it noun, verb, adjective or pronoun, most striking; and after any fine simile, noble metaphor, or other beautiful passage, a pause of some duration adds marvellously to the weight and power with which it falls on the ears of an audience, sinks into their hearts, and fixes itself in their memories' (p. 259):

Be not too *tame* – neither --- but let *your own* DISCRETION be *your* TUTOR --- suit the ACTION to the word --- the WORD to the ACTION --- with *this* SPECIAL observance --- that you o'erstep not the *modesty* of

NATURE ----- for anything so overdone is from the purpose of PLAYING --- whose *end* --- both at the *first* – and NOW ---- was --- and *is* --- to hold - - as 'twere – the *mirro*r up to NATURE ----- to show VIRTUE – her own *feature* ---- SCORN – her own image --- and the very *age and body of the time* his *form* and pressure.

So much for pronouncing it trippingly on the tongue! Although Plumptre disliked the habit, he recalled that Macready and Charles Kemble both tended to end-stop lines of blank verse regardless of the sense (p. 270). If this ponderous delivery was advocated for Shakespeare, then the delivery of high-flown rhetoric in melodrama must have been even more emphatic.

Yet, many actors deplored Elocution for making a mechanical science out of a living art. Most stock actors developed their voices on the job as apprentices, but others took formal lessons from older actors. Herman Vezin was a respected teacher, who was aquainted with the latest scientific developments. Gustave Garcia, brother to the prima donna, Malibran, taught both actors and singers, and invented a contraption of mirrors to observe his own larynx.[20] Rosina Filippi, half-sister of Eleanora Duse, became a teacher at Beerbohm Tree's Academy of Dramatic Art, and, although she advocated 'full vowels and sharp consonants',[21] she deplored the formalism of Elocution Teachers, who dictated pauses, emphases and intonations: 'I love Diction as much as I hate Elocution' (p. 3). She had learnt her pronunciation from Herman Vezin, whose technique was to sit facing his pupils and make them observe and copy his own delivery. He 'used to make me say words as if there were double consonants in them... Ggennerrally for "generly" and llibbrrarry for "libray"' (pp. 3-4). Filippi recalled how the Ghost of Hamlet's Father was always spoken in an 'old fashioned' way. This may have been because it was still performed with a 'tremolo mysterioso' backing, long after general musical accompaniment was dropped from Shakespeare productions, and this would have encouraged the actor (probably an older actor) to use his melodrama-voice: "Tis geeven ah-oot, that shleeping in min awchard – a shurpant scthung may' (p. 21).

Even with the aid of phonogaph cylinders, (Irving was first recorded in 1877)[22] it is impossible to reconstruct the Victorian actor's voice exactly, as the crude process of making a record encouraged excessive deliberation. Yet the evidence suggests that rhetorical delivery was essential in melodrama, and that, if actors were not careful, this affected their speech in naturalistic prose plays, and their delivery of Shakespearian verse. Each decade produced actors, whose voices were considered by contemporaries to be fine instruments, but whose delivery was characterised by the following generation as 'stagey' and artificial. However, throughout the century the declamatory melodrama-voice was recognised as part of the actor's art – a cultivated virtuosity comparable to that of an opera singer. In the same way as musical accompaniment encouraged, even forced, the actor to develop this rhetorical vocal style, so the sweep and rhythm of the music encouraged physical gesture on an almost balletic scale. Musical tempo – from 'agit' to 'lento' – determined the pace of playing, and supported the poise of the sustained gesture, and the suspension of a frozen 'picture'. Indeed musical accompaniment can help modern actors recapture the breadth, power and deliberation of melodramatic acting more than any other exercise or rehearsal technique.

Although melodrama as a genre remained popular throughout the century, styles of writing and performance inevitably changed; late Victorian melodramas were very different from those of the Romantic period: Charles Kean substituted business for gesture, and Boucicault, Reade and Taylor wrote conversations rather than speeches. Nevertheless, the self-conscious virtuosity of melodramatic acting continued as long as the pit orchestra supported scenes of action or emotion. To indicate something of these changes in both style and content, four climactic scenes can be compared with the finale of Fitzball's *Flying Dutchman*, and with Ducrow's scenes of dumb show, as discussed in Chapter 3. Each exploits the convention of wordless action accompanied by music, but there is a shift from rhetorical gesture to telling details, and from physical thrills to psychological distress.

Mme Celeste was a specialist in the pantomimic expression of emotion. Originally a dancer in Paris, she came to England in 1830 and by 1844 was joint manager of the Adelphi with Ben Webster. Her London acting debut had been as the dumb boy, Maurice, in J. R. Planché's *The Child of the Wreck* (Drury Lane, 1837). According to *The Times*, like Ducrow, 'her "dumb show"... is anything but inexplicable. She expressed by her varied and appropriate action, and by her swiftly changing features, the various passions of love, despair, indignation, and joy, with touching fidelity.'[23] In speaking parts, her French accent restricted her to roles like Miami, a half-caste French/Indian huntress of the Mississippi delta in J. B. Buckstone's *The Green Bushes* (Adelphi, 1845). When Miami witnesses the reunion between her lover, Connor, and his deserted wife, Geraldine, she is overwhelmed with jealousy:

> In a moment all her savage blood is roused. Half-a-dozen times is the rifle carried to her shoulder, and as often is the point let fall... At length, unable to control her fierce jealousy and passion, she fires, and Connor is shot through the heart. His wife frantically flies for assistance, and unknowing whence the fatal blow has been struck, supplicates on her knees the aid of her husband's assasssin... Miami stands by unmoved, the 'stoic of the woods'. With his last breath Connor entreats the murderer of the husband to protect the wife. He

dies. Miami leaps madly into the river, and the drop falls upon the scene of her rescue by a party of French soldiers.[24]

As the Victorian age succeeded that of the Romantics, such demonstrations of murderous passion were more frequently assigned to the 'outcasts' of society, mutes, idiots, drunkards, half-castes and foreigners.

The fascination with excessive emotion remained, but in 'gentlemanly' melodramas villains began masking their viciousness under a cloak of urbanity, and heroes and heroines developed stiff upper lips, with a tendency to swoon rather than rage. A performance of passionate dumbshow which concentrated on pathos rather than violence, was Charles Dillon's in *Belphegor* (Lyceum, 1856). The play was still constructed to demonstrate intensity of feeling, but:

> [Dillon] is no declaimer, but speaks naturally, and even on phrases of the highest passion is never noisy, substituting intention for stormy vehemence... His power over the feelings is extraordinary. In the first act of the present play he gradually melted his audience from scene to scene, and long ere the fall of the curtain every eye was moist with sympathetic tears.[25]

The *Saturday Review* felt he lacked versatility for the changes in circumstances from 'a wandering mountebank' to a 'fine chevalier', but 'the whole scene where Belphegor is deserted by his wife was finely acted. Profoundly touching, without the least violence or excess... Mr Dillon, greatly to his credit, never gives way to the melodramatic temptations of a part abounding in sudden transitions of moods and passions. He preserves, in the depths of his wrongs and sorrows, a gentleness as rare as it is piteous.'[26] The scene was less frenetic than the violent sensations of *The Flying Dutchman* or *The Green Bushes*, but it still depended on Dillon's silent performance, expressing emotion physically rather than verbally:

> His grief, from the first moment of bewildered, half-stupefying apprehension of his loss to the full agony of proof, was rendered not only with the most minute and subtle touches. A stifled cry as he entered the abandoned room, a sudden transformation as he turned from it, bowed in frame and feeble of limb, mute despair on his face, but no violence, showed fine restraint, no less than emotional intensity.

However from the perspective of 1890, Westland Marston concluded that:

> Mr Charles Dillon was an actor of great emotional gifts, but very deficient in intellectual ones. So long as he was under the impulse of feeling, gay or grave, he could act with great power, force, and delicacy... But it was the good taste begotten of feeling... and does not proceed from those dictates of judgement and reflection, without obeying which, in complex characters, the most passionate actor must be at sea. Charles Dillon often reached psychological truth by an impulse; he had, however, no psychological discernment.[27]

The conventions of melodrama

Dillon was more at home in the straightforward passions of melodrama than in the classics, where his concentration on 'feeling' seemed simplistic.

Another example of a passionate dumb-show is from one of the most extraordinary performances of the century, Charles Warner in *Drink* (Princess Theatre, 2 June 1879), adapted by Charles Reade from Zola's *L'Assommoir*. Although the play was a temperance tract, where the novel had been a sociological analysis, the climax of both was the descent into delirium tremens of the drunkard Copeau (see Plate IX (c)).

> His make-up is wonderful, and his voice, looks, and gestures are even horribly realistic. The unsteady walk, the thin yet bloated face, the wandering eyes, the lean, live fingers that clutch at nothingness and are never quiet, tell without need of spoken words the story of his fall... Copeau is left alone with the supposed bottle of claret... Shall he have half a glass just to warm him? The thought of the generous liquor infuses animation into his miserable body, and with trembling hands he unwraps the bottle and takes out the cork. 'What a body it has got for claret' he says, as he sniffs at it. Then a spasm of horrible delight thrills him as he makes the discovery that it is brandy. He recoils from it and crouches at the other end of the room, putting all the space possible between table and wall between him and the tempter... He will just taste it. With horrible gleaming eyes and convulsive fingers he approaches the table, seizes the bottle, and drinks. At first the spirit revives and strengthens him, and with new vigour he rushes out of the room, carrying the bottle with him. When he comes back his wife has returned, and finds him a raving maniac with the empty bottle. So he dies on the stage, the audience being spared no detail of delirium tremens. Whether this is legitimate art or desirable effect is a matter for individual opinion. but there can be no question of the power and intensity with which Mr Warner represents the most terrible scene ever presented on the English stage.[28]

The impact of such 'realism' cannot be doubted, though in his 'thrills', 'recoils' and 'crouches', Warner was still using traditional starts, transitions and attitudes to communicate his agony to the audience. Indeed, the explicit physicalisation of his being tempted by the bottle is very like the comically twitching fingers of Robson's *Daddy Hardcastle*. If Warner was being clinically accurate, it seems disturbingly like the sensational pathology of Mme Tussaud's Chamber of Horrors.

The scene of 'passionate action' in *The Silver King* by Henry Arthur Jones (Princess's, 1882), is not dumb-show but a soliloquy. Yet, the way it illustrates mental processes and transitions of emotion is very similar to the earlier scenes. The play starred Wilson Barrett, and it received an ecstatic review in *The Era*:

> In place of pantomimical, spectacular dramas, where the decorators and pictorial and mechanical effects are paramount... [it tells] a story of the present time in such a manner as to keep the attention chained by a succession of

original and striking incidents which serve to lay bare some of the vilest and most degrading of human passions, and to exhibit, in no over-accentuated, but in perfect natural colours, some of the loftiest and most delicate emotions of which human nature is capable.[29]

Barrett played Wilfred Denver, another drunkard, though one who is redeemable. At the end of the first act he awakes from a stupor in a strange room, and discovers the murdered body of his enemy Geoffrey Ware:

DENVER: *(Sits up and stares round him, tries to collect himself.)* What's up? What's the matter? *(Shakes himself.)* What am I doing here? This won't do! Get home! Get home you drunken scoundrel! Aren't you ashamed of yourself, Will Denver? Keeping your poor wife sitting up half the night for you – get home, d'ye hear, get home. *(Raises himself with difficulty and stares round and staggers.)* What's the matter with my head? I can't recollect! What place is this? *(With a sudden flash of recollection.)* Ah! Geoffrey Ware's room, I remember – yes, yes, I said I'd kill him and – Oh, my head, I'd better get home. Where's my hat? *(Gets up, takes candle, staggers, steadies himself, comes round table, sees WARE.)* What's that? It's Geoffrey Ware! What's he doing here? Get up, will you? *(Kneels down.)* Ah, what's this? Blood! He's shot! My God, I've murdered him. No! No! Let me think. What happened? Ah yes, I remember now – I came in at that door, he sprang at me and then we struggled. *(Looking at revolver)* My revolver – One barrel fired – I've murdered him. No, he's not dead, Geoffrey Ware! Is he dead? *(Eagerly feeling Ware's pulse.)* No, it doesn't beat. *(Tears down Ware's waistcoat and shirt, puts ear over Ware's heart.)* No, no, quite still, quite still. He's dead! Dead! Dead! Oh, I've killed him – I've killed him. *(Rising frantically, takes up revolver and puts it in his pocket.)* What can I do? *(With a great cry.)* Don't stare at me like that! *(Snatching off table cover and throwing it over body, his eyes fixed and staring at it unable to take off his glance.)* Close those eyes, Geoffrey – close them. Ah, yes, I murdered him – I've done it – I've done it – murdered him! *(Exit, his lips mechanically jabbering.)* I've done it! I've done it! I've done it! I've done it!

As written, the text seems merely banal, and one might wish Barratt had performed the scene in true dumb-show without the crude exclamations, but the speech does chart in detail each adjustment of the mental processes – gradual perception changing to horrified realisation – with each shift separated and underlined. This was the essence of melodrama acting and *The Era* described it as: 'A scene which for tragic intensity and marvellous inspiration has not been excelled in any drama of modern times.'[30] However, when it was revived in 1899 the artifice was painfully apparent. Perceptions had changed, but not all actors could change techniques. In seventeen years Barrett's mastery had turned into mannerism:

Of the acting it is difficult to speak with perfect fairness. In a play of this kind a robust, old-fashioned, conventional style is probably essential. Modern naturalism is out of place. To do Mr Barrett and his company justice, that touch of naturalism was completely absent. Even the most effective characters... were of the stage stagey... Mr Barrett's mannerisms have grown upon him to such an extent that his performances have ceased to bear any ascertainable relation to life. Voice, intonation, gesture, even facial expression are all modelled upon some extraordinary convention of his own, and the result is at times almost intolerable.[31]

Early in the century all actors, even in crude melodramas, used the same techniques as Siddons, Kean and Macready in Shakespeare. But by the end theatrical taste and theatrical techniques had diverged irretrivably. A performance like Wilson Barrett's, which grew out of the romantic tradition of demonstrating explicitly all that the characters felt, was considered by the cultured champions of naturalism to be contrived and artificial. This difference of perception made the 1890s a decade of controversy, even conflict. But before moving on to the arguments that raged around Henry Irving, let us consider a less controversial, though highly conventional, entertainment from the 1830s: the melodrama *Jack Sheppard*.

10

Jack Sheppard
by J. B. Buckstone

—————《O》—————

Adelphi Theatre, 28 October 1839

JACK SHEPPARD	Mrs Keeley
JONATHON WILD	Mr Lyon
BLUESKIN	Mr Paul Bedford
OWEN WOOD	Mr Wilkinson
DARRELL	Mr J. F. Saville
THAMES DARRELL	Mr E. H. Butler
Sir ROWLAND TRENCHARD	Mr Maynard
KNEEBONE	Mr H. Beverly
SHOTBOLT	Mr Wright
QUILT ARNOLD	Mr King
ABRAHAM MENDEZ	Mr Yates
Mrs WOOD	Mrs Fosbroke
WINNIFRED WOOD	Miss Allison
Mrs SHEPPARD	Miss M. Lee

The Action is set in London during the reign of George the Second

Act I: Epoch the first, 1703 – The widow and her child

Owen Wood, a carpenter, adopts two baby sons: Jack is the son of his journey-man, Thomas Sheppard, who has been hanged for theft; the other he rescues from the Thames, when the child's father is swept away under London Bridge having been pursued and shot by Sir Rowland Trenchard's men. During these adventures Wood crosses the path of Jonathon Wild, and his confederate, Blueskin, who rule the underworld of the Old Mint, Southwark.

Act II: Epoch the second, 1715 – The idle apprentice

Jack and 'Thames' Darrell are now apprentices to Wood. Jack is delinquent, and Thames exemplary – and beloved of Wood's daughter Winnifred. Jack has stolen a miniature from the house of Sir Rowland Trenchard. When Thames insists they return it, they discover Thames is a relation of Sir Rowland's. Jonathon Wild has meanwhile become a government informer, entrapping Jacobites like Captain Kneebone. He has found out enough of Sir Rowland's plot against the Darrell family to blackmail him. The two boys are arrested by Wild for the theft of the portrait, but Jack engineers their escape from the Round-house. Thames flees to France.

Act III: Nine years later, 1724

Jack, now a famous house-breaker, has escaped from Newgate. He meets up with Blueskin, his lieutenant, and his doxies in a 'Flash Ken'. Wild has become Chief Thief-taker to Sir Robert Walpole, and is determined to recapture Jack. He has also renewed his blackmail of Sir Rowland Trenchard, and, as Thames has now returned, threatens to kill the boy. Jack, disguised as one of Wild's henchmen, overhears Wild's schemes – and discovers that his own mother is also related to the Trenchards. He determines to assist Thames. Meanwhile Sir Rowland rebels against Wild's threats, and Wild murders him in the well-hole in his cellar. However Wild and his accomplice, Mendez the Jew, find they have locked themselves in the cellar.

Act IV

Jack is recaptured when he visits his mother's grave, and Blueskin starts to organise a rescue party, calling on Wood and Thames for assistance. Jack is visited in the condemned cell by Sir John Thornhill, William Hogarth and John Gay, all of whom are inspired to commemorate Jack in paint and on stage. Left alone, Jack makes his great escape attempt – from his chains, from the cell, and across the roofs of Newgate. The climax comes when Blueskin's gang burn Wild's house around him, while Jack is recaptured, as Wood, Thames and Winnifred look on in horror.

J. B. Buckstone adapted *Jack Sheppard* from Harrison Ainsworth's novel while it was being serialised in *Bentley's Miscellany* (January 1839 to February 1840). In October 1839 the novel was published in full, and before the end of that month eight different dramatisations were in performance. Ainsworth, and his illustrator George Cruikshank, gave particular help to the Surrey Theatre, but Buckstone's Adelphi production played longest, and was most often revived.[1] His script follows the novel extremely closely, reproducing whole speeches verbatim. If anything the play has fewer passages of high-flown sentiment than the novel. Sir Rowland Trenchard's guilty agonising illustrates the Gothic tone of Ainsworth's dialogue which Buckstone played down, excising the passage in parenthesis:

More blood! More blood! Shall I never banish those horrible phantoms from my couch – the father with his bleeding breast and dripping hair? – the mother with her wringing hands and looks of vengence and reproach? And must another be added to their number – their son? *[Horror! let me be spared this new crime! – And yet the gibbet – my name tarnished – my escutcheon blotted by the hangman! No, I cannot submit to that!]*[2]

The major part of Buckstone's editing consisted of speeding up the latter part of the plot, by cutting two of Sheppard's escapes from prison and Wild's escape from the well-hole. This led to some inconsitencies, but few that would have been noticed in the excitement of the action.

Both the novel and its dramatisations were comdemned for their sympathetic portrayal of a notorious criminal, particularly when a valet, convicted of murdering his master, blamed the novel for putting the idea into his head.[3] In 1840 the Lord Chamberlain refused licences to new plays about Sheppard, though the two scripts, including Buckstones's, which had been originally licensed could still be played. Several managers attempted to avoid the prohibition by using alternative titles:

> In order to evade the law, however, *Jack Sheppard* bobbed up in all sorts of versions and under all sorts of names!... including the following; *The Idle Apprentice; The Lost Apprentice; The Boy Burglar; The Young Housebreaker; The Storm in the Thames; Thames Darrell; Jack Ketch;* and *The Stone Jug.* In all these, of course Jack Sheppard had another name.[4]

Ainsworth's novel had appeared at the same time as Dickens's *Oliver Twist,* and these two 'Newgate Novels' were the climax of a whole series, which had started with Bulwer Lytton's *Paul Clifford* (1830). They spawned a host of 'transpontine' melodramas, and during the 1830s the Coberg, the Surrey and the Britannia presented several highwaymen: Captain Kyd, Claude Duval, Sixteen String Jack, Captain Heron and Dick Turpin. Murderers too were dramatised: William Corder, in *Maria Marten* (1829), *Jonathon Bradford* (1833), *Simon Lee* (1839), and ultimately Sweeney Todd, in Dibdin Pitt's *The String of Pearls, or The Fiend of Fleet Street* (1847). Of course, London had long been a hotbed of crime, but in the 1830s, efforts were being made to confront the problem, starting with Peel's Metropolitan Police Act of 1829. Keith Hollingsworth explains the appeal of 'Sheppardism' in the context of these changes:

> In certain persons, perhaps, a sense of injustice... might flow into a sympathetic identification with young Jack; but, despite some Chartist feeling in the populace, this was not the temper of the Sheppard enthusiasm, which was fundamentally gay... Sheppardism was not merely a working-class epidemic... The owners of Newgate had been forced to yield some of their power in 1832; the death-dealing laws had been swept away in the half-dozen years just preceding this novel and these plays; hangings had become few, the gallows less obtrusive; policemen walked the streets of a safer London. Prison reform was resepectable... A vast public could, at such a moment, permit itself to idolize a young thief – could see him as a victim of the old system or as a rebel against it, or could merely be entertained by a daring scamp who

loved his mother – without suffering a really inhibiting concern about the gravity of the issues.[5]

Against this defence of the play's innocuousness must be set the record of the Lord Chamberlain's censorship. His office maintained a close watch on all Newgate Drama, and in 1859 the newly appointed Examiner of Plays, William Donne, banned not only all plays based on *Jack Sheppard*, including Buckstone's, but those based on *Oliver Twist*. In 1868 Dickens's reputation was such that the ban on *Oliver Twist* was raised, but when Webster applied to revive Buckstone's *Jack Sheppard* at the Adelphi in 1873 he had to agree to the title *The Stone Jug*, change the names of the characters and remove Jack's 'two wives'.[6] In the late seven-

Figure 5. *Jack Sheppard*, frontispiece to the Webster edition, attributed to Pierce Egan, but in fact the Cruikshank illustration for Ainsworth's novel with the addition of the conventional frame of a proscenium arch

ties, after Donne's retirement, Newgate plays were licensed, but by then theatrical taste had changed, and the most popular version was a burlesque, *Little Jack Sheppard* with Nellie Farren and Fred Leslie at the Gaiety.

Hollingsworth may be correct in suggesting that Newgate novels romanticised the skill and bravado of the highwayman for the benefit of a middle-class readership, who had escaped into the new suburbs from the threatening violence of the East End, and Surrey-side rookeries, but the poor costermongers and sweat-shop labourers, who inhabited those districts, even if they were not criminal themselves, still saw the successful housebreaker or pickpocket as a class hero who robbed from the snobs and toffs. Those classes, who never read *Bentley's Miscellany*, but saw the melodrama versions, would have had a more personal response than the humanitarian novel-readers.[7] The fact that most thieves robbed their poverty-stricken neighbours was overlooked. But no such tolerance was extended to the criminal *exploiters*, – the gang bosses, fences, 'kidsmen' like Fagin, who ran schools of child pickpockets, and, above all, the informers, decendants of Jonathon Wild, who 'shopped' any petty criminal who fell behind with their protection money. Their activities were readily compared to those of the landlord, whose bailiffs could throw the most law-abiding citizen into the street, or even prison, for debt.[8]

Ainsworth's criminals were easily recognised a hundred years after Sheppard's death, and the plays' popularity suggests a 'contemporary relevance', yet, as a novelist, Ainsworth was remarkable for his research into historical manners and attitudes. The mounting and dressing of the play at the Adelphi was equally meticulous. Martin Meisel uses *Jack Sheppard* as a prime example of how stage design and *mise-en-scène* were used to 'realise' the illustrations from the published novel.[9] In this case they were by George Cruikshank, and at several points the note *'Tableau (see Illustration)'* appears in stage directions. As frontispiece to the Webster's acting edition, the Cruikshank engraving of Jack carving his name on the beam is printed within a proscenium arch frame, though it is described as 'an etching, by Pierce Egan, the Younger, from a drawing taken during the representation (see Fig. 5).[10] The acting edition describes the costumes in considerable detail, for example, Owen Wood's first dress is 'Plum coloured coat, gilt buttons, black smalls, old grey silk waistcoat, large shawl cravat, black George wig, three-cornered black hat'. How-ever, when compared with Ainsworth's own description of Wood's dress, the antiquarian accuracy of the stage costume seems merely conventional:

> The person, whose age might be forty, was attired in a brown double-breasted frieze coat, with very wide skirts, and a very narrow collar; a light drugget

waistcoat with pockets reaching to the knees; black plush breeches; grey worsted hose; and shoes with round toes, wooden heels, and high quarters, fastened by small silver buckles. He wore a three-cornered hat, a sandy-coloured scratch wig, and had a thick woollen wrapper folded round his throat. His clothes had evidently seen some service, and were plentifully begrimed with the dust of the workshop. Still he had a decent look, and decidedly the air of one well-to-do in the world.[11]

In another respect too, the play tended to generalise the authentic details of the novel: Ainsworth made extensive use of thieves' 'lingo', but the play restricted it to the most obviously vulgar character, Blueskin, while Sheppard and Wild adopt a more heightened style. Apart from this change in language, Buckstone could hardly make Ainsworth's characters more theatrical. The whole tone of the novel conveys the vivid style of melodrama characterisation: emotions are fully vocalised, and the physiognomy is crudely explicit. Blueskin is swarthy with a bottle nose, Abraham Mendez sports the long red beard of the stage Jew, and Wild's eyes are described as, 'small and grey; as far apart and as sly-looking as those of a fox. A physignomist, indeed, would have likened him to that crafty animal.'[12] The use of stereotyped characters did not imply a lack of detail, and one should not assume that even Jonathon Wild, motivelessly malignant though he is, would have been played as a caricature villain as parodied by Gilbert à Beckett or Jerome K. Jerome. Although the Webster edition lists a Mr Lyon as the first actor of Wild, O. Smith, the Adelphi's leading villain, soon took over the part.

Smith's most famous roles had been as supernatural creatures: Ruthven the Vampire, Vanderdecken the Flying Dutchman, and Frankenstein's Monster. Marston describes him as:

Celebrated for his deliniations in melodrama, both of villains and supernatural agents. That he could be very thorough in such presentations, suggesting at times by his voice, expression and make-up unfathomable wickedness, and again could freeze the spectator with his wierd appearance... I can still recall. He was, in a word, the nightmare of the stage.[13]

One of his most famous effects was his evil laugh, 'a taunting, deliberate basso profundo effect in three syllables... widely imitated in the profession and became a convention in the interpretation of villain roles'.[14] Another major role taken by an Adelphi stalwart was Paul Bedford's Blueskin. As a low comedian Bedford made more of the humour than the savagery of the part, emphasising geniality and gluttony. His rendition of 'Jolly Nose' was so popular that he sang it as a solo for years afterwards.[15] Frederick Yates, manager of the Adelphi, who specialised in playing grotesque eccentrics, played Mendez the Jew.

However it is in the playing of Jack Sheppard himself that the particular interest of this piece lies. The role was taken by Mrs Keeley, wife of the unctuous comedian Robert Keeley, Buckstone's foil in many Haymarket farces. Mary Keeley specialised in chambermaids, as in *Betty Martin* (Adelphi, 1855):

> Mrs Keeley converts the slight sketch into a work replete with life and truthfulness. The agonized terror with which she rushes on stage when she has just broken the clock, is all but tragical, and her weeping is such weeping that we feel could not exist in any other situation... The whole character is a complete creation from beginning to end.[16]

George Henry Lewes compared her with her husband: 'Keeley could play a gentleman; Mrs Keeley could never rise above the servant's hall. But, on the other hand, Mrs Keeley had a power over the more energetic passions which he wanted; she was an excellent melodramatic actress, and her pathos drew tears.'[17]

The cross-dressing of Jack Sheppard is a good illustration of the subversion described by Bernard Sharratt, by which the audience recognised the player 'intimately', but were 'distanced' from the fictitious character. This allowed them to identify with the personality without having to accept the moral reality of the play. A more well-known example of cross-dressing being used in this way is Cherubino in *The Marriage of Figaro*. Here potentially salacious adolescent lust is rendered innocuous, even charming, by a woman playing the part. A similar effect was achieved when Macheath was acted as a breeches-role in *The Beggar's Opera*, though this was usually considered to be an act of parody and burlesque. Perhaps the Macheath tradition suggested the cross-casting of *Jack Sheppard*, but there was no conscious parody in Buckstone's text or in Keeley's performance. Rather, her portrayal of the adolescent housebreaker was intended to help audiences warm to Jack's naive and charming qualities, and subvert his criminality. It is significant that in other 'respectable' theatres Jack was played by women – Mrs Honner at Sadler's Wells and Miss Rogers at the Queens – but in the 'lower-class' theatres men played the part, Hicks at the Victoria and E. F. Saville at the Surrey. 'Moral distancing' was less important here than in the West End. But this deliberate 'miscasting' of cross-dressing, which drew attention to the conventionality of the performance, was but an extreme example of what happened when audiences recognised other favourite actors in their stock roles: O. Smith leering and sneering as Wild, Paul Bedford boozing and singing as Blueskin, and Frederick Yates playing up the staginess of the stage Jew. All these performances displayed the same attractive ambiguity.

Mrs Keeley in no way played up the inappropriateness of the cross-casting. She acted with complete conviction, after meticulous preparation. Not only was her costume based on the Cruikshank illustrations, but she wore a short-cropped wig – there was nothing of the 'principal-boy' in her appearance – and although she often played in burlesques there was no conscious parody in her portrayal of Jack (see Plate VII(a)). There was none of the sexual titillation that Mme Vestris had brought to her performance of *Don Giovanni in London* in 1820. Obviously the casting of women as young boys must have had, at least subliminally, a certain sexual attraction, but often it was an 'innocent' convention to ensured the mature performance of immature characters. Dickens's response to Marie Bancroft's portrayal of Pippo in *The Maid and the Magpie* (Strand, 1856), which was a burlesque rather than straight role, was that 'it is perfectly free from offence... it [is] so exactly like a boy, that you cannot think of anthing like her sex in association with it'.[18] This kind of 'straight' cross-dressing was not the salacious exploitation of sexuality that it was to become later in the century, with female impersonators in the halls and principal boys in pantomime,[19] but the combination of realistic playing and artificial convention which was the peculiar appeal of melodrama. This very artificiality made the genre vunerable to parody, whether in the mockery of critics or the guying of burlesque. Yet even in *Little Jack Sheppard*, the Gaiety burlesque of 1885, the cross-dressing of Nellie Farren had a certain innocence: 'Nellie Farren was neither boy nor girl on the stage in her greatest performances, but a kind of sexless *espièglerie* – for there was no "sex-appeal" in her deserved fame.'[20] Although this refusal to acknowledge the appeal of androgyny seems ingenuous today, Frederick Robson had shown that burlesque offered scope for serious acting. Mrs Keeley certainly approached her melodrama role with exemplary seriousness.

In preparation for the performance she visited Newgate and was shown the very manacles from which Sheppard was reputed to have escaped, she was instructed in the use of plane and chisel by the stage-carpenter, and in the niceties of pugalism.[21] Her demonstration of these skills, especially that of escapology, reinforces Sharatt's analogy between popular theatre and spectator sport, as she made a particular point of playing them out to the audience:

> When I slipped [the handcuffs] off it was no stage slip, but a bona-fide operation. And it hurt me sometimes! But I contrived to squeeze my hands out by bringing the broad part together... I came down to the front, in full blaze of the footlights, so that the audience might fairly judge, and I always got an extra round of applause. I think I deserved it.[22]

When she picked Wild's pocket, dexterity was combined with drama, and, as in many suspense-scenes, the interplay between the reality of the physical skill and the fiction of the situation was of the very essence of melodrama:

> The abstraction of the documents from Jonathon Wild's pocket was so rapid and dextrous as to appear the accomplishment of a practiced hand at pocket-picking. Indeed, it looked so like the real thing that the audience were afraid lest the unwary thief-taker should turn round and catch the young culprit in the act, and there was quite a sigh of relief when Jack had safely landed the rightful proofs of his birth. The pickpocket incident was the result of careful study on the part of the actress, assisted by some instruction from an expert in the ways of thieves. The actor of Jonathon Wild seldom, if ever, felt the small, flexible hand of Mrs Keeley as it dived neatly into his pocket, and was hardly aware that the trick was done.[23]

Although Mrs Keeley maintained, and critical descriptions confirm, that she played the part 'realistically' and 'identified completely' with the character, in the more comical scenes she employed the 'arch' style of comic acting that 'impressed one with the idea that she was enjoying the joke quite as much as the audience, and yet was unconscious of being the cause of their merriment. This gave a spontaneity to everything she did or said, making her acts and words appear perfectly natural, or unstudied.' For instance, when Mendez said of escaping from handcuffs: 'Dat is no easy matter', Jack, who had just managed to file off his chains, replied in the same accent: '"No, dat it ain't" (holding up the handcuffs aside to the audience, who, of course, shout with laughter).'[24] In Jack's final escape from Newgate, Mrs Keeley once again displayed her technical mastery of loosening chains, yet she sang and danced as she did so. The ambivalence between the conventions of entertainment and the reality of the drama became exquisite when 'he dances in his fetters without his shoes. He suddenly stops, as if in pain, holds up his foot, and exclaims "A nail!"' This was then used to pick the padlock that held him fast.[25]

Mrs Keeley was equally capable of moving her audience to tears, as when Jack threw himself on his mother's grave, or in the final scene when he collapsed with exhaustion and despair. The year before *Jack Sheppard* she had triumphed in the most pathetic of all Victorian breeches-roles: Smike in *Nicholas Nickleby*. Edward Stirling had written this for the Adelphi in 1838, with Ben Webster playing Nicholas; O. Smith, Newman Noggs; Yates, Mantalini and Mrs Keeley, Smike. Dickens himself praised her performance: 'Mrs Keeley's first appearance beside the fire... and all the rest of Smike was excellent.'[26] At the first performance, however, there was a misunderstanding, which illustrated how the spectators thought they knew what to expect from a favourite performer, and how it took all Mrs Keeley's skill to retrieve the initiative:

> When Smike was seen for the first time, huddled up over the wretched fire in

the dimly-lighted kitchen of Do-the-boys Hall, the audience scarcely recognised the actress, and were for some time in doubt whether to laugh or weep at Smike's woe-begone appearance. At last they took a humorous view of the situation... and presently there was a roar of laughter in the house. But when the actress rose and walked totteringly to the footlights, where she remained still speechless and staring blankly at vacancy, the laughter gradually subsided, and long before Smike's opening lines were over, there was hardly a dry eye in the house. Then, when the lines came to an end, the walls of the Adelphi rang again and again with thunders of applause at the artistic conception of the character.[27]

The audience, recognising a 'point', responded, first by identifying with the feelings of the character, and then with applause for the actress. Emotional truth and theatrical conventions were in no way mutually exclusive: 'The desponding tones in which [Smike] pictured the approach of gloomy death... hushed the house into complete stillness, which was only broken by the most rapturous plaudits.'[28]

Mrs Keeley took her audiences with her, even when playing against her age and sex, which suggests that the actor's art in melodrama was to use a highly *conventionalised* technique to convey highly *convincing* emotion. The artificiality of the genre, both in texts and performance, was essential to its effect. Melodramas may have teetered on the edge of absurdity, but their appeal was not limited to the unsophisticated and gullible. They differed little in techniques and effectiveness from the great Victorian novels. Dickens was fond of mocking bad performances of melodrama, but in his novels – and indeed in his own public readings[29] – he revealed the power of *stylising* both grotesque comedy and sentimental pathos. Maybe the art that conceals art also defeats art – if the artist's aim is to touch the *feelings* of his public. To fully appreciate the power of Victorian melodrama one need only read an early Dickens novel; and to appreciate Dickens one must never forget his love of popular theatre. Literary critics who compare his finished novels with the bare scripts of the stage adaptions usually conclude they were crude failures: 'The dialogue in the novels is alive, but it can rarely stand alone, as a score of adaptations for the stage, in which the dialogue has been isolated and compressed into a play, plainly attest... Dickens rendered down into a play has seldom been Dickensian.'[30] Of course, much of his description, as well as his social comment, was lost, but the number and popularity of the dramatisations suggest that actors were not only capable of impersonating his extravagant characters, but, through their own emotional intensity, could give a sense of reality to many scenes, which on the page, not only of the playscripts, but in the novels themselves *read* as mawkish and sentimental.

11

The psychology
of acting

In 1830 Denis Diderot's essay on acting, *Le Paradoxe sur le comédien*, was published for the first time. It had originally been written in 1773 as a riposte to a French version, *Garrick, ou Les Acteurs anglais* by Antonio Sticotti, of John Hill's *The Actor* (1750), which I quoted in Chàpter 3: 'All the art in the world can never supply the want of sensibility in the player; if he is deficient in this essential quality... he will never make others feel what he does not feel himself.'[1] In his *Paradoxe* Diderot argued that the true art of the actor was precisely that he did not feel the emotions he portrayed, but reproduced the appearance of emotion by conscious imitation. He did not underrate the skill needed to learn and reproduce the symptoms of emotion, but argued that the process was one of observation – even of oneself – *followed* by imitation:

> He has rehearsed every note of his passion. He has learnt before a mirror every particle of his despair. He knows exactly when he must produce his handkerchief and shed his tears; and you will see him weep at the word, at the syllable, he has chosen, not a second sooner or later. The broken voice, the half-uttered words... the trembling limbs, the fainting, the bursts of fury – all this is pure mimicry... magnificent aping which the actor remembers long after his first study of it, of which he was perfectly conscious when he first put it before the public, and which leaves him... a full freedom of mind. Like other gymnastics, it taxes only his bodily strength.[2]

In *The Player's Passion* (1985), Joseph Roach sees Diderot's commentary as the most perceptive analysis of acting to date, pointing out that most twentieth-century theorist/practitioners eventually came to similar conclusions as to the essentially physical nature of performance, be it in Stanislavski's 'line of physical action', Brecht's 'gestus', Meyerhold's 'biomechanics', Artaud's 'athletics of the heart', or Grotowski's 'authentic action'. Inspiration comes from the dynamics of the body: stance, breath, energy and resonation. Roach perhaps exaggerates the influence of Diderot's arguments, in that many actors have vehmently rejected, even resented, them, but he is correct in pointing out that Diderot formulated the baseline for all future discussion.[3] In this chapter I want to follow the debate through the nineteenth century, and show how, despite Diderot, and despite the formality of their acting system, with its points, starts, attitudes and realisations, English actors continued to maintain that sensibility was the basis of their art. Even though it was not until the 1880s, with the translation of *The Paradox*, that these questions were formally discussed in England, in France the issues had been pursued throughout the century.

The tragedian Talma, writing in 1825, acknowledged the necessity for technical control, but, evoking the classic duality of Descartes, he attributed genius to a balance between emotion and reason. He certainly recognised the sensual excitement of 'inspiration': 'That faculty of exaltation which agitates an actor, takes possession of his senses, shakes even his very soul, and enables him to enter into the most tragic situations and the most terrible of passions as if they were his own.' However, 'The intelligence that accompanies sensibility judges the impressions which the latter has made us feel; it selects, arranges them, and subjects them to calculation.' As a practitioner, Talma's description of the creative rehearsal process carries more conviction than Diderot's:

> In the first place, by repeated exercises he enters deeply into the emotions, and his speech acquires the accent proper to the situation, of the personage he has to represent. This done he goes to the theatre not only to give theatrical effect to his studies, but also to yield himself to the spontaneous flashes of his sensibility and all the emotions which it involutarily produces in him. What does he then do? In order that his inspiration may not be lost, his memory, in the silence of repose, recalls the accents of his voice, the expressions of his features, his action – in a word the spontaneous workings of his mind... His intelligence then passes all these means in review, connecting them and fixing them in his memory, to re-employ them at pleasure in succeeding representations.[4]

Note how Talma separated the mental functions of feeling and judging, imagining and remembering, just as the Romantic actors used their formalised gestures to represent clearly differentiated 'dramatic passions'.

The English actor who most closely resembled Talma was Macready. The French themselves noted the similarity when he performed *Virginius* in Paris in 1828. Although Macready was unacquainted with either Talma's or Diderot's theories, his partnership with Helen Faucit, which started in 1837, illuminates the whole question of identification, improvisation and emotional involvement. Helen Faucit was born into a theatrical family in 1819. Her actress mother lived with William Farren, the Haymarket comedian, and her 'uncle' Percy Farren trained the young girl: 'To him and him only could I confide, with the assurance of perfect sympathy, all my devotion for the heroines of Shakespeare. He taught me the value of the different metres in blank verse and rhyme... he made me understand the value of words, nay, of every letter of every word, for the purpose of declamation.' But it was not only on her technique that Farren worked; his response to her first professional performance, as a thirteen-year-old Juliet (Richmond, 1833), had been disappointment because 'I was not in the character throughout, and he found I had not the true artistic power to lose myself in the being of the character.'[5]

The desire to lose herself in the character remained with Faucit throughout her career – even in her last performance of Juliet, aged fifty-two, she fainted, 'overcome with the reality of the "thick-coming fancies"'.[6] No doubt her deep sense of involvement recommended her to Macready, who inherited her services when he took over Covent Garden from Charles Kemble in 1837. It was a quality that she admired in Macready : 'There is such an earnestness and meaning about everything he does, even the most trifling word or action, that carries such truth with it.'[7] At first Faucit did not enjoy acting with him as much as with Charles Kemble, 'there is something cold and distant almost repulsive in his manner', and when he led her on for a curtain call she felt 'he thought it a great bore'.[8] She changed her mind on both points: within two years she had fallen in love with Macready, much to his embarassment,[9] and came to agree with him that 'calls' were destructive to the art of acting, particularly if taken during the play:

> How offensive to right feeling, as well as to every rule of art, it is, for example, to see Claude Melnotte lead on Pauline, when the curtain has just descended on their separation... or, more intolerable still, where Juliet has taken the potion, been mourned over by her kindred as dead, and Romeo is, as we think, far away in Mantua, to see her advance hand in hand with him at the end of the act in answer to the summons to the unthinking few! Who can care what becomes of them after? The spell is broken, the interest destroyed.

In the previous chapters I argued that an audience's enjoyment could encompass the skill of the performer as well as the suspense of the drama, but to the actress who wished to 'lose herself in the character' such an interruption was intolerable:

> On the occasions when the... clamour of the audience left me no choice, and I have gone before them (I fear very ungraciously), I have never been the same afterwards, – never able to lose myself in full measure in the illusion of the story... It was ever my desire to forget my audience. Little did they... know how much they took from my power of working out my conception when they forced me in this way out of my dream-world.[10]

On the first night of her performing Pauline, in *The Lady of Lyons* (15

February 1838), she learnt the danger of losing herself entirely, when Macready told her off for introducing a burst of hysterical laughter:

> Which came upon me, I suppose, as the natural relief from the intensity of the mingled feelings of anger, scorn, wounded pride, and outraged love, by which I found myself carried away. The effect upon the audience was electrical because the impulse was genuine. But well do I remember Mr Macready's remonstrance with me for yielding to it. It was too daring, he said; to have failed in it on a first representation might have ruined the scene (which was true). No one, moreover, should ever, he said, hazard an unrehearsed effect.[11]

Macready too could be carried away by an emotional scene, but it seems that he was capable of indulging his feelings at the same time as controlling his performance. Sensibility and intelligence seemed to function simultaneously, rather than consecutively, as Talma had described. At the climax of *The Winter's Tale*, Hermione appears as a statue and 'comes to life' when kissed by Leontes. Macready embraced Helen Faucit with unwonted vehemence:

> He was Leontes' very self! His passionate joy at finding Hermione really alive seemed beyond control. Now he was prostrate at her feet, then enfolding her in his arms... The hair, which came unbound, and fell on my shoulders, was reverently kissed and caressed. The whole change was so sudden, so overwhelming, that I suppose I cried out hysterically, for he whispered to me, 'Don't be frightened my child! don't be frightened! Control yourself!' All this went on during a tumult of applause that sounded like a storm of hail.[12]

Another amusing account of spontaneous 'inspiration' involving Macready comes from John Colman, when he was playing Othello to Macready's Iago:

> I sprang upon Iago, and seized him by the throat. I remembered nothing until I found I had literally flung him bodily down upon the stage, and stood above him, erect and quivering with wrath. On his part, he growled like an angry lion. The incident was as unprecedented as it was unpremeditated, and its effect on the audience was electrical. They got up and cheered.

When Colman excused himself to Macready after the play, explaining he had been carried away, Macready answered gruffly: 'Remember the next time you play this part with me, confine your excitement to your mind, and not to your muscles!'[13] Diderot and Talma would have considered all these lapses into emotion examples of bad acting, and would have agreed with George Henry Lewes when he argued: 'All art is symbolical. If it presented emotion in its real expression it would cease to move us as art... [the actor] is feigning and we know he is feigning.'

However Lewes formulated a rather different paradox than Diderot's:

> If the actor lose all power over his art under the disturbing influence of emotion, he also loses all power over his art in proportion to his deadness to emo-

tion. If he really feel, he cannot act; but he cannot act unless he feel... As in all art, feeling lies at the root, but the foliage and flowers, though deriving their sap from emotion, derive their form and structure from the intellect. The poet cannot write while his eyes are full of tears... but he must have felt, or his verse will be a mere echo... he is a spectator of his own tumult; and though moved by it, can yet so master it as to select from it only those elements which suit his purpose. We are all spectators of ourselves; but it is the peculiarity of the artistic nature to indulge in such introspection even in moments of all but the most disturbing passion, and to draw thence materials for art. This is true also of the fine actor.

As for sudden flashes of 'inspiration', Lewes insisted the intellect needs to judge whether their suggestions are really appropriate: 'Trusting to the inspiration of the moment is like trusting to a ship wreck for your first lesson in swimming.'[14] The subtlety of these distinctions tended to be lost on Romantic actors whose whole concern was to excite the feelings of the audience, and as all these 'lapses' had provoked tumults of applause, it is not surprising that the vehement expression of emotion, even if expressed 'symbolically', often led performers to experience the feelings themselves.

Most psychological theories of the time, such as those of Darwin, Herbert Spencer, Alexander Bain and William James, concentrated on the physiological basis of emotion. Darwin wrote that 'Most of our emotions are so closely connected with their expression, that they hardly exist if the body remains passive.'[15] Lewes himself had argued along these lines in his *Physiology of Common Life* (1859), and in his major study of psychology, *Problems of Life and Mind* (1874-79), even calling one of the volumes 'The Physical Basis of the Mind'. His thinking on psychology was much influenced by experiments on the nervous system, in which electric stimuli were used to activate supposedly dead muscles. Given Lewes's conclusion from such evidence that 'it is the man and not the brain that thinks; it is the organism as a whole, and not one organ that feels and acts',[16] it is not surprising that he placed equal emphasis on the sensory experience of feelings, likening it to the vibrations of an electric current, and on the selective control of these sensations, transforming them into 'artistic symbols', which he attributed to the 'idealising' power of the intellect. But, unlike Talma, he did not propound a Cartesian division between mind and body. 'Rather', according to Roach:

> Lewes sees a rapid alternation of attention from one level of consciousness to another, not unlike alternating current in standard electrical devices. In searching out a metaphor for this version of double or multiple consciousness, Lewes shows that at least one sort of theatrical performance was foremost in his mind: 'When Ducrow rode six horses at once he pressed the reins of each alternatively, now checking, now redirecting.'[17]

The psychology of acting

One implication of this physological bias was the suggestion that internal sensations could be naturally stimulated by adopting the external expression. However, the mutual interconnection between physical expression and emotional sensation does not depend entirely on the realistic accuracy with which the outward symptoms are adopted. A symbolic representation can be equally 'affective'. Singers, dancers and mimes, as well as 'naturalistic' actors, have all found that the process of performing can stimulate what Talma called 'the faculty of exaltation'.

It was not until the 1880s that the psychological debate was joined by the actors themselves, specifically by Henry Irving and Constant Coquelin. In 1880 Coquelin, a star of the *Comédie Française*, baldly stated that he considered Diderot's Paradox 'to be literal truth; and I am convinced that one can only be a great actor on condition of complete self-mastery and ability to express feelings which are not experienced, which may never be experienced, which from the very nature of things never can be experienced'.[18] In 1887 he went on to present his own theory of 'The Dual Personality of the Actor', which was even more Cartesian than Talma's: The actor 'has his first self, which is the player, and his second self, which is the instrument. The first self conceives the person to be created... and the being that he sees is represented by his second self. This dual personality is the characteristic of the actor.'[19] He then described how he prepared his own characterisations from detailed observation. He particularly criticised actors who let their 'second self' dominate and thus perform all their roles as minor variations on their own personalities.

Coquelin may have been influenced in this argument by his compatriot François Delsarte (1811-71), who was the most philosophical acting teacher of the nineteenth century. Unfortunately Delsarte himself left no written accounts of his work, but, through his disciples, he profoundly influenced both American Modern Dance – one of the most complete expositions of his theory being by the dancer Ted Shawn, who learnt of Delsarte from Steele MacKaye[20] – and the classical French mime of Decroux. It has also been claimed that Delsarte taught Rachel and Coquelin, but most of Delsarte's pupils were not actors but opera singers and musicians, like his nephew Bizet. The basis of Delsarte's theory, unlike Coquelin's dualism, was triadic: the psyche was defined as Body, Soul and Mind, and its functions as Vital, Emotional and Intellectual. From this triad he devloped a highly complex system, which correlated psychological impulses with particular zones of the body. For instance, gesturing to or from the breast indicates intellectual idealism, to the plexus indicates spiritual aspiration, and to the gut indicates sensory appetites.

Despite his attempts to integrate mystical experiences, creative intuition and religious faith into his analysis, the 'Delsarte System', as taught by his disciples, remained fundamentally mechanistic, and in practice his categorising of physical gestures was as prescriptive as the technical handbooks of 'passions'. Incidentally, in 1886 Professor Moses True Brown of Tufts College described the system as 'semiotics' in what may be the earliest application of the term to the art of theatre: 'The term is an excellent one in the technique of expression. It signifies the appropriation of the sign to the idea. Give the sign and you suggest the mood. This fitting the gesture to the idea is Delsarte's discovery.'[21]

More original than Delsarte's semiology of physical signs and gestures were his 'Laws of Motion'. Most teachers exhorted actors to be 'graceful', 'emphatic' or just 'expressive', and usually taught these qualities through dancing and fencing, and occasionally as 'deportment'. Delsarte's systematic analysis of movement and his development of a sense of scale and style anticipated much of Laban's work in this area. As well as considering the position or attitude, he analysed the strength, pace, direction, rhythm and balance of gestures as they are formed, as part of a succession or pattern of movement.

However, the influence of this impressive French teacher on English acting must be acknowledged as slight. British actors were suspicious of any excessive systematisation, though certain Delsartian principles appeared in an article by Henry Neville on 'Gesture' in *Voice, Speech and Gesture: A Practical Handbook to the Elocutionary Art*, published in 1897. However, Neville's instructions are clumsily schematic and lack the underlying philosophy of Delsarte:

To the three main sections [of the arm] may be attributed three zones:
The VITAL   Which is the upper arm.
The VOLITIONAL Which is the forearm.
The MENTAL   Which is the hand.
Grace of motion flows from the brain and operates on the shoulder and arm, and there can be no force in the arm if the muscles of the shoulder are neglected... The shoulder intervenes in all forms of emotion:-
The COLLOQUIAL   The RHETORICAL   The EPIC.
It determines the degree of warmth, of intensity, though it does not specify their nature, but it undoubtedly shows by association with the face whether love, hate, contempt, or indifference are the inspiring cause of motion.[22]

Beyond these rather vague principles, there is no evidence that the Delsarte System was 'taken up' in England as it was in America, not only by Steele MacKaye, who had studied with him in 1871, but by David Belasco, certain silent movie actors, dancers such as Isadora Duncan, Ruth St Denis and Ted Shawn, and a host of lecturers on elocution and expression, who made the craze of 'Delsarte' as fashionable across America

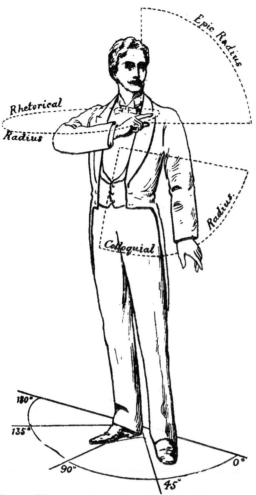

Figure 6. 'Zones of Gesture', Henry Neville's chapter 'Gesture' in *Voice, Speech and Gesture*, edited by Hugh Campbell, 1897

as 'The Method' or 'Aerobics' have been in the twentieth century.[23]

It was during his 1884-85 tour of America that Henry Irving was invited to address Harvard University on the subject of 'The Art of Acting'. Much of his lecture was a commonplace recital of anecdotes, and Irving's usual plea for actors' social respectability. It was probably prepared for him by his publicity agent, Austin Brereton, and/or his business manager, Bram Stoker.[24] However Irving made one significant observation, which I emphasise by italics:

> It is necessary to warn you against the theory expounded with brilliant inge-
> nuity by Diderot, that the actor never feels. When Macready played
> Virginius, after burying his beloved daughter, he confessed that his real expe-

rience gave a new force to his acting in the most pathetic situations of the play... It is necessary to this art that *the mind should have, as it were, a double consciousness, in which all the emotions proper to the occasion may have full swing, while the actor is all the time on the alert for every detail of his method.*[25]

What Irving had noticed was that, as with Macready in *The Winter's Tale*, sensibility and technical control can be exercised at the *same time*. It is not a question of 'either/or' but 'both'. Coquelin's devision of the self into two 'personalities' is persuasive as a means of critical analysis, as is Lewes's image of Ducrow's horses, but Irving's recognition of 'layers of consciousness' coincided more accurately with the new psychology of Theodule Ribot and Sigmund Freud than with the physiological theories of Lewes or Delsarte. Doubtless Irving was ignorant of the works of all these men, except the theatrical criticism of Lewes, and perhaps too much emphasis can be placed on a single remark in an occasional address, but the concept that feelings, behaviour and even personality are formed and controlled by unconscious layers of 'motivation' was to be crucial in twentieth-century theories of acting, particularly those of Stanislavski and the American Method. English actors have never been renowned for theoretical analysis, but as Dion Boucicault remarked in 1887: 'The Frenchman acquired his principles before he acquired his experience. The Englishman acquired his practice from which he deduced his principles.' He also made the sensible observation that Coquelin's objectivity suited his comic acting, while Irving was more at home in tragedy and melodrama: 'Comedy is largely a physiological study, tragedy is largely pathological.'[26] Whether or not Irving was a perceptive theorist of psychology, there is no question that as an actor he was a master of the pathological.

Victorian actors employed a basically emotional analysis of character. Of course there were reasons why characters felt different emotions at different times, and expression varied with personality and social background, as well as with the style of the play, but they seldom seemed to be driven by *unconscious* motives. Guilt was not suppressed, but was indulged as an agony assuaged only by further crimes. Although some characters were presented as 'naturally' good or 'naturally' evil, the reasons for these propensities were unambiguous. The same quality can be found in the early Victorian novels of Ainsworth, Dickens, Wilkie Collins and Thackeray, but later, in the works of Meredith, George Eliot, Henry James and Thomas Hardy, the psychological complexity increases; characters behave according to 'instincts' or 'conditioning', of which they are hardly aware. When Dickens lashed out at hypocrisy in the 1840s, he implied evil men knew they were being evil: it was only in his later novels, and those of other writers in the 1870s and 1880s, that unconscious hypocrisy was recognised. Richard Altick, in *Victorian Studies in Scarlet*, describes the change:

> Bulwer-Lytton, Dickens, and Collins had sometimes dignified their use of murder by attempting to depict 'the criminal mind', a topic which understandably had a special attraction for the Victorians. But they did so only to the extent of describing the mind's operation... not concerning themselves with its origins or development. Normally they did not think it necessary to convince the reader that the murderer was psychologically bent to be a murderer, or that murder would have inexorably ensued from the circumstances described. To them, as to most of their contemporaries, the criminal was a man apart. Novelists like Eliot and Hardy, however, were concerned with the forces that lay behind the criminal act, with the development of the murderer, or would-be murderer, from the ordinary human being under the irresistible pressure of circumstance and passion. They tend to use homicide, meditated or actual, to probe the psychology of ordinary men and women and illustrate the personal and social forces that caused basically well-disposed human beings to commit criminal acts. Instead of studying the criminal personality, in short, they studied the personality which became criminal.[27]

Modern critics of early Victorian fiction have, of course, found that when behaviour had been realisticly observed, it is possible to recognise a character's 'psychology', but that diagnosis was unavailable to the readers, and even writers, at the time. Actors interpreting such characters inevitably distanced themselves even further from the original 'realistic observation' of the author. Of course, as contemporary audiences shared the same assumptions as the actors, their interpretations may well have satisfied, but all too often a second-hand quality became apparent to new generations, who questioned the old assumptions. To them the performances seemed simplistic and outdated. Clement Scott scorned the melodrama of the 1850s and championed a new generation which included not only well-made society plays, but the 'new' melodrama style of Irving. In their turn, however, Scott and Irving were to be the whipping boys of the next wave of Naturalists led by Bernard Shaw and William Archer.

All sorts of new ideas and artistic movements emerged in the last quarter of the century, but the dogmatism of earlier years continued. There was little tolerance and much outrage. The old was castigated as prejudiced and bland, the new as immoral and ugly. The certainties of the 1860s – when capitalist enterprise and Imperial expansion had been seen as processes of enlightenment and civilisation – were being undermined. In the 1870s, as the balance of political power lost its equilibrium, so too dangerous '-isms' challenged the cultural and intellectual equilibrium: Darwinism, Socialism, Atheism, Impressionism, Naturalism. Although few of these ideas were presented explicitly in the theatre – English audiences have seldom found didacticism entertaining – there were changes that reflected new ideas, even within the conventionalised form of melodrama.

The Bells, as performed by Henry Irving in 1871, was a new kind of psychological melodrama. Interestingly, although created by Talien in the original, *Le Juif Polonaise* by Emile Erckmann and Pierre Alexander Chatrian (Théâtre Cluny, 1869), the part of Mathias was also performed by Coquelin. H. Chance Newton describes how Irving and Coquelin differed fundamentally in their interpretations of the man haunted by the memory of a murder he had committed years before:

> No two performances could be so opposed to each other as Coquelin's and Irving's. Irving gave a romanticised and inescapably magnetic performance that haunted one for many a day and night after seeing him. Coquelin made this innkeeping murderer a bullet-headed bully of the most matter-of-fact criminal description. The Irving 'Mathias' was in continual terror at the idea of detection, whereas Coquelin gloried in his gory crime and laughed and chuckled over it... Irving and I talked to Coquelin about this strange disparity of view concerning the homicidal licensed victualler. Coquelin, admitting that Irving's was a very great, penetrating performance, asserted roundly that nevertheless it was totally unlike the French murderer that he represented. Coquelin added, 'I play Mathias as I know such murderers to be in parts of my country; Irving's is a great assumption, but not a bit like the real thing.'[28]

Coquelin studied the external appearance of the character, Irving revealed his inner turmoil. Coquelin's approach was sociological, Irving's psychological.

Irving followed the convention of melodrama, explicitly demonstrating his tortured feelings, but there was no chance of his being overheard by some comic villager or sinister gypsy. His torment was concealed from those on stage, however vividly they were conveyed to the audience. The climax of the play is Mathias's dream, when, under a hypnotic spell, he re-enacts his crime before a ghostly court of law. The dream is so vivid that Mathias dies, half asleep half awake, crying, 'Take the rope from my neck!' The final line of the play – not always delivered because it was lost in the applause for Irving's death throes – was, 'Be comforted. He was a noble fellow, while he lived – and he has died without pain.' With or without the line, the murderer's secret died with him; no one in the play ever knew of his guilt.[29] Although this concealment was hardly the unconscious suppression of a Freudian trauma, it did suggest disturbing ideas: reality cannot always be recognised from appearances; the mind can never truly suppress a haunting memory; and blameless behaviour cannot expiate unacknowledged crime.

Irving conveyed Mathias's feelings with a combination of traditional gestures – starting in horror, quivering in fear – which he employed freely during the dream sequence, and telling details of the more naturalistic style, such as when someone mentioned the 'Polish Jew's winter':

> Irving pretends to pick cork from his glass with his little finger, slowly saying 'Oh, you were talking of that, were you?' He then brushes his finger three times against his waistcoat and repeats, 'You were talking of that.' Irving took his time. It was all done with his face and eyes. You knew what he was thinking.[30]

It was then that he heard the sound of the ghostly sledge-bells. Although he acted one of the villagers in the scene many times, Edward Gordon Craig, in his biography of Irving, confused this moment with an earlier one, when Mathias reacted to the mention of the itinerant mesmerist, which occured as he was changing his boots. Nevertheless, despite doubts as to the precision of Craig's memory, his account vividly evokes Irving's method:

> Now you might think that the act of taking off some boots could be done in one way only – but the way Irving did it had never been thought of till he did it, and has never been done since. It was in every gesture, every half move, in the play of his shoulders, legs, head, and arms, mesmeric in the highest degree... Irving was buckling his second shoe, seated, leaning over it with his two long hands stretched down over the buckles. We suddenly saw these fingers stop their work; the crown of the head suddenly seemed to glitter and become frozen – and then, at the pace of the slowest and most terrified snail, the two hands, still motionless and dead, were seen to be coming up the side of the leg... the whole torso of the man, also seeming frozen, was gradually, and by an almost perceptible movement, seen to be drawing up and back, as it would straighten a little, and to lean a little against the chair on which he was seated. Once in that position – motionless – eyes fixed ahead of him and fixed on us all – there he sat for the space of ten to twelve seconds which, I can assure you, seemed to us all like a lifetime, and then said in a voice deep and overwhelmingly beautiful: 'Oh, you were talking of that – were you?' And as the last syllable was uttered, there came from afar off the regular throbbing sound of sledge-bells.

Eventually having looked anxiously round the room, and at the quiet groups of villagers drinking and smoking,

> He glides up to a standing position... suddenly he staggers and shivers from his toes to his neck; his jaws begin to chatter; the hair on his forehead, falling over, writhes as though it were a nest of little snakes. Everyone is on his feet at once to help... and one of the moments of the immense and touching dance closes – only one – and the next one begins, and the next after – figure after figure of exquisite pattern and purpose is unfolded, and then closed, and ever a new one unfolded in its wake.[31]

This description indicates the exciting originality of Irving's style, yet he was only developing traditional melodramatic techniques. The process was conceived of as 'moments... figure after figure', and in this Irving was, in his way, making a sequence of passionate 'points', each one of which was greeted on its completion with a round of applause. Craig, by calling this a 'dance', emphasised the physical nature of the expressive gestures. They were not the semiological gestures prescribed in the handbooks or by Delsarte; Irving concentrated on the sensation rather than the sign – the qualities that Desarte had identified in his Laws of Movement: energy, tension, rhythm, direction. Indeed Irving's movement seemed to bear out Lewes's assertion that it was the body rather than the mind that feels emotion, the vibrations of the nervous system were made tangible in his angular, fervid squirming, and in the intensely personal vocal style.

This made Irving's appeal highly ambivalent. Although the intensity of his passionate interpretations seemed simplistic, as did his policy of reviving melodramas from the fifties and sixties, the impression he gave on stage – and equally off it – was of subtlety and intelligence. As with many aspects of the *fin de siècle*, there was an extreme individuality, almost oddity, in Irving's performances and in his personality. In 1876 William Archer had castigated these peculiarities in a pamphlet, *The Fashionable Tragedian*, but later he came to recognise the actor's extraordinary originality:

> I began to understand his language with tolerable ease, and his movements amused instead of afflicting me... It seemed as though locomotion with Mr Irving were not a result of volition, but an involuntary spasm, complicated by extraordinary sidelong and backward skirmishing, reminding one of the movement of a napkin-ring shot out from under the forefinger... he can on occasions speak with perfect purity, but how seldom these lucid intervals occur... not a vowel but has undergone a change into something new and strange, not a consonant but is jerked out with a convulsion of the throat or a spasm of the jaw... [However, if] Edmund Kean read Shakespeare by flashes of lightning; Mr Irving reads him by the students's midnight oil... by intellect he makes us forget his negative failings and forgive his positive faults. By intellect he dominates the stage.[32]

Shaw would not even allow Irving his intellect: 'the stupidest man I ever met. Simply no brains – nothing but character and temperament.'[33] Although Shaw could always find stupidity in unexpected quarters, his more serious description contradicts Archer's suggestion that Irving was a thoughtful actor: 'The condition in which he works is a somnambulistic one: he hypnotizes himself into a sort of dreamy energy, and is intoxicated by the humming of his words in his nose.'[34] Shaw no doubt considered this a damning criticism, but it suggests total absorption, like the 'faculty of exaltation' that Talma attributed to the inspired actor. Each performance revealed, as did his whole career, that Irving's entire personality was dedicated to the art of acting. He was intrigued by this himself, and remarked to Ellen Terry: 'I was thinking how strange it is that I should have made the reputation I have as an actor, with nothing to help me – with no equipment. My legs, my voice – everything has been against me. For an actor who can't walk, can't talk and has no face to speak of, I've done pretty well.'[35] He also asked her:

> 'What makes a popular actor? Physique! What makes a great actor? Imagination and sensibility.' I tried to believe it... After the lapse of years I began to wonder if Henry was ever really popular. It came naturally to most people to dislike his acting. They found it queer, as some found the art of Whistler queer. But he forced them, almost against their will and nature, out of dislike into admiration. They had to come up to him, for never would he go down to them. This is not popularity.[36]

In a book about acting techniques, it may be a dereliction to merely conclude that an actor had a magical 'star quality', but there was more to Irving's hold over his public than originality or stagecraft; there was a 'psychological' quality, not only in that he drew on his own unconscious creativity, but that his performances touched the unconcious needs of his spectators. I believe he did this by embodying those extremes the Victorians admired in fiction but suppressed in real life. The Victorian gentleman, unlike the Regency buck or Restoration wit, showed his breeding by restraining his emotions; clamped into his frock-coat and starched collar, he cultivated a stiff urbanity, and in the same way his wife and daughters, in corset and bustle, pretended that they could not comprehend any 'unpleasantness'.

There were, of course, rebels against bourgeois attitudes, but respectable ladies and gentlemen thoroughly disapproved of such 'Bohemians'. But in the theatre it was different, here emotions could be safely indulged. A certain moral latitude was even extended to actors: the marital irregularities of Ellen Terry were overlooked, even when her illegitimate son, Gordon Craig, appeared on the same stage. Irving himself seemed a perfect gentleman off-stage. He lectured to universities and religious societies, he was a welcome member of London clubs. Like Bancroft, Hawtrey and Alexander, he was 'one-of-us'. And yet he acted with such abandon, and acted such abandoned characters: Mathias, Eugene Aram, Dubosc, even Mephistopheles; though there were his saintly portraits of Thomas à Becket, King Charles the martyr and the Vicar of Wakefield. Irving seemed to encompass opposites – particularly in *The Bells*. Mathias embodied kindness and criminality, was mayor and murderer, was punished and yet not found out. His portrayal touched the psyche of the age. As Irving was an actor and these portraits were not *really* real, audiences took him to their hearts as a great artist. But to those whose respectability really cracked no such affection could be extended: on the same day as Irving received his knighthood, Oscar Wilde was convicted at the Old Bailey.

Irving approached Shakespeare in the same way: he found redeeming qualities in evil men; his Macbeth had a conscience, his Othello was cultivated, his Lear was loving and his Shylock tragic. The essence of these interpretations, like that of his melodrama villains, was moral ambiguity. Irving's whole style evoked mystery and an almost eccentric individuality. The darkening of the Lyceum auditorium throughout a performance not only enhanced the 'Rembrant-like' gloom of the settings, within which Irving's heroes gleamed in the isolation of a personal follow-spot, but isolated the spectators one from the other, the response of each one seeming, as Shaw had written of the actor, 'somnambulistic... intoxicated by the humming of his words'. The Lyceum audience could respond *en masse* with rounds of applause, but even this corporate expression had, according to Craig, a certain mystical, one might say hysterical, quality to it:

> In *The Bells*, the hurricane of applause at Irving's entrance was no interruption. It was no boisterous greeting for a blustering actor – it was something which can only be described as part and parcel of the whole, as right as rain. It was a torrent while it lasted. Power responded to power. This applause was no false note, whereas silence would have been utterly false; for though Irving endured and did not accept the applause, he deliberately called it out of the spectators. It was necessary to them – not to him; it was something they had to experience, or to be rid of, or rather released from, before they could exactly take in what he was going to give them.[37]

This ritualistic response indicates the therapeutic catharsis that was evoked by the strange magical quality of Irving at his greatest. As Terry wrote, it was something more than 'popularity'.

Popularity of the straightforward kind was awarded to a very different actor, whose appeal to conservative playgoers is more easily explained. Wilson Barrett, though short of stature, was the sort of actor Irving had in mind when he attributed popularity to 'physique'. Barrett was the theatrical embodiment of the 'muscular Christianity' with which conservatives sought to combat the insidious '-isms' threatening their cultural hegemony. He could play the passions in the traditional manner, as described above in *The Silver King* (1885), but Clement Scott was excited not just by the acting, but by how both performance and play combined to to teach a moral lesson: 'Wilson Barrett set an excellent example. His first act was as fine an exposition of the weakness that leads to dissipation and drunkenness, which is the pathway to crime, as could well be presented in a modern homely play.'[38] Barrett had urged the author, Henry Arthur Jones, to reject the questionable morality of the French drama – Dumas, Sardou and Zola – and write:

> A pure English comedy, with a pure story, in which the characters shall be English, with English ideas, and English feelings, honest true men, and tender, loving women, from which plague, pestilence, adultery, fornication, battle, murder, and sudden death be banished... The characters must not preach virtue, let them act it, not spout self-denial, but show it.[39]

Having eliminated virtually all scope for drama, Jones was unable to produce such a play in *The Silver King*, but, by making Denver innocent of the crime he thinks he has committed, they almost managed to have their cake and eat it.

The Barrett repertoire was in fact spectacularly hypocritical, and, although he had none of the mischievous irony with which Irving's vices payed homage to virtue, his melodramas too evoked a dreamlike suspension of moral realism, because they preached one morality and displayed another. Having made a provincial reputation in domestic melodramas like *East Lynne*, Barrett's first London successes were labelled 'The Gospel of Rags'. *Lights o'London* (10 September 1881) and *The Romany Rye* (10 June 1882) by George R. Sims, a journalist with a sentimental social conscious, were followed by *The Silver King* (16 November 1882). Barrett's acting was hailed, like Irving's, as the antithesis of the new 'society drama' of the West End: 'The best protest I know of against that "tea-cup and saucer" school of acting... I appreciate the "strength" of your performance at the striking points... but the heartfelt earnestness from first to last is what I value most.'[40]

However the clash of moral values was not in a complex central character, but in the melodramatic conflict between Barrett and his regular villain, E. S. Willard. Of the two Willard was the more subtle, witty actor. He presented unrelieved malevolence to match Barrett's 'heartfelt earnestness', but did so with such sophistication that audiences were excited as much by his villainy as by Barrett's pathos. As 'The Spider' in *Lights o'London* his 'cool, white livered, and coldly satirical villain, took everyone by surprise... This was no traditional stage villain, but a wholly new contribution to character.'[41] In *Hoodman Blind* (1885), by Barrett and H. A. Jones, Austen Brereton felt that the honours fell to Willard. 'Although Lezzard is a scoundrel, he is a very different type of man to the "Spider" of *The Silver King*... whose life is destroyed by a hopeless passion. He carries despair and hate in his face, in his voice, in his bearing. The impersonation is full of thought, it is determinate, incisive, picturesque, and nervous.'[42]

The highlight of Wilson Barrett's career was a remarkable production, in which, by a spectacular exploitation of moral symbolism, the 'double standards' of the late Victorian psychology were amply satisfied. *The Sign of the Cross* combined the moral decadence of lavish orgies in Nero's court, with a sanctimonious portrayal of the early Christian martyrs. Barrett played a redeemed voluptuary, Marcus Superbus, who was inspired to espouse the faith of those he persecuted by the innocent purity of a Christian maiden, whom he had tried to seduce, and with whom he eventually advanced hand-in-hand into the arena (see Plate VIII). The hypocrisy of Barrett was that he titillated the audience with his villainy, then reassured them with a miraculous conversion. Irving's villains were more disturbing, they too inspired a sensual fascination, but did not repent. Indeed, G. R. Sims, author of Barrett's 'Gospel of Rags' plays, had castigated Irving as morally corrupting: 'The prime mover in a series of dramas which, carried by you to the utmost point of realistic ghastliness, have undermined the constitution of society, and familiarised the masses with the most loathsome details of crime and blood.'[43]

Barrett recognised that *The Sign of the Cross* might have proved controversial, despite his own high moral purpose, and first tried it out it in mid-West America (St Louis, 27 March 1895), followed by a provincial tour of England. Its reception was awesome:

> An audience, notoriously addicted to the frothiest and most frivolous forms of entertainment, [was] hushed to silence, spell-bound and thrilled by dramatic pictures of the gradual purification by love and faith of a licentious Pagan, and the ecstatic exaltation of the early Christian martyrs. The whole house, it was apparent, was unable to resist a certain undeniable spiritual charm evolved from an atmosphere of unassaillable purity, simplicity and faith, pervading the crucial scenes of the drama. The exquisite language of Holy Writ – frequently pressed into the dramatist's service – was listened to with a reverence that bordered on awe... When the curtain fell, and after a moment's silence a great roar of cheering went up.[44]

The play was so successful that several companies were set up to perform it under licence, on the principle established by Boucicault's *Colleen Bawn*. James Thomas estimates 70,000 spectators saw one or other of these touring productions each week.[45] This exploitation of a theatrical blockbuster resembles the simultaneous releases of the cinema. Indeed, both style and content anticipated the biblical epics of D. W. Griffith and Cecil B. DeMille – who made a film of it in 1932.

Barrett claimed that his evangelical drama was not inspired by showmanship, but was 'the best way of combating the unwholesome tendencies of the so-called "problem play". These "sex pieces" were frightening family people from the theatre. I wanted to bring wives and daughters to it, and at the same time bridge the gulf dividing regular theatre goers from the class which avoids the playhouse from religious motives.'[46] Although the play did little to undermine the popularity of the new 'sex pieces', Barrett did succeed in filling his theatre with those who had long been prejudiced against it. As well as patronising the provincial productions, church groups from all over the country organised special excursions to London to see the original performed by Barrett himself. Today the script seems mawkish and sentimental, and the exploitation of the virginal heroine seems masochistic. Yet the 'moral' success of Barrett's sanctimonious production must be given as much credit as the 'artistic' success of Irving, and the 'intellectual' success of the New Drama, in achieving, as the century drew to a close, the accolade of respectability that had been denied to the leaders of the early Victorian theatre, Macready, Kean and Phelps.

12

Trilby
by Paul Potter, after Du Maurier

———~~~~~⦿~~~~~———

Haymarket Theatre, 30 October 1895.

SVENGALI	Mr Herbert Beerbohm Tree
TALBOT WYNNE, 'Taffy'	Mr Edmund Maurice
SANDY McALISTER, 'The Laird'	Mr Lionel Brough
WILLIAM BAGOT, 'Little Billee'	Mr Patrick Evans
GECKO	Mr C. M. Hallard
ZOUZOU	Mr Herbert Ross
DODOR	Mr Gerald Du Maurier
Rev. THOMAS BAGOT	Mr Charles Allan
TRILBY O'FERRALL	Miss Dorothea Baird
Mrs BAGOT	Miss Frances Ivor
Mme VINARD	Miss Rosina Filippi

The action is set in Paris during the 1850s

Act I

Three British art students share a studio in Paris. 'Taffy' Wynne and Sandy McAlister are attracted by the young Irish model Trilby O'Ferrall, but 'Little Billee' Bagot wishes to marry her, even though he is upset by her posing nude. She has refused him because she thinks herself 'unworthy of him'. Svengali, a neighbouring Jewish piano player, demonstrates his hypnotic powers over Trilby, curing her migrane. He claims he could train her voice, even though she is tone-deaf. The Act ends with Taffy persuading Trilby to accept Little Billee's proposal.

Act II

The night before the wedding, Little Billee's mother arrives unannounced. Svengali tells her of the marriage and poisons her against Trilby. Mrs Bagot forbids the marriage. Little Billee's friends propose an elopement, but Svengali, when alone with Trilby, mesmerises her to write a letter of farewell. The protests of his companion, the violinist Gecko, provokes Svengali into a heart attack, but he recovers and leaves with Trilby. The friends return, Billee reads the letter and is heart-broken.

[162]

Trilby

Act III

Five years later, the British friends return to Paris and attend the Circus des Bashibazouks. They are horrified to discover 'Madame Svengali', the newly famous concert soprano, is actually Trilby. In the interval they see her in the foyer, and realise she is in a trance. Taffy attacks Svengali, as he follows Trilby to the platform. The musician has a heart attack and dies cursing. Uproar is heard from the theatre as Trilby's marvellous voice is transformed back to tunelessness. She is led into the foyer in a state of collapse.

Act IV

Trilby has been brought back to the old studio to help her recover mentally and physically from her experiences. She remembers nothing of her singing career, and Billee has proposed to her again. A Christmas present is delivered addressed to Trilby – it is a portrait of himself ordered by Svengali. When Trilby looks on it she lapses into a trance, and having sung a few notes of her favourite ballad of Ben Bolt, she collapses and dies in the arms of Little Billee.

Trilby was one of the 'sex pieces' of which Wilson Barrett so disapproved. Du Maurier's novel had set his story of a fallen woman's exclusion from 'society' in the Latin Quarter of Paris; but *Trilby* was more risqué than *The Second Mrs Tanqueray* or *The Woman of No Importance* in that her moral indiscretions were not in the past. She happily admits to the three British artists that she models in 'the altogether', and, somewhat less happily, that she has slept with artists for whom she posed. However, this last fact was cut from the play, which concentrated on the mesmerist Svengali, who transforms the innocent *grisette* into an international singing star. She can only sing whilst in a trance, and when Svengali dies in the middle of a concert she returns to her normal state of tone-deafness. Trilby achieves fame and respectability, but it is at the cost of losing her own identity.

This psychological rape has obvious significance in relation to the movement for sexual emancipation, but it also reveals a particular attitude to Art. The beauty of Trilby's literally mindless singing is attributed to the 'personality' of her voice, so that banal ditties, like *Ben Bolt* and *Malbrouk va-t'en guerre* become infused with intense but vague emotion. Formal beauty and intensity of feeling are more important than the meaning of the songs. This also applied to her vocal rendition of a Chopin's *Impromptu*, which Du Maurier described in extravagantly 'innocent' terms:

Suddenly, without words, as a light nymph catching the whirl of a double skipping-rope, La Svengali breaks in, and vocalises that astounding piece of music that so few pianists can even play: but no pianist has ever played it like this; no piano has ever given out such notes as these! Every single phrase is a string of perfect gems, of purest ray serene, strung together on a loose golden thread! The higher and shriller she sings, the sweeter it is; higher and shriller than any woman had ever sung before.[1]

This rhapsody on the pure beauty of form and expression was the essence of aestheticism, as championed by Pater, Swinburn and Wilde.

In Paul Potter's dramatic version of Du Maurier's novel the emphasis was shifted from the misalliance between Trilby and Little Billee to the psychic powers of Svengali. In turn this prompts the question of how 'mesmeric' was Beerbohm Tree's own performance. How far can the late flowering of Romantic Acting in the 1890s be attributed to the 'unique personality' of stars like Tree, Irving, Terry, Bernhardt and Mrs Patrick Campbell? In performance Tree seemed to be transformed, not only by skilful make-up, but by the intensity of his identification. Similarly, he excited his audiences' imaginations, not just by naturalistic scenery, but by the aesthetic sensuality with which he composed the whole production. Michael Booth, discussing Tree's *Henry VIII* (1910), suggests that

> The pace of production, the particular uses of mass, colour, light, and costume, the technique of the actor – all these elements of spectacle really have no parallel on the Western dramatic stage of today. The world of spectacle has gone, but in its time it provided a rich visual feast the like of which the English stage had never known before and has never equalled since.[2]

Tree's 'inspired' performances and his extravagant productions both displayed an anti-intellectual aestheticism. It was as if the rationality of the ego was suppressed – as in hypnosis – and a dreamlike symbolism was evoked.

Both the novel and the play reveal a moral suppression, similar to the 'double standards' of Wilson Barrett's Muscular Christianity, but whereas Barrett's libidinous fantasies were cloaked in religiosity, Du Maurier's prejudices were masked by an apparently broad-minded aestheticism. He had been an art student in Paris himself in the 1850s, and, in his subsequent career as a Punch cartoonist, he had gently mocked the vulgarity and affectations of drawing-room society. Eventually, however, he adopted the values of those he satirised. In the novel he described the innocence of Trilby's attitude to nudity, but then made her dissolve in shame when Little Billee saw her posing; he expounded Billee's agnosticism at length, but then let traditional 'Christian' values triumph unchallenged, when Trilby is killed off by the wasting away which dispatched so many fallen women. Even more offensive to the modern reader are Du Maurier's chauvinistic assumptions, both sexual and racial. He describes Little Billee's snobbery as 'moral scruples'; Trilby's skivvying as 'selfless'; Svengali's Jewishness as 'sinister'; Taffy's muscular physique as 'British decency'; and Zouzou's marrying an heiress as a 'crime' because she is ugly.

Du Maurier had been encouraged to write by his friend Henry James, but he had none of the American's ironical insight into the contradictions of society and the complexities of relationships. James noticed that, although Du Maurier ridiculed the 'Aesthetes' in his Punch cartoons, his own judgement were swayed by physical appearances: 'The world was, very simply, divided for him into what was beautiful and what was ugly, and especially into what looked so.'[3] This concern may be understandable in a cartoonist, but *fin-de-siècle* society as a whole seemed to judge by appearance, and confuse morality with aesthetics. Victorian actors had always believed in a coincidence between inner reality and external expression, but in the nineties this straightforward coincidence was being challenged. Appearances could not be trusted, though they must be maintained. In Society this was seen in the hypocritical shock which greeted the exposure of the 'secret vices' of public figures like Charles Dilke, Charles Parnell and Oscar Wilde – it was not the vice that shocked but the publicity: the violating of appearances. In art there was a more subtle exploration of appearance and reality. The novels of George Eliot, Thomas Hardy and Henry James revealed that motives for action were not always those professed, or even believed in, by their characters. In poetry and the visual arts the Symbolists suggested a more than metaphorical relationship between image and substance: if appearances were interpreted imaginatively, they might reveal a deeper significance: an unconscious meaning.

The redefinition of 'the unconscious' by psychologists during the later years of the century had important implications for the art of acting. Not only did they suggest that motives may be unconscious, but they explored the mechanism by which unconscious motives affected personality. The unconscious had, of course, been recognised earlier in the century, but its relationship with consciousness was considered as mechanical rather than symbolic – a physiological rather than psychological relationship. The theory of mesmerism, which featured so largely in *Trilby*, clearly indicates this shift, in both expert and popular patterns of thought.

The Austrian, Franz Anton Mesmer, attributed his hypnotic powers to a 'subtle etheral fluid', which he called Animal Magnetism. In 1784, at his clinic in Paris, he treated patients with a mechanically created 'magnetic influence'. In seance-like gloom, to the accompaniment of gentle music, they joined hands and made contact with Mesmer's *banquet*, a kind of battery with metal terminals. Mesmer then excited the magnetism of his subjects by stroking and touching them. This intimacy often produced hysterical reactions. A commission, which included such luminaries as Lavoisier, Benjamin Franklin and Dr Guillotin, examined Mesmer's methods, and concluded that 'Imagination works wonders; magnetism yields no results', attributing his powers to 'suggestion'.[4] However, the desire to find a physical explanation for the manifestations continued to inspire belief in the psychic power of magnetism. The unconscious was seen as an external influence, and not intrinsic to the mind itself.

Maria M. Tatar, in a study of mesmerism and literature, traces the phenonomon from Mary Shelley's *Frankenstein*, through Dickens and Poe, to Henry James:

> In the literature inspired by mesmerism, amateur scientists and psychologists usurped the power of gods and demons to become agents of good and evil. Having mastered the secrets of a cosmic fluid, they were able to control the human mind. These men of science... could take advantage of that fluid to establish a mental rapport with other people. They could turn the men around them into instruments of their own will or into mediums of a higher intelligence.[5]

Mathias in *The Bells*, forced to re-enact his dreadful crime, was an *instrument* of the mesmerist's will, whilst Trilby was a *medium* for the musical genius of Svengali. Maria Tatar sees Henry James's *The Bostonians* (1886) as the first 'modern' explanation of these telepathic powers, in that he suggested that it was the unacknowledged *desire* of the subject, rather than the extraordinary power of the mesmerist, that was the true cause of apparently irrational behaviour:

> The narrator makes it abundantly clear – first by satirising the claims of mes- merists and spiritualists, then by punctuating his narrative with psychological insights – that a quite natural explanation can account for Verena's receptivity to the affluent Bostonian and her impoverished cousin... [their spells] are in the end no more satanic and no more devine than human nature.[6]

As people became aware that they engendered their own irrational and erotic desires, and were not necessarily 'inspired' by the influence of others or the impersonal compulsion of some 'ethereal fluid', so, as moral responsibility could no longer be shifted onto external causes, there was a greater pressure on individuals to suppress their 'baser instincts'. The results of this kind of suppression were described in the *Studies in Hysteria* published by Breuer and Freud in 1895. Breuer used hypnosis in his 'cathartic therapy' to overrule the censorious control of the ego, thus allowing his patients – like Mathias – to retell or re-enact their suppressed fears and guilt. Freud rejected hypnosis and developed his own psychoanalytical technique, which interpreted the 'symbolic' meaning of his patients' dreams and the images produced in free-associ- ation exercises. Thus we find in psychoanalysis the two elements that exemplify the 'psychological melodrama' of the 1890s: firstly, the liberation of unconscious fears, or creative faculties, under the influence of mesmerism, and, secondly, the suppression of 'unacceptable attitudes' – conventional value-judgements or prejudices – that reveal themselves, not directly, but through the symbolic conventions of the dramatic form: the poetic justice of the narrative; the stereotyping of the characterisation; and, in Du Maurier's case at least, the dreamlike assumption that the beautiful is good and the ugly is evil.

The conventionality of these assumptions in *Trilby* led Beerbohm Tree to recognise that although Paul Potter's dramatic adaptation was 'hogwash',[7] it would appeal to a West End public. His production opened in Manchester in October 1895, and at the Haymarket on 2 November. It ran until the following July, when Tree moved from the Haymarket to the newly built Her Majesty's. *Trilby*'s success did much to finance that lavish investment. The *Manchester Guardian* wrote of the first performance that the design and casting faithfully 'realized' many of Du Maurier's illustrations, and these reminders of the novel embued the melodrama with greater significance (see Plate IX). The critic thought the dramatist was wise to play down 'the "dame aux Camélias" in another setting... at all events till the stage has been a good deal futher Ibsenised'.[8] In London *The Era* particularly praised Tree's own performance:

> Svengali towers above his companions with the pride of Lucifer and the malice of Mephistopheles... How weird are the bursts of Svengali's merriment, what authority there is in his magic, what intensity in his rage, his agony, his ambition! Two scenes of Mr Tree's it is hard to erase from one's memory. The first is that in which Svengali, believing himself to be on the point of death, cries to the 'God of Israel' for mercy. The second is the awful death scene in the last act... so awful is the sight of that hideous corpse, half inverted on the table. Mr Tree's Svengali is so grand an impersonation that the question at once suggests itself – when will he play Shylock?

Of the two actors whose looks were chosen to realise Trilby and Little Billee, Dorothea Baird 'charmed her audience as the real Trilby charmed the three students', but 'Mr Patrick Evans, beyond looking like the Billee of the book, did little to help matters. His performance was decidedly amateurish.' Above all, *The Era* suggested, the play wisely did not try to satisfy 'a purient itch for forbidden fruit', but, by 'gliding gently over some little bits of thinnish ice', presented an 'atmosphere of friendship, love, and loving kindness'.[9] Even William Archer enjoyed the 'fantastic fairy-tale... Not for nothing does Svengali wear the features of a gargoyle from some medieval minster. He is lineally descended from the Devil of the Miracle Plays.'[10] But before considering

Archer's more considered appraisal of Tree, let us consider how the actor approached his art.

Herbert Beerbohm was born in 1852, son of a successful German merchant, who had settled in London in 1830. Although he always wanted to become an actor, he worked in the City for some eight years, so that when he became a professional in 1878, he was one of the many 'amateurs' with no family grounding in the theatre. According to Michael Sanderson's statistics, during the 1880s 58.7 per cent of new actors came from the Professions, Commerce and Industry (i.e. a total of 91), but from 1890 to 1913 the proportion was 69.8 per cent (132). Unlike Bancroft or Kendal, Tree did not marry an established actress, but a stage-struck college student, Maud Holt. Her professional debut in 1883 helped swell Sanderson's statistics for actresses: only 29.4 per cent (10) of actresses acting through the 1880s, did not have theatrical origins, while during the 1890s the proportion rose to 62.8 per cent (59).[11] Thus the theatrical profession had changed considerably by the time Tree built Her Majesty's in 1896. Whilst he had been manager of the Haymarket, from 1887, his position was like that of John Hare at the Court, but Tree was not just a gentleman character actor, he was more flamboyant, and his ambition was to inherit the mantle of Irving.

Both of Tree's daughters, Viola and Iris, acted with him, and they give a vivid picture of their father's approach. Both stressed his spontaneity: he seldom seemed to study, and often introduced new effects during performance. According to Viola,

> He was always an adventure, an excitement, one never knew quite what he would do; but it was always the right thing to give inspiration to one's next line... He actually became the part he was playing – that is why he was never the same from night to night, and why sometimes he appeared to be 'walking through his part'. With him it was everything or nothing: he was either living the part over again, or else completely out of it.[12]

Iris remarked on his dynamism during rehearsals: 'building his productions with such loving eagerness, raging, commanding, almost mesmerising people to perform his will', and on stage:

> I am sure he had genius, although, perhaps, unaided by great technique or intellectual knowledge... one could criticize his acting, but no one could deny the power and wizardry that he exercised over the imaginations of his audience... It was in those parts of sinister fancy, of whimsical humour, of nightmare and dream, that he let his spirit loose, leaving the audience haunted and bewitched. He had the strange faculty for stirring the imagination by little touches, as in Fagin's asthmatic cough before the opened window, which made one almost feel the fog rolling in from the river... the clenched, awkward gestures of Beethoven; the thin, slightly affected voice of Richard II, which gave a strange, pitiful beauty to his weakness; the snarling woes of

Shylock, whose passions seemed tearing at themselves rather than at his ene-
mies.[13]

It was the same quality that made a success of Svengali: the power of
personality rather than technique.

The same impression is given by both William Archer and Bernard
Shaw, neither of whom really approved of such self-indulgence. Archer
criticised Tree's Svengali precisely because it was all spontaneous effect
with very little preparation:

> It stands on a low plain of art, because it is not an effort of observation and
> composition, but of sheer untrammelled fantasy. Mr Tree is simply doing
> what comes easiest to him, luxuriating in the obvious and violent gestures
> and grimaces... To revert to a former illustration, the carvers of Gothic gar-
> goyles were artists in their way, but we do not class them with Michael
> Angelo.[14]

Shaw on the other hand got more fun out of Tree's performances,
even if only as a butt for scurrilous wit: 'Mr Tree only wants one thing to
make an excellent Falstaff, and that is to be born over again as unlike
himself as possible.'[15] 'One of the most moving points in his Richard [II]
was made with the assistance of a dog who does not appear among
Shakespeare's dramatis personae, When the dog – Richard's pet dog –
turned to Bolingbroke and licked his hand, Richard's heart broke';[16]

> In Pygmalion the heroine, in a rage, throws the hero's slippers in his face... I
> knew that Mrs Patrick Campbell was very dexterous, very strong, and a dead
> shot... The effect was appalling. He had totally forgotten that there was any
> such incident in the play; and it seemed to him that Mrs Campbell, suddenly
> giving way to an impulse of diabolical wrath and hatred... The worst of it was
> that it was quite evident that he would be just as surprised and wounded next
> time.[17]

Desmond MacCarthy confirmed the impression that Tree ' believed
in inspiration. He was to the last an improvisor, trusting to the emotions
of the moment.' It led to success in 'exaggerated situations', but, 'astonishingly effective as his Svengali and Fagin were, such parts did not show
what was most moving in his acting – his fantastic humour and the
extreme delicacy of his insight into the pathos of certain characters and
situations'. This sensitivity was seen in *Enemy of the People* when Dr
Stockmann, complaining about the insularity of bourgeois homes, 'put
his hand for a second on [his wife's] shoulder. It is hard to describe a gesture that is exactly right, but this one at that moment said as plainly as
words: "Of course, my dear, that is not a hit at you." That momentary
gesture expressed perfectly the relation between husband and wife.'[18]

Tree would probably have understood more than any previous English actor the views of Stanislavski, who, almost contemporaneously, was struggling with the problems of 'living his parts', and revealing, by a similar 'delicacy of insight', the sub-text of Chekhov's naturalistic masterpieces. Stanislavski, like Tree, was tempted by 'exaggerated situations', delighted in elaborate make-up, and preferred to discover original gestures and intonations from his own personality, rather than use the 'clichés' of traditional acting – and, coincidentally, both actors recognised that Dr Stockmann was 'almost his favourite part'.[19] Tree, like Stanislavski, tried hard, with a similar lack of success, to involve himself with modern drama, from the Naturalistic *Pygmalion* and *Enemy of the People* to the Symbolist *False Gods* by Brieux and *L'Intruse* by Maeterlinck. He invited William Poel's 'Experimental' Elizabethan Stage Society to contribute to the Shakespeare Festivals mounted at His Majesty's, and in 1913 he even visited the Moscow Arts Theatre to see Craig's famous *Hamlet*. Though neither Stanislavski nor Tree were ever comfortable dealing with modernist ideas, they both tried to move with the times. Had Tree been able to follow Stanislavski in overcoming his taste for romantic melodrama, and rigorously examined by what 'method' he achieved his instinctive identification with a role, then the Academy of Dramatic Art, which he founded in 1903, might possibly have done for English acting what Stanislavski's studio did for the Moscow Arts Theatre.

But, of course, Tree was no Stanislavski, like many pragmatic English actors he 'did not believe acting could be taught',[20] and instruction at the Academy concentrated on voice production, dancing and fencing. In 1893 he had given a lecture on acting to the Royal Institution, and, published as *The Imaginative Faculty*, it was a statement of extreme anti-Diderot views – technique was a necessary chore, while sensibility was the key to real acting:

> Acting, in fact, is purely an affair of the imagination... Children are born actors. They lose the faculty only when the wings of their imagination are weighted by self-consciousness. It is not everyone to whom is given the capacity of always remaining a child. It is a blessed gift of receptive sensibility which it should be the endeavour (the unconscious endeavour perhaps) of every artist to cultivate and to retain... The actor must be capable, of course, of pronouncing his native language, and of having a reasonable control over the movement of his limbs; but thus equipped, his technical education is practically complete.[21]

Tree believed so strongly in the innocent eye of childhood that he deplored 'the pernicious habit of reading books', and warned against a University education: 'The point of view is apt to become academic, the academic to degenerate into the didactic'; as well as 'a too prosperous society', which may 'hinder rather than to foster the growth of this sensitive plant, which will often flourish in the rude winds of adversity, and perish in the scent-laden salons of fashion'.[22]

Stanislavski was never so anti-intellectual, but the opinions expressed in *The Imaginative Faculty* suggest that Tree would have wholeheartedly agreed with the Russian when he wrote:

> The actor must first of all believe in everything that takes place on the stage, and most of all he must believe in what he himself is doing... I speak of the truth of emotions, of the truth of inner creative urges which strain forward to find expression... Scenic truth is not like truth in life; it is peculiar to itself. On stage truth is that in which the actor sincerely believes... For this it is necessary for the actor to develop to the highest degree his imagination, a child-like naiveté and trustfulness.[23]

Stanislavski felt impelled to consider his own acting because he found it impossible to maintain the same involvement when playing a part for a long time – he discussed this with particular reference to his performance of Dr Stockmann – and his 'system' was developed specifically to ensure creative involvement in every performance. Tree would certainly have benefited from that. It was notorious how his performances fell away during a long run. His remedy was to vary his repertoire by performing matinees of past successes or new plays, unlikely to survive a long run of evening performances. Otherwise, like the young Stanislavski, he tended to overplay and force up the emotional temperature by improvising during performances.

The only role that seemed ever fresh when he performed it was Svengali, partly because it was virtually impossible to overplay. Archer considered it an 'easy' performance for Tree, an elaboration of his own extravagant personality, but the American critic John Rankin Towse recognised the skill as well as the eccentricity of the actor:

> The swift, noiseless, cat-like movements, watchful eyes, and ghastly face, incessant restlessness, and the curiously skilful blending of fawning and arrogance, contributed to an abnormal, but not wholly incredible, individuality... The egotism, meanness, cynical selfishness, and innate ferocity of the creature were vividly exposed; but in all its viciousness and degradation – and herein lay the special excellence of the portrayal – there was the constant imitation of the artistic sense, the love of music for its own sake as well as its rewards, which was the villain's one redeeming grace. In this fantastic creation Mr Tree came nearer to the establishment of perfect illusion than ever before. It was a wonderful performance of its kind, but it should be noted that it involved no manifestation of the higher kind of emotional eloquence, nor the embodiment of any great ideal.[24]

However, 'great ideals' and 'the higher kind of emotions' were perhaps no longer relevant. The Classical concept of universal ideals and the Romantic notion of the nobility of passion, which had inspired artists throughout the century, were now seen as suspect or affected. Emotional intensity, as in Svengali, was dangerous and destructive, nobility, as in Tree's Richard II and Hamlet, was a sign of weakness and pathos. Tree's 'instinctive' response to character acting revealed a twentieth-century subjectivity, in which originality of perception, nervous and immediate, rather than any grand design, replaced the moral certainties for which the Victorians had striven. Unfortunately Tree did not have the insight to recognise that his impulsive improvisatory approach was inappropriate to his attempt to emulate Irving as an actor, or Saxe-Meiningen as a stage director. His talent was more Expressionistic than Classical. He should have performed the king in Wilde's Symbolist *Salome*, as the poet had suggested,[25] rather than in Stephen Phillips's *Herod* (1900), a historical romance in the tradition of *Richelieu* and *The Sign of the Cross*. For most of his career he was (forgive the pun) barking up the wrong tree.

It is difficult to decide whether to admire Tree's personal originality, or to feel frustrated at his inability to focus his talents into a modern system. As W. L. Courtney wrote before Tree's final American tour in 1917:

> You will remind me that I am describing the qualities of an amateur, not of a professional. I do not shrink from the conclusion. Tree had all the best points of an amateur, and some of his triumphs were gained just for that reason. He was a glorified amateur who dared things which a professional never would have dared, and won a shining victory. He mistrusted all talk about technique. 'I have not got technique,' he once said: 'it is a dull thing. It enslaves the imagination.'[26]

The late nineteenth century saw the traditional art of acting wither in the hands of 'amateurs' like Beerbohm Tree and Mrs Patrick Campbell. Their inventive originality and 'animal magnetism' certainly made technique seem dull, but they could teach their fellow actors little. Combine the personality playing of these *glorious* amateurs with the undemonstative elegance of the *casual* amateurs – such as Charles Wyndham, Gerald Du Maurier and Lily Langtry – and the experimental approaches of the *earnest* amateurs – Craig, Shaw, Poel and Barker – and it is easy to see how the old Victorian professional technique of 'performing the passions' not only became unfashionable in the Edwardian theatre, but was to be ridiculed as the mark of a clichéd, dead and absurd theatricality.

13

Shakespearian
interpretation

That theatrical circumstance and audiences attitude should have affected the style and performance of nineteenth-century plays is self-evident,
but, because Shakespeare is the most regularly performed author of our
own age as well as theirs, it is easy to fall into the error of assuming that,
because the Victorians performed the plays differently, they were mis-
guided, insensitive and wrong. Even J. L. Styan in his otherwise excellent study of twentieth-century approaches to interpretation, *The
Shakespeare Revolution*, condemns the Victorians for 'misplaced ingenuity', 'recalcitrant traditions' and 'the hacking and plastering of
Shakespeare for the stage'. He should have taken note of his own comment that: 'any true interaction between study and stage... points as
much to the history of taste as of perception'.[1] He explains how scholarship from the 1880s onwards revealed the Elizabethan-ness of both the
form and content of Shakespeare's plays, and how this made an impact
on twentieth-century theatre practice: Poel and Guthrie redesigned the
theatre's architecture, Barker, Atkins and Bridges-Adams produced
unabridged versions with fluidity and speed. But some of the new criticism, which concentrated on sub-textual psychology or supra-textual
imagery, has prompted all kinds of experiments, from 'relevant'
modern-dress to 'archetypal' abstraction, so that today we are embarrassed by the number of 'original' ways there are of producing
Shakespeare. We still feel the plays can speak to us, but there seems to
be little unanimity as to what their meaning might be. One thing is certain: they are not contemporary plays, they need 'interpretation' and
virtually every new production tries to discover a different style in which
to perform these 'distanced' texts.

This was not a problem for the Victorians. Although many nineteenth-century scholars deplored the disparity between the plays as performed and the texts as read – the most notable being Lamb's

contention that 'the plays of Shakespeare are less calculated for performance on a stage than those of almost any other dramatist whatever'[2] –
actual *performances* of Shakespeare, mangled as the texts may have been,
spoke directly to Victorian audiences. Of course the plays were set in the
past, but then so were most serious plays being written before the 1870s.
The vogue for 'costume dramas', such as *Virginius* and *Richelieu*, was to a
great extent due to the reverence in which Shakespeare was held, and if
little respect was extended to the fluid structure of his dramaturgy, poets
and playwrights throughout the century found it natural to express
themselves in blank verse – though today much of it reads like a parody
of their chosen model.

This taste had, as it were, a reverse influence on the appreciation of
Shakespeare. If 'good theatre' was assumed to be a historical intrigue in
five acts, with accurate costuming and lavish scenery, then it seemed only
natural to edit the playing texts of Shakespeare to accomodate the same
format. Modern critics and theatre historians may look back scornfully
at the 'hacking and plastering' this involved, but the Shakespeare of the
Victorian stage was far more 'their contemporary' than he is today; so
much so that his plays underwent the same editorial 'management' that
Sheridan Knowles had invited Macready to apply to *Virginius.* But the
actor-managers did not do this with the modern attitude that *'chaque
texte n'est qu'un prétexte'.*[3] They had too much respect for the traditions
of Shakespearian production, or, as they would have put it, for
Shakespeare himself. Any alteration was considered as something the
author would have adopted himself, given modern theatrical conditions
– and can we be so certain that he would not?

What then was the appeal of Shakespeare to the nineteenth century?
To read Lamb's view that the plays should not have been performed,
which was echoed by Coleridge and Hazlitt, one might suppose that
there was a dichotomy between literary critics and theatrical practi-
cioners. In fact, Victorian scholars, actors and spectators had more in
common with each other, than any of them have with our own critical
relativity. An examination of why Lamb came to his conclusion may help
illustrate what actually appealed to them. Lamb's essay *On the Tragedies
of Shakespeare* was written in 1812, but, as an extreme statement of
Romantic Criticism, most of his assumptions still held true early in
Victoria's reign.

His main concern was that actors concentrated on the passions of a
scene rather than the motives of their characters:

> The glory of the scenic art is to personate passion and the turns of passion...
> [but] to know the internal workings and movements of a great mind, of an
> Othello or a Hamlet for instance; the when and the why and the how far they

should be moved... seems to demand a reach of intellect of a vastly different extent from that which is employed in the bare imitation of the signs of these passions in the countenance or gesture, which signs... indicate some passion... *generally*. But of the motives and grounds of the passions... of these the actor can give no more idea by his face or gesture than the eye (without a metaphor) can speak, or the muscles utter intelligible sounds (p. 28).

Few actors would have disputed Lamb's contention that their prime task was to 'personate the passions', but they might have argued that it was the words of the text, not the subtlety of the performer, that provided the 'whys and wherefores', and, furthermore, that in denying theatre its 'metaphor' Lamb misunderstood its method. However a few, Kemble or Macready perhaps, might have been perturbed by Lamb's criticism that, by concentrating on the passion rather than the motive, little distinction was made by actors between the passions of 'high' drama, such as Shakespeare, and of 'low' melodrama, and that Mrs Siddons played Mrs Beverley in *The Gamester* in the same way as Lady Macbeth. But surely it was right to present both characters as *real* people, moved by the same emotions of guilt and grief? Lamb's point was that Shakespeare's characters were not like other people – Macbeth was not George Barnwell:

So little do the actions comparatively affect us, that while the impulses, the inner mind in all its perverted greatness, solely seem real, and is exclusively attended to, *the crime is comparatively nothing*... The state of sublime emotion into which we are elevated by those images of night and horror which Macbeth is made to utter... seems to belong to history, to something past and inevitable, if it has anything to do with time at all. The sublime images, the poetry alone, is that which is present to our mind in reading.

So to see Lear acted – to see an old man tottering about the stage with a walking-stick, turned out of doors by his daughters in a rainy night, has nothing in it but what is painful and disgusting. We want to take him into shelter and relieve him... The greatness of Lear is not in corporeal dimension, but in intellectual... On the stage we see nothing but corporeal infirmities and weakness, the impotence of rage; while we read it, we see not Lear, but we are Lear – we are in his mind (p. 30, my italics).

When this argument is set beside the practice of the actors, with their concentration on 'scenes of affective passion', it becomes clear that they actually shared Lamb's concern for 'the inner world', 'the intellect' and even 'the sublime images'. They valued these aspects more than the contrapuntal action of Shakespeare's plots, or the moral implications of the plays' 'world picture', which are aspects emphasised in our own century. Both critics and actors placed authentic passion before moral judgement. This may seem a strange assertion to make of the puritanical Victorians, but when related to their admiration of the unique creativity of the romantic artist, and the individual enterprise of the 'great men of history', it is easy to see how the grandeur of Shakespeare's language led them to believe in the grandeur of his heroic characters – or rather their 'sublimity'.

This quality had been defined in 1756 by Edmund Burke in his *Essay into our Idea of the Sublime and the Beautiful*. Here the classical aesthetic of art – the harmonious expression of general truths, to please and to instruct – was challenged by a theory of sublime art, which surpassed the harmony of the merely beautiful and the worthiness of the merely good, and which aimed, above all, at an emotional response. As terror is the most violent emotion, Burke concluded that 'terror is in all cases whatsoever the ruling principle of the sublime'.[4] Thus he made an equation between aesthetics and emotion. Siddons's sleepwalking and Kean's Giles Overreach both achieved sublimity in that they inspired terror in their audiences. Sublimity also implied the contemplation of superlatives, so that, when applied to Shakespeare, his characters were defined in terms of extraordinary greatness, rather than placed in the context of normal social intercourse. The concept of sublimity also contributed to, and helped justify, the domination of the stage by the overwhelming presence of the star actor.

One might think it was the actor–manager system that had led to Shakespeare's tragedies being used as star vehicles, but the heroic characters themselves appealled directly to Victorian taste. For example, *Othello*, which depends on the centrality of the hero and the sublimity of his passion, has proved very difficult for twentieth-century actors. Both black and white performers have felt uncomfortable, when the passion is characterised as 'primitive', and even the best actors have over-compensated for the raw emotion: Paul Robson was considered too dignified, Olivier too exotic. Many modern productions have presented convincing Iagos and impressive Desdemonas, but, as Julie Hankey asked of the 1970s: 'Where in this did Othello stand? He was as elusive as ever. He did not flourish in this new world. At worst he became something of an embarrassment, and eccentric guest, stumbling in on an intelligent conversation, out of another period, another play.'[5] That we now refuse to accept Shakespeare's world unquestioningly may be a moral advance, but, from a purely theatrical point of view, the Victorians were more able to fulfil the intentions of the text, because actors played the passion rather than the person. They were thrilled and moved by many different kinds of Othello, from the cat-like fascination of Edmund Kean, through the pathos of Macready, the vigour of Gustavus Brooke, and the agony of Ira Aldridge, to the overwhelming savagery of Salvini.

But if the actor–managers could handle Shakespearian tragedy, the organisation of their theatre and the taste of their audience were ill-suited to presenting the comedies with any kind of 'authenticity'. There is no place in comedy for the sublime, and its concern for social morality demands an ensemble playing rarely found in the Victorian theatre. Because the plays were difficult both to appreciate and to stage, the Victorians produced some extremely perverse interpretations. However, as this very perversity reveals the taste of the age, I intend to consider performances of *The Taming of the Shrew*, *As You Like It*, and *The Merchant of Venice*, and leave tragic performance for the final chapter. These three plays are particularly significant because their portrayal of women would seem to have been radically at odds with typical Victorian attitudes.

As one might have expected, the Victorians generally approved of the conclusion to *The Taming of the Shrew*, but the bawdy brutality of the actual taming upset their sense of propriety and their ideal of romantic love. However the text usually performed was a version made by David Garrick, and revised by J. P. Kemble, called *Katharine and Petruchio*. The play had been shortened into a two-act afterpiece by cutting the Induction and the subplot of Kate's sister Bianca. Although Garrick had written his 1756 version for the vivacious Kitty Clive and the swaggering Henry Woodward, the general effect is well described by Tori Haring-Smith:

> In transforming Shakespeare's play into a moral farce, Garrick removed all ambiguities from Shakespeare's text. His characters' simple, explicit motives eliminate the tension in Shakespeare's play. Garrick's gentlemanly tamer is no real threat to his bride, and his shrew is clearly tamed but not beaten... Shakespeare's play raises questions; Garrick's only offers pat answers.[6]

Kemble's 1810 revision increased the low comedy of Grumio and the servants, while his own unbending style made Petruchio even more gentlemanly, and Mrs Charles Kemble's elegance made Katharine more ladylike. George Daniel wrote of Kate, in his Introduction to the Kemble version: 'With a wayward temper, she has a good heart, and an excellent understanding; and at the close, she calls forth the noble attributes of her sex, with a dignity and feeling that unfold the beauties of her mind, no longer enthralled by the fury of her passions.'[7] This text baldly supported the ideal of the patriarchal marriage.

In 1844 Ben Webster, manager of the Haymarket, was persuaded by J. R. Planché not only to revive Shakespeare's original text, but to perform it using the conventions of the Elizabethan stage. One might have hoped that, by restoring the 'objectifying' elements of the subplot, in which the demure Bianca manipulates her suitors better than her headstrong sister, and the play-within-a-play convention established by the

Induction, that the ambiguity of Shakespeare's original would have been regained, but in fact, if Katharine emerged the stronger character, it was due more to the acting of Louisa Nisbett than to Planché's production concept. Planché wanted to revive the Elizabethan staging conventions more as an experiment in antiquarian reconstruction than a disruption of the actor/audience relationship to effect the meaning of the play. The Induction was given a 'realistic' setting, so as to 'transport' the audience back to Tudor times, within which *The Shrew* was performed in front of a draped tapestry with placards announcing the location, so as to illustrate the quaint customs of the time (see Plate XI(a)). Planché seemed rather surprised that 'the revival was eminently successful, incontestably proving that a good play, well acted, will carry the audience with it, unassisted by scenery.'[8] Not everyone considered it so successful, some critics found both the convention and the restored text 'tedious'. Perceptively, *The Examiner* considered the experiment 'needless pedantry... This very absence of scenery, in an age when scenes are every-day things, becomes in its turn a scenic effect. More persons came to see how a stage was fitted up in the sixteenth century, than for any other purpose whatever. Let a series of plays on the same principle be acted, and observe the result.'[9] This critic was undoubtedly right: the scenic conventions of the nineteenth century were not accidental, they answered a cultural need of the period, and so too did the fact that the certainties of *Katharine and Petruchio* continued to be more popular than the ambiguities of *The Taming of the Shrew*.[10]

Nevertheless the nineteenth-century theatre had its own kind of ambiguity, its own sense of the artificiality of performance. While Buckstone played Grumio with his 'usual gusto', Louisa Nisbett brought to the playing of Kate the up-front drollery and archness that were the hallmark of the comic actress. Miss Nisbett, who had created Lady Gay Spanker in Boucicault's *London Assurance*, had a quality of audience rapport which Westland Marston compared with that of Mme Vestis:

> [It was] less her wont than that of Vestris to indulge in those little acts of pantomime by which an actress appeals personally to her admirers... [but] if the latter beat her in seductive charm of look and manner, and in the art of sending telegraphic glances, she had not that delight in mirth and those boundless animal spirits which, with Miss Nisbett created an infection of enjoyment.[11]

Clement Scott described how in *London Assurance* she 'was accustomed to deliver the lines close to the footlights, with eyes fixed on the audience',[12] and the *Theatrical Journal* pointed out how in *The Shrew* her infectious laughter, and the flashes of outrage, which she shared with the audience at the expense of Petruchio, helped subvert her submission in the last act: 'She did not suddenly sink into the abject slave of her husband's whim, but now and then broke out into the short ebullitions of hasty temper she was wont to indulge in.'[13] Her vivacity was further heightened, perhaps unintentionally, by an encomical performance from Webster as her tamer: 'This stirling actor had few faults; perhaps the chief of them was a certain heaviness and sombreness in playing young heroes of comedy. Thus his Petruchio seemed really violent and angry, and showed little enjoyment of the part in which he was masquerading.'[14]

However, even if Nisbett proved more attractive than the heavy Webster, it does not necessarily follow that the audience rejected the Victorian reading of *The Shrew* as Shakespeare's endorsement of male superiority. As Haring-Smith points out, Webster suffered from 'the critical assumption that a truly Shakespearean hero/lover should be genteel. Because he violated the public's expectations (however ill-founded), he was censured.'[15] Even when confronted with a text, much of which had not been staged for two hundred years, and presented in a revolutionary non-scenic setting, audiences still believed that they 'knew their Shakespeare'. They might look for new acting points and changes in the emphasis of a characterisation, but they knew nothing of 'original interpretation' of the kind with which modern directors seek to illuminate – or subvert – the meaning of Shakespeare's text.

The other 'great' Victorian Katharine conformed to a very different gender stereotype. Where Louisa Nisbett had been vivacious and lightweight, Ada Rehan was dignified and formidable. Augustin Daly's 1887 production was not intended to subvert patriarchal assumptions, but Rehan's Kate can be recognised, from our distance, as a richly ambiguous 'New Woman'. Graham Robertson thought there was something of a Trilby/Svengali relationship between the Irish actress and the American stage director. In society she 'she was shy and (off the stage) intensely self-conscious' and on meeting her he wondered:

> How was it possible that this remote creature whose chief desire was to creep into a corner and hide herself could nightly flare forth into the incarnation of terrible vitality, the 'Tiger burning bright', the flower of flame that was her Katharine the Shrew? I marvelled and still marvel, for I never solved the mystery of Ada Rehan, to which, I think, Augustin Daly alone held the key.'[16]

That Rehan was Daly's mistress was not the whole mystery of his influence, nor even that he rigorously rehearsed her, but, that having recognised her abilities as well as her attractions, he doctored the text to exploit both. According to Haring-Smith, Daly 'placed the actor above the script and rearranged the play to give curtains and other dramatic moments to these principles. Daly delayed Rehan's first entrance as Katharine until the opening of the second act, teasing the audience until then with descriptions of this remarkable shrew.'[17] Daly was as dictatorial a director as Pinero or Jones, both of whose plays he presented in America, but he was ultimately more interested in the acting than the text. Robertson, in accordance with his Svengali theory, decided 'Daly must have been a great actor who could not act... but in Ada Rehan he found his means of self expression... with her gentle good nature which he could mould to his will',[18] and Clement Scott quoted his son's opinion that 'Mr Daly made each play a monologue, with himself as principal performer.'[19] Such directing skills have become less unusual in the twentieth century.

Yet, however well Daly had prepared the ground, Rehan's own stage presence was remarkable. Ellen Terry was delighted by her sense of humour, and suggested she had something of the archness that Nisbett had used to keep the audience on her side: 'Directly she came on I knew how she was going to do the part. She had such shy, demure fun. She understood, like all great comedians, that you must not pretend to be serious so sincerely that no one in the audience sees through it.'[20] But apparently most people (or was it just the men?) did not recognise this sense of fun, and found her scarlet woman, with flaming hair and a deep red dress, 'A termagant in temper; haughty; self-willed; imperious' (see Plate X(b)).[21] Rehan herself looked on her 'as a grand creature – a very noble nature – of high breeding – a spoiled, wilful child who had always had her own way with every one'. She also 'found Katharine a very exhausing part to play. Her first entry demands a height of passion, which in most other plays would be the climax of an evening's work. The force has to be sustained throughout two acts; indeed almost to the end of the play.'[22]

Clement Scott thought first-night tension made her first London performance particularly exciting:

> It was as it should be a double Katharine. It was the Katharine of a whirlwind and the Katharine of a calm. The nerveous tension of the actress at the outset was almost painful. She screamed under Petruchio's insults like a wounded animal caught in a trap. Her eyes flashed the fire of indignation. She was one magnificent tremble. Her nails were dug into her clasped hands till it seemed as if they must have bled. Her anger was not vulgar, mean, degrading; but magnificent, superb, like a tempest rushing through a forest; and then gradually, very gradually, exquisitely toned, came the calm, and the peace, and the advent of the real woman, whose nature was always there, but only became dignified under this terrible punishment and trial.

The vitality of the performance was such that even Scott, who, the following year, was to be so outraged by Ibsen's *Doll's House*, had to admit 'to tell the truth, the humiliation of such a Katharine is a little painful to the beholder. We admire her power so much that we regret the necessity of her punishment.'[23] As when Lamb had felt that Macbeth's 'crime is comparatively nothing' when set beside his 'sublime emotion', Scott did not question the 'necessity of her punishment', but was bowled over by the splendour of her passions. When Daly took the production to Paris in 1889, *Le Figaro* was less blinded by ingrained assumptions as to the meaning of the play: 'The treatment of a rich, beautiful, elegant and virtuous young woman – taking her faults into consideration – like a wild animal does not cause merriment with our nation.' The critic then claimed that Ada Rehan's 'stature and singular beauty present the image of a Scandinavian divinity of the Valhalla'.[24] His description was taken up by Joseph Daly in his brother's biography: 'Her raving became that of a goddess, or one of those unconquerable women whom the Vikings worshipped and dreaded.'[25] Would it be fanciful to suppose that Rehan's Kate embodied something of the destructive quality which Ibsen attributed to the trolls, and portrayed in Hedda Gabler, Ellida Wangle and Rebecca West?

John Drew's Petruchio certainly seems to have been as mismatched as Helmer, Tesman and Dr Wangle. In many modern plays he and Rehan played against each other perfectly in their 'battle of the sexes':

> They give and take like masters of the foils, parry and thrust with such skill and grace... The foils are the brightest and sharpest; the touch is so light, the flash of them so dazzling, as to confound the spectators and leave them without pity for the defeated gallant who has drawn sword with a woman and come out of the fray pierced and bleeding... They know the heights and depths of each others powers, and one helps the other like generous comrades.

But L. Clarke Davis qualified his praise of Drew; he seemed wrong in doublet and hose, and 'must be seen in the modern morning frock-coat, with a bouquet in his button-hole, and a glove to play tricks with'.[26] A. B. Walkley, who did not much like Rehan's 'animalism' with its 'shrieks and grunts', thought that 'everything that can be done is done by Mr John Drew to soften and humanize the part of Petruchio... [as] such a part can only be made palatable by an air of obvious insincerity'.[27] All these criticisms leave us with an impression that the production had an ambivalent, even shocking, effect on its audience. It is unlikely that this was the conscious intention of Daly or his performers, but does indicate how the ambivalence of Shakepeare's play, which Haring-Smith suggests was lost in Victorian productions, did in fact disturb the collective conscience of the 1880s, when the relationship between the sexes was newly under question.

In 1892 Oscar Wilde offered the script of *A Woman of No Importance* (under its original title of *The Good Woman*) to Daly, suggesting Rehan played Mrs Erlynne, the 'woman with a past'. In the light of their secret liaison it is not surprising Daly turned down the offer. But Bernard Shaw too saw the potential of Ada Rehan in the new socially-responsible drama, and attempted to rescue her from Daly, just as he tried to prise Ellen Terry away from Irving's reactionary clutches. At the time of *The Shrew*'s first London performance he wrote a spoof letter to *The Pall Mall Gazette:*

> I am an Englishwoman, just come up, frivolously enough, from Devon to enjoy a few weeks of the season in London, and at the very first theatre I visit I find an American woman playing Katharine in The Taming of the Shrew – a piece which is one vile insult to womanhood and manhood from the first word to the last. I think no woman should enter a theatre where that play is performed... Of course, it was not Shakespear [sic]: it was only Garrick adulterated by Shakespear. Instead of Shakespear's coarse, thick-skinned money hunter, who sets to work to tame his wife exactly as brutal people tame animals or children – that is, by breaking their spirits by domineering cruelty – we had Garrick's fop who tries to 'shut up' his wife by behaving worse than she – a plan which is often tried by foolish and ill-mannered young husbands in real life, and one which invariably fails ignominiously, as it deserves to. The gentleman who plays Petruchio at Daly's – I neither know nor desire to know his name – does what he can to persuade the audience that he is not in earnest, and that the whole play is a farce, just as Garrick before him found it necessary to do; but in spite of his fine clothes, even at the wedding, and his winks and smirks when Katharine is not looking, he cannot make the spectacle of a man cracking a heavy whip at a starving woman other than disgusting and unmanly. In an age when woman was a mere chattel, Katharine's degrading speech about 'Thy husband is thy lord...' might have passed with an audience of bullies. But imagine a parcel of gentlemen in the stalls of the Gaiety Theatre, half of them perhaps living idly on their wives incomes, grinning complacently through it as if it were true or even honourably romantic.[28]

In his own person Shaw accused Shakespeare of 'immaturity', declaring the last scene to be 'altogether disgusting to modern sensibility'.[29] When he reviewed Daly's *Midsummer Night's Dream* in 1895, he appealed directly to Ada Rehan not to continue sacrificing her talent to 'artificial entertainment' and the 'self-culture' of grace and diction, which 'seems to have isolated her instead of quickening her sympathy and drawing closer her contact with the world', unlike Duse or Achurch, who seem to speak 'for all women as they are hardly ever able to speak and act for themselves'. With Rehan, 'we admire, not what she is doing, but the charm with which she does it. That sort of admiration will not last... I am afraid this means avoiding the company of Mr Daly.'[30]

Unfortunately, Graham Robertson understood Ada Rehan better than Bernard Shaw. In 1899 Daly died in Paris, in the presence of both wife and mistress, and Rehan seemed to lose her ability to act: 'She appeared a few times in America in some of her old parts but with small success:

she was brought out as Beatrice, a character that should have fitted her like a glove, and achieved complete failure.'[31]

Rehan had, however, made a great success of Rosalind in Daly's *As You Like It* in December 1889, as had Mrs Nisbett, who had appeared in Macready's production of 1842. Both actresses relied on their stage charm, Rehan seeming graceful and vivacious, while Nisbett 'followed the "Saucy lackey" tradition',[32] but the most significant portrayal of Rosalind in the nineteenth century was that of Helen Faucit, who interpreted the role in an impeccably Victorian manner. Faucit had made a close study of Shakespeare's tragic heroines from her earliest youth, under the tuition of Percy Farren, but when Macready planned a production of *As You Like It*, in 1839, to follow their performance together in *Richelieu*, she was worried by not having studied the comedy:

> I did not know the words, nor had I even seen the play performed, but I heard enough of what Mrs Jordan and others had done with the character, to add fresh alarm to my misgivings... The performance was received with enthusiasm. I went home happy... but there a rude awakening awaited me. I was told I had been merely playing, not acting, not impersonating, a great character. I had not, it seemed to my friends, made out what were traditionally known as the great points of the character... It was only when I came to study the character minutely, and to act it frequently, that its depths were revealed to me.[33]

Nevertheless, Theodore Martin claimed that, although his wife's interpretation may have 'deepened' over the years, she had, from the start, rejected the 'air of hoydenish audacity heretofore given to the character of Rosalind'.[34] Mrs Jordan in the early years of the century had revelled in the wit of the role as a breeches-part, and Mrs Nisbett had followed that tradition, but Faucit could not understand the 'stage perversion' of casting 'actresses whose strength lay only in comedy':

> Even the joyous, buoyant side of her nature could hardly have justice done to it in their hands; for that is so inextricably mingled with deep womanly tenderness, with an active intellect disciplined by fine culture, as well as tempered by a certain native distinction, that a mere comedian could not give the true tone and colouring even to her playfulness and wit. Those forest scenes between Orlando and herself are not, as a comedy actress would be apt to make them, mere pleasant fooling. At the core of all that Rosalind says and does, lies a passionate love as pure and all-absorbing as ever swayed a woman's heart.[35]

Faucit interpreted the play as a testing of Orlando by Rosalind, who, having no doubt of her own love, seeks to discover the depth of his affection.

In true nineteenth-century fashion, the actress ensured the audience were never in doubt as to the character's real feelings, but she did not attempt to signal that she was playing with Orlando by asides or arch glances at the audience. Instead she used delicate by-play, as when after the wrestling-match: 'she has taken a chain from her neck, and stealthily kissing it – at least I always used to do so – she gives it to Orlando'; or by letting emotions overwhelm her in a burst of tears and trembling, as when Celia first tells Rosalind she has seen Orlando in the forest (pp. 247 and 258). At the height of the game, when Ganymede gets Orlando to propose to him, Faucit experienced 'a trembling of the voice and the involutary rushing of happy tears to the eyes, which made it necessary for me to turn my head away from Orlando' (p. 274). By the 1860s some critics found her meticulous 'pointing' too deliberate: the *Atheneum* (12 November 1864) described her Lady Macbeth as: 'elaborately studied and carefully illustrated with sculpturesque attitudes, which are sometimes too painfully realized'.[36] Henry Morley too saw her as 'an actress trained in the school of the Kembles, careful to make every gesture an embodiment of thought; too careful sometimes'.[37]

But despite the explicitness of her technique, Faucit had no difficulty in sharing the emotions of a part. Although she was able to describe minutely the shift of mood and motivation of a character, she admitted that her written accounts could not reveal exactly 'what I did upon the stage, or how I did it, for this is more than I myself could tell'. However, the purpose of her playing was very clearly stated as an 'endeavour to present a living picture of womanhood as divined by Shakespeare, and held up by him as an ideal for women to aspire to and for men to respect'.[38] It was this idealisation of Rosalind that led to a portrait that was noted for sentiment rather than comedy. It was a Romantic Victorian idealisation, typified by dignity and propriety, as can be seen from a panegyric written by Herman Merivale, who acted Touchstone in a final benefit performance in 1879, when Faucit was sixty-two:

> She is all Rosalind. The sweet round voice, the statuesque and gracious attitudes, the perfect tenderness of conception and the sustained tone of the *Grand dame de par le monde*, as Brantôme has it, who never forgets her royalty for a moment in the lovely garnish of a boy... the abiding charm of this Rosalind is its perfect ladyhood.[39]

No doubt by 1879 Faucit was herself an ideal Victorian lady, wife of Sir Theodore Martin – Edinburgh solicitor, Parliamentary agent and biographer of Prince Albert. However, unlike Louisa Nisbett, who had retired from the stage when she became Lady Boothby, when Faucit married Martin, 'it had been understood between us that she was to be free to continue the practice of her art. To her it was the very life of life.' In her husband's opinion, by the way she combined her duties as mistress of her household and as a working actress 'she opened a new view of womanhood' (p. 230). That her portrayal of Rosalind, wittily testing the quality of her man, sentimentalised as it may seem today, was also taken as an ideal of womanhood, should make us wary of considering the generation of women that preceded the emancipation movement, as irretrivably domesticated.

The technique Faucit adopted to present her 'ideal of womanhood' was to identify her own emotions with those of the character. Memories of her youthful passion for Macready, who was twenty-four years older, married, and unbendingly respectable,[40] may have informed her later performances of Rosalind as the 'ideal lover'. They were not playful and high-spirited, but shot through with a certain wistfulness, which critics described as 'purity':

> [She] charmed us by the simplicity, the delicacy, the purity of the delineation. The character, like the play itself, is ideal, and therefore requires a spiritualization in the performance, without which it is apt to become gross and sensual. It is not because she assumes masculine habiliments, and instructs her lover how to woo her, that *Rosalind* is to be taken as a hoyden. In the real world this would undoubtedly be the case, but not in the Forest of Arden, where, as Hazlitt justly says, 'nursed in solitude, under the shade of melancholy boughs, the imagination grows soft and delicate, and the wit runs riot in idleness, like a spoilt child that is never sent to school'. This softness and delicacy we never saw more beautifully represented than in Miss Faucit's performence of Rosalind – the caprice of the part never more ethereally embodied.[41]

At the height of her unrequited passion, Macready, rather ingenuously seeking to concentrate her mind on her career rather on than himself, wrote her a memorandum of rules for acting (Diary; 9 January 1840). They advocated emotional identification, but without sacrificing clarity or effectiveness:

> Be always in earnest, though seldom emphatic.
> Passion does not require a loud tone of voice, nor wide, nor violent gesticulations.
> Let Passion have full possession of the bosom before attempting to speak its language...
> Passion facilitates the delivery, except when choking with emotion...
> Distinctly mark the necessity for time in the transition from one passion to another...
> Most watchful care required in articulating, particularly vowel sounds.[42]

Robert Lowe described how Faucit's desire for identification led to an almost Stanislavskian analysis:

> To her, Juliet, Rosalind, Desdemona were real personages; she was not satisfied with the study of their emotions as they were stirred in the play; she

sought, in ever line of their speech, in every thought they gave utterance to, in every allusion to them by others, clues to enable her to understand their previous history and the influences that had moulded their character. She was not an actress, playing a part, so much as a woman, realizing in the abstract the joys and sufferings of her sex.[43]

This approach is revealed in her book *Some of Shakespeare's Female Characters*, written after her retirement in 1880. Her method was to define what Stanislavski was to call the 'given circumstances' of her role. She imagined what had happened to Rosalind before the play: she had lost her mother, and 'when her father was deposed she was yet a girl, little likely, perhaps, to appreciate the change from the princess of a reigning, to a princess of a dethroned house'. She even considered the political circumstances:

> The beauty and gentle bearing of Rosalind, as the years went on, made her dear to the people, who had probably found out by this time that they had made a bad exchange in the 'humorous Duke' for the aimiable and accomplished ruler whom he had supplanted... Celia's father, holding his place by an uncertain tenure... did not fail to observe this feeling among his subjects. It was dangerous to let it grow to a head;... before the play opens, the thought had been present in his mind that Rosalind must stay no longer at his court.[44]

Though much of this is based on an expository speech from the courtier LeBeau, the fact that Faucit took note of the speech of a 'walking gentleman' indicates a thoroughness of preparation and exercise of imagination unlikely to have been undertaken by Mrs Jordan or Miss Nisbett. It was much more in line with the critical interpretation of Shakespeare by Anna Jameson (*Shakespeare's Heroines* [1832]), and the reconstructions of *The Girlhood of Shakespeare's Heroines*, written as novellas by Mary Cowden Clarke (1850-52). In the descriptions of all three – actress, critic and novelist – Shakespeare's characters were approached as very real people, living real lives, and moved by real emotions. The artifice of the pastoral convention was ignored, and, although managers such as Macready and Phelps found the role of Jaques more 'meaty' than Orlando or Duke Senior, his melancholy cynicism was so out of tune with Victorian romantic idealism, they portrayed him as an affected, disagreeable and ugly grotesque to set off the youthful high spirits of Rosalind and Orlando.

Actor–managers much preferred Shylock as a portrayal of male malignancy contrasted with female purity, as it provided an splendid opportunity for passionate acting. It had been one of Edmund Kean's greatest successes – see Chapter 3 for Hazlitt's description of 'the conflict of passions' and 'the rapidity of his transitions from one tone and feeling to another'.[45] In the later nineteenth century, however, attitudes towards Jews was changing, and downright villainy was no longer an acceptable interpretation. The appreciation of Portia too had changed since Hazlitt had complained of her 'affectation and pedantry'. Mrs Jameson rejected this, as well as Schlegel's sneering description of Portia as 'rich, beautiful and clever'. In her essay she stressed the 'womanly' nature of Portia's intellect, which is 'modified by sympathies and moral qualities', and concluded

> that Shylock is not a finer or more finished character in his way than Portia is in hers. These two splendid figures are worthy of each other – worthy of being placed together within the same rich framework of enchanting poetry and glorious and graceful forms. She hangs beside the terrible inexorable Jew, the brilliant lights of her character set off by the shadowy power of his, like a magnificent beauty-breathing Titian by the side of a gorgeous Rembrandt.[46]

The metaphor indicates a visual appreciation of Shakespeare typical of the Victorians. If Edmund Kean had revelled in the conflicting passions of Shylock, his son Charles luxuriated in the spendour of a reconstructed Venice. His 1858 production restored Portia's suitors Morocco and Aragon, who were usually cut, but did so at the expense of Bassanio's casket-scene, which was cut by about three-quarters, as Kean's real interest was in the variety of setting and costumes that these scenes provided.[47] This production gave eleven-year-old Ellen Terry her first experience of the play. She appeared in St Mark's Square – 'painted from drawings taken on the spot' – as an urchin carrying a basket of doves, which she was firmly convinced 'was the principal attraction of the scene'.[48] Seventeen years later, in 1875, she played Portia at the Prince of Wales's under the Bancrofts. This too was a highly visual interpretation of the play.

At the age of seventeen Ellen had been married to the Pre-Raphaelite painter G. F. Watts, though he was thirty years her senior. Two years later they separated, and in 1868 Ellen eloped with another artist, the architect William Godwin, to whom she bore two childen. There have been several recent studies of Ellen Terry, which examine the social and psychological implications of these tangled relationships, and all agree on the one aspect that I wish to emphasise when considering Terry's performances: her close involvement with artists contributed to her own vivid sense of visual style.[49] In 1875, a year after her return to the stage, the Bancrofts asked her to play Portia, and Godwin to design the play.

As one might expect of the Prince of Wales's, the production aimed to be 'naturalistic', in that extravagant passions were played down, and the scenic environment was meticulously represented. Godwin's analysis of

his designs explains an aspect of Victorian production which is very alien
to our own theatre:

> It is essential first of all that the Scene-painter should bear well in mind that
> in 1590 Venice was neither a city of palaces nor a city of ruins, and that along
> her canals and streets two great styles of art, broadly speaking, prevailed, and
> a third was gradually usurping the place of both... the Byzantine, the Gothic,
> and the Renaissance... if we desire to realize the Venice of Shakespeare, we
> shall have to cover most of the brick work with veneers of marble, either
> plain or in coloured diaper, or with stucco decorated with painted diapers,
> and the few exceptions to this rule would be the very smallest and poorest
> houses and the ealiest Byzantine works.[50]

Molwyn Merchant has pointed out that Godwin did not combine all
these architectural styles in a single street-scene just to display his erudi-
tion or painterly skills: 'scholarship is here wholly subordinated to critical perception... this flexible and complex setting he has designed as a
miniture conflation of the three styles he has analysed, a meeting-point
of the grandure and accelerating decadence of Shylock's Venice'.[51] The
architectural styles are used almost as characters in the play: the ancient
Byzantine reflects the Lavantine traditions of the Jew, the brilliant
Gothic proclaims the civic pride of the Doge's court, and the elegant
Renaissance implies the humanistic sympathies of Shakespeare's own
generation. According to the same principle Portia's Belmont was
depicted as a Palladian villa.

In his description of the costumes, Godwin reveals the same sensitivity to visual symbolism allied with a rather prosaic consideration of the
characters as 'real people': 'Portia would do her shopping probably at
Padua, and would therefore follow the fashions of the mainland.'[52] This
attitude typifies exactly the 'cup-and-saucer' approach to the classics. So
too did Charles Coghlan's performance as Shylock, which, according to
all the critics, was the cause of the production's failure. Clement Scott
was appalled at Coghlan's lack of expression:

> If Shylock is to express no feeling toward Antonio one way or the other; if he
> is to describe insults levelled at him with no energy; if he is to show no love
> for his daughter, no greed for his gold, no eagerness for his revenge, to take
> up no position at the trial, and appear merely as a moody, sulky, and uninter-
> esting person, it would be difficult to say what value there is in *The Merchant
> of Venice* as a stage play. This new throry of natural acting will not hold water
> for an instant.[53]

Dutton Cook was more generous in recognising that:

> Mr Coghlan has proved himself on frequent occasions an actor of intelli-
> gence... [but] by accident or intention, Mr Coghlan makes Shylock a man of
> indistinct character, weak and irresolute of mind... slow of speech, much

addicted to muttering, and incapable of investing his utterances with anything like incisiveness of tone or pungency of sarcasm... all [was] delivered in
the same dreary monotone, the blank verse broken up into prose, and the
scene generally disturbed by long pauses and imperfect management of the
voice.[54]

It remained to Ellen Terry to rescue something from this disappointing
production. She did so by exploiting the two qualities most appreciated
in the Victorian theatre: visual charm and sentiment.

It is not surprising that Terry had attracted the attention of Watts and
Godwin: her whole appearance was splendidly 'Pre-Raphaelite'. Unlike
the chaste dignity of Faucit, or the jaunty chic of Marie Bancroft, Terry
had the angular grace of a young animal. Watts had Holman Hunt
design her a brown silk wedding-gown, Julia Cameron photographed
her in Grecian *décolletage*, and Godwin had dressed her in a kimono to
match their Japanese decor. Nina Auerbach explores at length the psychological influences of such costumes on Terry's real-life roles of child-
bride and unmarried mother, but her ability to inhabit her stage
costumes and settings with an awareness of aesthetic effect was recognised throughout her stage career. In *The Merchant of Venice* Alice
Comyns-Carr, who was to become Terry's chief costume designer at the
Lyceum, enthused about the 'tall and slender figure in a china-blue and
white brocade dress, with one crimson rose at her breast... [whose]
greatest effect was when she walked into the court in her black robes of
justice'.[55] In Henry Irving's production this black robe were exchanged
for an even more striking red one (see Plate X(a)). Beerbohm Tree
remembered the Lyceum Portia as looking 'like one of Leighton's
women, queen-like.'[56]

Terry herself especially remembered the almond-blossom dress
Godwin had designed for her, and considered that the Prince of Wales's
production was 'a more gorgeous and complete little spectacle' than had
ever been staged:

Veronese's 'Marriage in Cana' had inspired many of the stage pictures... I
played the part more stiffly and slowly at the Prince of Wales's than I did in
later years. I moved and spoke slowly. The clothes seemed to demand it...
The aesthetic movement, with all its faults, was responsible for a great deal of
enthusiasm for anything beautiful. It made people welcome the Bancrofts'
production of 'The Merchant of Venice' with an appreciation which took the
practical form of an offer to keep the performances going by subscription, as
the general public was not supporting them... The audiences may have been
scanty, but they were wonderful. O'Shaughnessy, Watts-Dunton, Oscar
Wilde, Alfred Gilbert and, I think, Swinburne were there. A poetic and artistic atmosphere pervaded the front of the house as well as the stage itself.[57]

But if the aesthetic elements of the production were caviare to the general, Terry's personality captivated everyone. Where Coghlan's lack of traditional technique had led to a blurred, almost invisible, characterisation of Shylock, Terry was able to combine the skills she had learnt from Mrs Kean, with a nervous energy that made the critics uncertain of where her talents lay. Dutton Cook wrote that she 'is singularly skilled in the business of the scene... with great care and inventiveness in regards to detail';[58] Scott thought her 'so fresh and charming... no traces of the stage were there, no renewal of old business, no suggestion of immemorial traditions... the very poetry of acting', and yet 'Miss Ellen Terry's complete success was constantly threatened by a paralysis of nervousness which was resisted with extreme difficulty';[59] Henry James, in line with his usual criticism of Bancroft productions, concluded, 'most of the actors at the Prince of Wales's... struck me as essentially amateurish, and this is the impression produced by Miss Ellen Terry... [and her sister Kate] The art of these young ladies is awkward and experimental; their very speech lacks smoothness and firmness.' He did, however, enumerate Ellen's 'amateurish' attractions at some length: 'Miss Terry is picturesque; she looks like a preRaphaelite drawing... She is intelligent and vivacious, and she is indeed, in a certain measure, interesting. With great frankness and spontaneity, she is at the same time singularly delicate and lady-like, and it seems almost and impertinence to criticize her harshly.'[60]

Amateurish Terry may have been, but she was professional enough to know when she had control over her audience:

> Never until I played as Portia at the Prince of Wales's had I experienced that awe-struck feeling which comes, I suppose, to no actress more than once in a life-time – the feeling of the conqueror. In homely parlance, I knew that I had 'got them' at the moment when I spoke the speech beginning, 'You see me, Lord Bassanio, where I stand'.[61]

Perhaps it should be no surprise that the audience were captivated by this speech, rather than the more famous appeal for mercy, for in it Portia offered up her person and her wealth to the successful suitor Bassanio – Auerbach describes her here as 'a more accomplished and polished Katharina'.[62] As Charles Cowden Clarke admitted in *Shakespeare Characters*, 'There is a class of my own sex who never fail to manifest an uneasiness, if not jealousy, when they perceive a woman verging towards the manly perogative; and... the trial-scene would induce this prejudice against her.'[63] Maybe the speech to Bassanio rang true because Terry had twice given herself up to men who did not truly appreciate her – Godwin was to desert her shortly after her return to the theatre – and this gave the sentiment added poignancy.

It may also have been that she could not make the most of the trial-scene because of Coghlan's uninteresting Shylock. When she played the role with Irving in 1879, the opposite was true: the trial was the climax to Irving's revolutionary interpretation, and Portia's triumph was overshadowed by Shylock's tragedy:

> Henry Irving's Shylock necessitated an entire revision of my conception of Portia, especially in the trial scene... I had considered, and am still of the same mind that Portia in the trial scene ought to be very quiet. I saw an extraordinary effect in this quietness. But as Henry's Shylock was quiet, I had to give it up. His heroic saint was splendid, but it wasn't good for Portia.[64]

There is not space to examine Irving's interpetation in detail – Alan Hughes does this excellently in *Henry Irving, Shakespearean*[65] – but as the drama focused on the defeat of Shylock, Portia emerged as lacking the mercy she recommended. Terry herself noted that the famous appeal was used as bait in her trap, and concluded that she cheated Shylock by a legal quibble, 'However one looks at it one cannot admire it. It has an unattractive element of moral deceit – of the dangerous doctrine that the means is justified by the end.'[66]

For most of the century actors and actresses had experienced little difficulty interpreting Shakespeare according to their own lights, however much we might disagree with their interpretations. They had no compunction in cutting what they felt to be Shakespeare's lapses in taste. For instance the general disapproval of Jessica in *The Merchant* – Cowden Clarke calls her 'flimsy, thoughtless, unstable'[67] – led them to cut her poetic scene with Lorenzo in Belmont. Charles Kean deleted it altogether and it was only partially restored at the Prince of Wales's; in neither case did cast or critics complain. However, with Irving's production of *The Merchant* we seem to enter into a familiar world of controversy and ambiguity. Scholarly 'purists' were horrified when Irving cut the final act. He did this only once or twice, but the myth arose that he always finished the play with Shylock's defeat. But even when presented uncut, the Lyceum's *Merchant* was perceived as a self-conscious reinterpretation. Contemporary attitudes to such things as Jews and marriage were seen to be at odds with the Elizabethan playwright. Henry Arthur Jones recognised that Irving had tried to accomodate these new attitudes: Shylock's heart-broken exit was 'undoubtedly a great piece of acting. It was however, quite ex-Shakesperean, if not anti-Shakespearean.'[68] The *West End Review* agreed: 'Before a persecuted Hebrew prophet for hero, a dull ill-mannered Christian for villain, and an incomparable Portia flinging in her lot with the might-is-right party, Shakespeare retired discomfited.'[69] Thus, in the last decades of the century, theatre historians and literary critics combined to undermine the naive confidence of the stock-theatre Shakespearians.

14

Hamlet
by William Shakespeare

———❦———

St George's Hall, Landham Place, 16 April 1881
Presented by The Shakespeare Society, directed by William Poel

CENTINAL	Mr F. Boon	MONTANO	Mr A. Rogers
BARNARDO	Mr R. Templeman	ROSSENCRAFT	Mr W. Waterton
HORATIO	Mr W. L. Hallward	GILDERSTONE	Mr J. B. Partridge
MARCELLUS	Mr D. Robinson	DUKE	Mr D. Glover
KING	Mr H. Stacke	PROLOGUE	Mr A. Rogers
QUEEN	Miss Zoe Bland	LUCIANUS	Mr. Templeman
HAMLET	Mr William Poel	FORTENBRASSE	Mr D. Robinson
LAERTES	Mr J. B. Partridge	CAPTAIN	Mr A. Rogers
CORAMBIS	Mr F. J. Lowe	CLOWNE	Mr G. Battiscombe
CORNELIA	Mr Matthey	ANOTHER	Mr R. Templeman
OFELIA	Miss Helen Maude	A BRAGGART	Mr F. Powell

AMBASSADORS FROM ENGLAND   Mssrs Spendlove and Boon

Lyceum Theatre, 11 Sepember 1897
Presented by Johnston Forbes Robertson

HAMLET	Mr Forbes Robertson	HORATIO	Mr Harrison Hunter
GHOST	Mr Ian Robertson	OSRIC	Mr Martin Harvey
GERTRUDE	Miss Glanville	GRAVEDIGGER	Mr Willes
POLONIUS	Mr J. H. Barnes	CLAUDIUS	Mr Cooper Cliffe
LAERTES	Mr Bernard Gould	OPHELIA	Mrs Patrick Campbell
	(Bernard Partridge)		

Graham Brown, Franklyn Dyall, Fisher White

This book has made much of the entrance of 'amateurs' into the theatrical profession. To begin with, newcomers were obliged, like Henry Irving, to pick up professional techniques in the rough and tumble of the stock theatre. Later actors, like Hare, Alexander, Wyndham and Tree, established their style in London based long-runs, as did most of the actresses from non-theatrical families, such as Marie Tempest, Stella Campbell and Julia Neilson, who entered the profession in the late 1880s. As they acted mostly in well-made plays, which demanded a fairly restrained 'naturalistic' style, they were to a great extent responsible for the demise of the passionate 'melodramatic' style, even in Shakespeare.

Few commercial managements in the 1890s were prepared to mount Shakespearian productions, and, as provincial stock theatres were replaced by touring houses, Shakespeare became a speciality of a few companies. In London Irving's Lyceum was the only theatre that consistently performed Shakespeare; sometimes in long runs, like *Henry VIII*, which ran throughout 1892, but also as revivals from the repertoire at the end of seasons or on tour. Wilson Barrett managed a decent run of *Hamlet* at the Princess in 1884, but, during the nineties, Beerbohm Tree was Irving's only regular rival in London. Both Tree and Irving concentrated on the centrality of their own performances and the scenic splendour of their productions. Their acting style was not very different in Shakespeare from the eccentric romanticism they brought to 'modern' roles like Mathias or Svengali, but their Shakespeare no longer seemed like 'a contemporary'. Productions tended towards the operatic: the texts were like libretti, scaffolds to support virtuoso soloists and lavish scenery. After the failure of Irving's 1888 *Macbeth* – a genuine attempt at a psychological reinterpretation – all his later Shakespeare productions concentrated on scenery: *Henry VIII*, which the Victorians always treated as a pageant, *King Lear*, set in Ford Madox Brown's Pre-Raphaelite Ancient Britain, and *Cymbeline* and *Coriolanus*, both designed with the aid of Alma Tadema. 1900 saw Tree's gorgeous *Midsummer Night's Dream*, with its infamous rabbits and fairies with electric lights all over their costumes. Thus, if any genuine reassessment of how to perform Shakespeare was to be found, it was from outside, or on the fringes of, the theatrical profession.

Two companies were started in the 1880s, which were to maintain something of the stock theatre approach to Shakespeare well into the twentieth century, through a policy of touring a repertoire of plays performed by actors at the start of their careers. Ben Greet's Woodland Players performed in the open-air as a fashionable entertainment for country-house parties, while Frank Benson's company specialised in employing university graduates, many of whom did not intend to become true professionals. In fact both companies launched several actors who were successful in the 1900s, and the 'Bensonians' eventually evolved into the Stratford Memorial Company. But the most revolutionary Shakespearian of the 1880s was William Poel, who stage-managed for Benson in 1884, and whose production of the First Quarto *Hamlet* is the starting-point of this chapter.

This production may have been revolutionary, but it was hardly immediately influential. Poel had started acting in 1875 under the veteran comedian Charles Mathews, but the following year he was reduced to trudging on foot round James Scott's North Yorkshire fit-up circuit, where the average houses were less than ten pounds a night. Returning to London he took acting lessons from Edward Stirling, who as a youth had acted in *The Iron Chest* with Edmund Kean. From Stirling Poel learnt something of the old 'professional' style of speech, and an appreciation of the verse lacking from Irving's psychological interpretations. The young Poel respected Irving, but from the start disliked his approach to Shakespeare, finding his pictorial style, with its curtain tableaux, ' sensational and stagey'. Later in his career, when asked 'What do you think of Irving?', he replied, 'I wouldn't give him five pounds a week.'[1]

In 1878 he toured the provinces giving solo readings of Shakespeare. Such public readings were fairly common, even by established actors, and tended to appeal to the earnest middle classes, who prefered 'rational entertainment' to the not entirely reputable theatre. Macready gave readings in Workingmen's Institutes as a deliberate contribution to 'social betterment'; Irving usually accompanied his readings with a plea on behalf of the theatre's respectability; Fanny Kemble, having left her American husband in 1847, made a career of solo readings. The impact of a reading without settings could have a revelatory effect on regular theatre-goers; audiences were often moved to tears, as they were by Dickens's public readings. Frederick Pollock was astonished by the effect of Macready's *Hamlet*:

> Much, of course, is lost by the abscence of all stage effect, but, on the other hand, much is gained by having every part finely rendered. Polonius is no longer a buffoon, Laertes becomes a gentleman, and Horatio a fit companion for Hamlet. The Ghost was very grand, and the effect was increased by the expression of the face and fixed stare of the eye.[2]

Although her readings were limited to an hour, Fanny Kemble wanted to use them to revive correct Shakespeare texts, and she built up a repertoire of twenty-four plays, concentrating on the 'beauty of the plays as poetical compositions'.[3] Rather like a radio production, a non-scenic reading appealed to the imagination of its audience, rather than the illusion of the stage.

Poel's own solo readings led to a tour by 'The Elizabethans', a small company of 'professional ladies and gentlemen whose efforts are special-ly directed towards creating a more general taste for the study of Shakespeare',[4] and whose readings were given in costume. Although they included several popular plays – *The Hunchback, The Iron Chest, Eugene Aram* – the emphasis remained on *the study* of Shakespeare. This led Poel to compare modern acting editions with the original texts, and in 1880 he gave a paper on why the acting editions were so corrupt to the Shakespere Society. Here Poel learnt that the Society's president, Dr F. J. Furnivall, was soon to publish facsimile editions of the First and Second Quartos of *Hamlet*.

In 1881 Poel persuaded Furnivall to support a performance of the First Quarto on a bare draped stage in St George's Hall. The purpose was to demonstrate, or rather test, the theory that this 1603 edition was closer to Elizabethan stage practice than the fuller texts of the 1604

Figure 7. Henry Irving reciting Thomas Hood's poem *Eugene Aram* at the Arts Club, Manchester, 1881

Quarto and the Folio of 1623. The experiment was announced in the *Academy* of 12 February 1881:

> A member of the New Shakespere Society, Dr W. Pole [sic], and some amateur friends have resolved on giving what Shakespere students and critics have long desired to see, a performance of Shakespere's first sketch of his *Hamlet* as represented by the first quarto of 1603, preserving its order of scenes, following its stage directions and omissions, and correcting only the manifest blunders of its text.[5]

Apart from Poel himself, the company was entirely amateur if one includes Bernard Partridge, the *Punch* cartoonist who regularly illustrated Lyceum programmes, and Maud Holt (stage-name Helen Maude), who was to marry Beerbohm Tree in 1883.

Despite Robert Speaight's claim that the occasion was 'obscure to the point of clandestinity',[6] several critics attended, though few had anything positive to report. The *Standard* considered the acting so bad that 'perhaps no more effective way of destroying interest in the quartos could have been discovered'.[7] *The Stage*, pretending to some scholarship, concluded, 'The 1603 quarto edition is botched, bedraggled, and bold enough to try the energy of the finest company of actors to make sense of it; but here it was in the hands of incompetent duffers.'[8] The *Morning Post* mocked Poel's own performance:

> The knight of the woeful countenance who impersonated the Prince of Denmark struggled valiantly with the drawbacks of an unsympathetic voice, a tendency to tears, and a see-saw delivery of the lines, and in one or two scenes, aided by the classical leanness of his nether limbs, he soared into mediocrity.[9]

Only the *Academy*, whose critic was probably a Shakespere Society member, appreciated what Poel was trying to do:

> The First Quarto play 'went' admirably, and was finished in the orthodox two hours and a-half of Shakespere's time. . . The impression that the entire performance left on the hearer was that Quarto 1 was distinctly the representation – through whatever clouds – of a whole, a complete play that could and did stand alone; and that this play was not merely a distorted version of the authorized text of Quarto 2 when completed by the Folio, but a drama differently motivated in which revenge was more prominent, the Queen clear of guilt, and Laertes less treacherous.[10]

However, the originality of the staging was more significant than the effectiveness of the text, or the shortcomings of the actors, as this became the basis of Poel's life-long campaign for 'authentic' Shakespeare. Firstly, the actors were dressed as Elizabethans, unlike the quasi-Vikings introduced by Charles Kean and Fechter; secondly, there was no attempt at scenic illusion, although a curtain was drawn briefly five times to set and strike simple props; thirdly, by not adding any 'business', keeping the moves to a minimum and speaking the verse swiftly, the whole text was performed, apart from the cutting of a few 'indecencies'.[11] This meant the return of Fortinbras, who he had been banished since the days of Betterton, so that now, according to Poel, he could 'appear like Richmond in *Richard III* as the hero who will restore peace and order to the distracted kingdom'.[12] By combining the appeal to the imagination of a reading without scenery, and the appeal to the intellect of scholastic authority, Poel was launched into a career of theatrical antiquarianism very different from that of Irving or Tree. When he next performed the First Quarto almost twenty years later in 1900 he reconstructed an Elizabethan stage, employed an all-male cast, with a competent Hamlet in Richard Hoodless, and got the Dolmetsch consort to provide period music.

The development of scholarship in these years was, of course, not Poel's alone. Furnivall's Shakespere Society was committed to historical research as well as critical analysis. Amongst the influences that effected Poel's productions were the historical research of Sidney Lee, who drew parallels between the plays and the politics of Elizabethan England; the textual criticism of W. W. Greg, which included the publication of the early quartos and the Henslow Diaries; the discovery of the De Witt drawing of the Swan Theatre, which was published in 1888; the research of E. K. Chambers, leading to *The Medieval Stage* of 1903; and the musical reconstructions of Arnold Dolmetsch. The publication in America from 1871 of H. H. Furness's *Shakespeare Variorum Editions* brought together textual variants, a scholarly gloss on original meanings and detailed accounts of different stage interpretations. Anyone who kept abreast of this scholarship must soon have realised that there were many more ways than one of producing Shakespeare.

For some years after 1881 Poel concentrated on making his living, but his experience as manager for Emma Cons at the Royal Victoria Coffee Hall (the Old Vic), as stage-manager for the Benson Company, and as director of his own Little Comedies Company, which provided drawing-room entertainments for *soirées* and At Homes, ensured that he did not lose touch with the professional theatre while pursuing research and, from 1887, working with the Shakespeare Reading Society. Shaw found their performances very instructive: 'From these simple recitals, without cuts, waits or scenery, and therefore without those departures from the conditions contemplated by the poet which are inevitable in a modern theatre, I learn a good deal about the plays which I could learn in no other way. What is more, I enjoy myself.'[13] Entertainment value was not one of the Shakespeare Readers' first priorities, and Poel's crusading spirit was always tempered by a Victorian earnestness.

In 1893 he hired the Royalty Theatre and erected a reconstruction of the Fortune Playhouse for a production of *Measure for Measure*, the success of which led to the foundation of the Elizabethan Stage Society in the following year. Although the setting was not a three-sided platform thrust out into the audience, it did allow for continuous playing, without scene changes, using upper and inner stages with traverse curtains (see Plate XI(b)). To an extent, by presenting an Elizabethan stage, complete with stage-sitters, behind a Victorian proscenium arch, this experiment resembled Webster's *Taming of the Shrew* (1847), but Poel's approach to acting on such a stage was very different:

> It was just for acting's sake that the Elizabethan Stage Society was born. Some people have called me an archaeologist, but I am not. I am really a modernist. My original aim was just to find out some means of acting Shakespeare naturally and appeallingly from the full text as in modern drama. I found that for this the platform stage was necessary and also some suggestion of the spirit and manners of the time.[14]

So also was a reform of verse speaking, which led Poel into voice training. He always prefered to work with 'unformed' actors – students and amateurs – even to the extent of casting women in male roles. Over the years he worked with many actresses, who were to have very successful careers, such as Lillah MaCarthy, who was to marry Granville Barker; Rosina Filippi and Elsie Fogerty, who, as voice teachers, passed on Poel's training; and Edith Evans, whom he recruited from a milliner's shop in 1912. The essential quality Poel wanted was rapidity, and to achieve this his actors needed clear enunciation, physical expressiveness, and 'inner repose'.[15] Poel believed the plays made sense through their poetry, not through the emotional intensity of the actors. He rejected the pauses indulged in by Macready and advocated in Dr Plumptre's Elocution of 1880 (see above, p. 127), and demanded a fluidity of intonation 'on the line and through the line'. Norman Marshall's rather caustic account of Poel's work in *The Producer and the Play* concluded that 'Poel had a remarkable understanding of how Elizabethan verse should be spoken. The trouble was that he taught them rather than produced them':

> He began his rehearsals by 'teaching the tunes' to the company. Every line was analysed as a series of musical notes. Then Poel would himself 'give the tune' with deliberate exaggeration. The actor had to repeat it with the same exaggeration over and over again until it was firmly fixed in his mind. Only then would Poel allow the actor to speak the lines without exaggeration. All this took time. Usually from two to three weeks were spent with the company sitting in a room concentrating entirely on the music of the verse. The short time that was left for rehearsing on the stage was spent chiefly on arranging very simple moves and groupings while the actor did his best to

characterise his part and deliver his elaborately learned 'tunes' with an air of sponaneity.[16]

Poel insisted he was not just after the 'music' but the sense. As he explained in 1909, one must find the key-word of each sentence:

> As with the other arts, so it is with good acting, its excellence lies in restraint and in knowing what to surrender. If elocution is to imitate nature, a dozen or more words must be sacrificed so that one word may predominate and thus give the keynote to the tune of the whole sentence. In this way only can the sound be made to echo the sense. But the last thing, apparently, the actor cares to do is to give up making every word tell.[17]

He advocated the rapid delivery of continental actors, such as Rachel, Salvini and Coquelin. Indeed, his method of teaching 'the tunes' was much like the technique of *détailler* used by the doyens of the Comédie Française to instruct their pupils in rhythm and inflection.[18] Poel's concern for artistry and discipline rather than spontaneous inspiration echoed G. H. Lewes's analysis of the 'symbols' of the actor's art, and his view of acting as an craft to be taught by masters to apprentices owed much to the Utopian Socialism of Ruskin and William Morris, which fuelled his contempt for commercialism:

> It has often been said by foreigners that the English people lack the aesthetic instinct, that moral sense which unconsciously supplies a standard of true and false art. And this is easily explained. Business is the strongest passion of an Englishman's mind, and art gives way before it with morbid liberality. There is no power, in our average playgoer, to discriminate between the art which knows its sentimental patrons, and the art which is derived from a close study of the resourses of the art. The quality of the actor's art is gauged by the number of encores and recalls; the standard of theatrical advancement is determined by the number of theatres built and of those who pay to go into them.[19]

Poel then was not just an antiquarian eccentric, as he has sometimes been portrayed, nor did he just rediscover some (certainly not all) of the techniques of the Elizabethan theatre, but, as the bland naturalism of the late Victorian theatre declined into the even blander commercialism of Edwardian entertainment, he forged a link between the artistry of the old 'grand manner' and new anti-naturalistic experiments. Poel was never really a modernist, like, say, Gordon Craig, but, just as the rediscovery of the Commedia dell' Arte inspired the European modernists Meyerhold, Reinhardt and Copeau, so his rediscovery of Elizabethan stagecraft inspired Granville Barker, Yeats and the Old Vic productions of the 1920s.

Yet it would be wrong to conclude this study of Victorian acting with the impression that all was decadence and decline in the established theatre, and that progress could only be expected from the 'earnest amateurs'. The last new interpretation of *Hamlet* of the nineteenth century was in many ways the finest. It was produced at the Lyceum in 1897 by Johnson Forbes Robertson. Robertson was born into an artistic, though not specifically theatrical, family in 1852. He studied at the Royal Academy as a painter, and became an actor to help support the large family, of which he was the eldest. After some small parts in long-runs in London and on tour, he was employed by Charles Calvert in Manchester, where he acted Prince Hal to Phelps's doubling of Henry IV and Justice Shallow. The veteran took the young actor under his wing as part of the small nucleus of actors with whom he toured the dwindling stock theatre circuit.

In 1874 John Hollingshead mounted a season of 'legitimate drama' at the Gaiety during which Forbes Robertson acted with Herman Vezin as well as Phelps, the two actors to whom Robertson attributed his admired vocal technique. Shaw was to describe his voice in 1895 as 'an organ with only one stop: to the musician it suggests a clarinet in A, played only in the chalumeau register; but then the chalumeau, sympathetically sounded, has a richly melancholy and noble effect.'[20] In *Hamlet* two years later, Clement Scott felt it had more range, 'capable of every tone and modulation... alternately deep and tender. It reminds one of the moan and wail of the cello.'[21] During the later 1870s Forbes Robertson acted in drawing-room drama with the Bancrofts, the Kendals, and Geneviève Ward, but he always wished to be a classical actor, and in 1882 he was engaged by Irving as Claudio in *Much Ado About Nothing*. William Winter's description of him as Orlando in a Stratford Memorial performance in 1885 conveys the elegance, intellect and restraint which Irving valued as a foil to his own idiosyncratic style:

> Forbes-Robertson's embodiment, a little grave and severe and somewhat too intellectual, was, nevertheless, instinct with the right feeling... His air of high breeding and his perfect taste commended him to cordial sympathy... There was no lack of ardour, but the ardour was coloured and controlled by manifestation of that hallowing adoration with which true love sublimates passion and consecrates the object it adores.[22]

In all his interpretations Forbes Robertson revealed a similar 'idealising' approach to Shakespeare's characters, in the tradition of Macready and Faucit, rather than that of Irving and Tree.

In 1895 John Hare invited him to act opposite Mrs Patrick Campbell in Pinero's *The Notorious Mrs Ebbsmith*, which was intended to repeat her success in *The Second Mrs Tanqueray*. During the production the couple fell in love, and it may have been Mrs Pat who pushed Forbes Robertson rather reluctantly into management:

I would gladly have remained an actor pure and simple, to be called off the ranks, so to speak, by anyone who wished to engage me... I had acted with all the leading people of that time, and, though at periods being very hard worked, I had comparatively no anxieties. The very speculative and gambling nature of theatrical management was distasteful to me... On the other hand, several actors, younger than I, had taken up management very much earlier in their careers, ant there was nothing for it but to take a theatre if I was to maintain my place.[23]

Although he was now forty-three and well established, Forbes Robertson was once again helped by a master of the previous generation: Irving leased him the Lyceum on very favourable terms whilst he was on tour in America. The first production, *Romeo and Juliet*, was, according to Kate Terry Gielgud, 'a worthy successor to the Irving Shakespeare revivals – in excellent taste, never overdone', and although Forbes Robertson looked 'a trifle too ascetic... he can speak blank verse admirably'.[24] William Archer, however, pointed to the essential difference between the two lovers: 'the one has skill without temperament, the other temperament without skill. Mr Robertson can act Romeo, but cannot look or feel the part; Mrs Campbell could be Juliet if she only knew how to act it.' He went on to deplore her lack of traditional technique, and reflected on the general decline in 'the art of Shakespearian acting – its traditions will be lost more hopelessly than ever, and no one will believe that there are really great and vivid and poignant emotions to be got out of Shakespeare on the stage.'[25]

It was not that Mrs Campbell was a poor actress – in the right parts, Pinero's Paula Tanqueray and Agnes Ebbsmith, Sardou's Fedora, Maeterlinck's Mélisande and even Yeats's Deirdre, she was excellent – but she was modern: her emotions seemed uncontrolled and erratic, or, rather, they smouldered in the sub-text of the part before bursting forth with incoherent violence. As Juliet she looked stunning – young and Italianate – A. B. Walkley could not imagine 'a more delicious embodiment of Juliet',[26] but Kate Terry Gielgud put her finger on the problem:

Passion, the deep tragedy of the classic stage, she cannot touch; she is too *fin-de-siècle*, too much the morbid, introspective modern woman. She seems unable to conceive and represent the broader, less civilised nature that shows its feelings, loving, hating, despairing with equal intensity; an intensity none the less deep that it wears no mask.[27]

Craig described this 'masking', or refusal to show explicitly the emotions of each moment, as 'incompetence – an incapacity to understand that everything has to be clearly explained to the spectators' (see p. 123). Forbes Robertson always made his feelings clear in the handling of the lines, but Mrs Pat knew she lacked his classical technique. She wrote frantically to her sister Louise for help:

Are the tears there when I weep real?... was the fall right & the language delivered simply enough – or would tears in the voice be better there?... Where are the exact points when I seem too much the woman and to lose the girl's anger?... to keep the rhythm I accentuated *such* [in the line 'Here such a coil'] & the meaning is clearer if I accentuate *Here*... Yes, it is the grandioso note that is wrong. I *must* keep it *all* simple... I DREADED being a *sentimental* Juliet.[28]

Early in her career she had ruined her voice by having to shout her way through Rosalind in a Ben Greet open-air production, and had never really mastered the voice production needed for a large theatre.[29] In fact Mrs Pat was the quintissential amateur as described by Archer: all temperament and little technique.

In 1897 Forbes Robertson took over the Lyceum again while Irving was in America, and this time Irving not only leased him the theatre, but personally suggested that he should play Hamlet, and lent him the Lyceum scenery without charge (see Plate XII). In this respect at least Robertson's *Hamlet* was typically Victorian in that he was acting in borrowed 'stock' scenery. Irving's Hamlet had been a neurotic introvert, whose self-contemplation led to agonies of doubt, which in turn led him to rail viciously against the two loves of his life, his mother and Ophelia. The morbidity of this interpretation had suited the dungeon-like scenery, half hidden in the gloom of Irving's subtle gas-lighting, within which Ellen Terry's Pre-Raphaelite Ophelia gleamed with the fragility of a candle flame. Forbes Robertson's Hamlet, however, seemed out of place in the Viking halls; his inspiration was Elizabethan. His Prince was an outsider in the court of Elsinore, not because of psychological incompatibility, but because he had the idealising sensitivity of a Renaissance scholar, which in nineteenth-century terms meant a Christian gentleman. It was not until his final performances of the role at Harvard University in 1916, that he acted in an 'Elizabethan' playhouse. George Pierce Baker had constructed a small-scale version of the Fortune, and Forbes Robertson was delighted with the economy and intimacy of the performance.[30]

Earlier in his career his physical technique had been stiff and awkward: 'too apt to throw his head back, and gesticulate too freely, and to wave his arms and legs in an eccentric manner'. Like an 'antique semaphore' he seemed a caricature of Irving's gawkiness,[31] but now he had begot a smoothness in gesture as well as in speech. William Archer missed Irving's febrile excitement, describing Robertson's Hamlet as 'an admirable performance', that brought out 'the grace and distinction of Hamlet, his affability... his melancholy, his intellectual discursiveness', but in which 'he slurs and almost ignores the nervous excitability on Hamlet's part which merges so naturally, nay, almost indistinguishably, into his pretended madness'.[32]

J. T. Grien was also struck by Hamlet's affability and humour, and felt that although he was alienated from the court, it was by philosophical detatchment:

> Yet I hardly dare complain that I was diverted rather than harrowed while witnessing this performance, so fresh, so young *[Forbes Robertson was forty-five]*, so full of true humour. The delicate lights and shades, the cordiality displayed towards Horatio, the diplomatic civility towards Rosencrantz and Guildenstern, the gentle contempt for Polonius, the paternal tone towards Ophelia, the unconcealed hatred for the king, the sympathetic attitude towards the Queen – all were harmonized as in a fair mosaic; and through all this beamed the smile of the thinker who regarded the whole world as a pretty stage, and all its inhabitants as players[33]

The third great 'modern' critic of the nineties, Bernard Shaw, was inspired to one of his finest and most perceptive reviews. He had discussed the play with Forbes Robertson beforehand, and, indeed, the intellect, humour and irony of the interpretation could be described as Shavian. Shaw's analysis shows how the actor combined traditional skills with contemporary insights:

> Mr Forbes Robertson is essentially a classical actor... What I mean by classical is that he can present a dramatic hero as a man whose passions are those which have produced the philosophy, the poetry, the art, and the statecraft of the world, and not merely those which have produced its weddings, coroners' inquests, and executions. And this is just the sort of actor that Hamlet requires... Mr Forbes Robertson takes the part quite easily and spontaneously. There is none of that strange Lyceum intensity which comes from the perpetual struggle between Sir Henry Irving and Shakespear. The lines help Mr Forbes Robertson instead of getting in his way at every turn... He does not superstitiously worship William; he enjoys him and understands his methods of expression. Instead of cutting every line that can possibly be spared, he retains every gem... He does not utter half a line; then stop to act; then go on with another half line; and then stop to act again, with the clock running away with Shakespear's chances all the time. He plays as Shakespear should be played, on the line and to the line, with the utterance and acting simultaneous, inseperable and in fact identical.[34]

Because of his swift and easy playing, and his appreciation of the music of each line and of the play as a whole, Forbes Robertson not only spoke as William Poel would have liked, but was able to play in three and a half hours a more complete text than any Victorian predecessor. Not only were Reynaldo, Voltimand and Cornelius restored, but, most significantly, Fortinbras. In the final moments of the play Hamlet struggled to the throne, where he died sitting upright like a king, Fortinbras and his soldiers entered to do him homage.

Although Shaw was pleased by Mrs Patrick Campbell's convincing madness as Ophelia, most critics agreed with Kate Terry Gielgud that it was curious that the production was so satisfying, 'since, with the exception of the Hamlet, none of the parts are well cast'. She dismissed Mrs Pat as 'a mere, tiresome, walking-lady until the mad scene, and that, since we cared not a fig what became of the said walking-lady, became a mere excrescence upon the play'.[35] Thus we must conclude that the production as a whole was poised between two worlds: Forbes Robertson, as director, had performed a generally authentic text, but had staged it with inappropriate scenery, which was too traditional, and an inappropriate supporting cast, whose style was too modern; yet, as an actor, he triumphed over these disadvantages. This was possible not only because of his mastery of traditional verse speaking, which he had learnt from Phelps and Vezin, but because his audience still accepted the dramaturgical conventions of the Victorian stage that focused on the personality and passion of the heroic individual, and could overlook lapses in ensemble playing that twentieth-century audiences would have found intolerable.

As the irrepressible spokesman of the modern theatre, it is fitting to give Shaw a final word in looking back on Victorian styles of acting, and how they had been determined by the organisation of their theatre. At his second visit to Hamlet, when it had run for two months, he felt that:

> Mr Forbes Robertson's exhausting part had been growing longer and heavier on his hands; whilst the support of the others had been falling off; so that he was keeping up the charm of the representation almost singlehanded just when the torturing fatigue and monotony had made the task most difficult.

This prompted him to reflect on the respective problems of stock theatre and the long-run:

> The truth is, it is just as impossible for a human being to study and perform a new part of any magnitude every day as to play Hamlet for a hundred consecutive nights. Nevertheless, if an actor is required to do these things, he will find some way out of the difficulty without refusing. The stock actor solved the problem by adopting a 'line': for example, if his 'line' was old age, he acquired a trick of doddering and speaking in a cracked voice: if juvenility, he swaggered and effervesced... he 'swallowed' every part given him in a couple of hours, and regurgitated it in the evening over the footlights, always in the same manner, however finely the dramatist might have individualised it... A moment's consideration will shew that the results of the long-run system at its worst are more bearable than the horrors of the past... The best system, of course, lies between these extremes.[36]

Of course! However, I hope this study of the 'bad old systems' has revealed that, although both stock and long-run had their failing, there were Victorian actors who not only learnt to 'find a way out of the difficulty', but actually mastered the essential conventions of their art so as to give their audiences theatrical experiences of a profundity and vividness such as we might envy a hundred years later.

Notes

Chapter 1: Tradition and change

1 T. J. Seale, *The Players* (London, 1847), II, 307.
2 Edward Stirling, *Old Drury Lane* (London, 1881), I.
3 Elliston to unnamed correspondent, 22 May 18--, Harvard Theatre Collection, *Autographs*, I, A-F.
4 Macready to George Macready, 10 Aug. 1832, Princeton University Library.
5 Macready to Bristol Manager, 28 Aug. 1836, Princeton University Library: AM 18339.
6 11 Dec. 1834, W. C. Macready, *Diaries*, edited by W. Toynbee (London, 1912), I, 208.
7 John Colman, *Players and Playwrights* (Philadelphia, 1890), I, 66.
8 *The Manchester Courier*, 21 June 1864; cited with details of Irving's preparation and performance, Laurence Irving, *Henry Irving, the Actor and his World* (London, 1951), p. 117.
9 *Ibid.* pp. 242-9; for the 1874 Hamlet see A. Hughes, *Henry Irving, Shakespearian* (Cambridge, 1981), chapter 2, pp. 27-87.
10 James R. Anderson, *An Actor's Life* (London, 1902), pp. 255-6.
11 *Ibid.* pp. 322-3.
12 See D. Bradby, L. James and B. Sharratt, *Politics and Performance in Popular Theatre* (Cambridge, 1980); C. Barker, 'A Theatre for the People' in K. Richards and P. Thomson (eds.), *Nineteenth Century British Theatre* (London, 1971), pp. 3-24.
13 Kellow Chesney, *The Victorian Underworld* (London, 1970), p. 119.
14 Michael Baker, *The Rise of the Victorian Actor* (London, 1978), p. 146, paraphrasing The Report of the Select Committee on Theatre Licenses and Regulations, *Accounts and Committees*, 1866, XVI, 1.
15 Dion Bouciault, 'Barnstorming; or, the Lost Art of Acting', *New York Herald*, 1883.
16 Allardyce Nicoll, *A History of English Drama, 1660-1900* (London, 1970), IV, 222-33; Frederick and Lisa Lone Marker, 'A Guide to London Theatres', *The Revels History of English Drama* (London, 1975), VI, l-lxii; Leman Rede, *The Road to the Stage* (London 1836), pp. 12-13.
17 Peter Paterson, *Glimpses of Real Life* (London, 1864), p. 93; James Grant, *Sketches of London* (London, 1838), p. 169.
18 Michael Baker, *The Rise of the Victorian Actor,* p. 225.
19 Alfred Bunn, *The Stage: Both Before and Behind the Curtain* (London, 1840), III, 229-39.
20 See Alan S. Downer, *The Eminent Tragedian* (Harvard, 1966), pp. 147-9.

21 Haymarket advertisement, 1843, quoted Allardyce Nicoll, *The Development of the Theatre* (London, 5th ed., 1966), p. 159.
22 C. E. Pascoe, *The Dramatic List* (London, 2nd ed., 1880), p. 187.
23 E. G. Craig, *Henry Irving* (London, 1930), p. 100.
24 *The Examiner*, 26 July 1835.
25 Westland Marston, *Our Recent Actors* (London, 1888), p. 166.
26 W. C. Macready [21 Aug 1839], *Diaries*, edited by W. Toynbee (London, 1912), II, 22.
27 John Colman, *Players and Playwrights*, I, 285.
28 Quoted Alan S. Downer, *The Eminent Tragedian*, pp. 199-200.
29 W. C. Macready, *Diaries*, 13 Sept. 1840, II, 80.
30 J. R. Planché, *Recollections and Reflections* (London, 1901).
31 W. Appleton, *Madame Vestris and the London Stage* (New York, 1974), pp. 51-62.
32 J. R. Planché, *Recollections and Reflections*, p. 180.
33 *The Times*, 5 March 1841, in *Dramatic List*, p. 50.
34 Henry Morley, *The Journal of a London Playgoer* (London, 1891), pp. 69-70.
35 Michael Baker, *The Rise of the Victorian Actor*, pp. 140-1.
36 M. Glen Wilson, 'The Career of Charles Kean: a Financial Report' in K. Richards and P. Thomson (eds.), *Nineteenth Century British Theatre* (London, 1971), pp. 39-50.
37 *Theatrical Journal*, 25 May 1844; quoted S. S. Allen, *Samuel Phelps and Sadler's Wells Theatre* (Middletown, Conn., 1971), p. 76.
38 Henry Morley, *London Playgoer*, p. 129.
39 *Ibid.* p. 138.
40 *Theatrical Journal*, 23 Aug 1845; quoted S. S. Allen, *Phelps*, p. 97.
41 *Weekly Dispatch*, 21 Nov. 1858.
42 S. S. Allen, *Phelps*, Appendix I, pp. 314-15.
43 *Theatrical Journal*, 6 Dec. 1845.
44 John Colman, *Players and Playwrights*, I, 182.
45 *Punch*, 26 Nov. 1862.
46 William Archer, 'Samuel Phelps', *Actors and Actresses of Great Britain and the United States*, edited by B. Matthews and L. Hutton (New York, 1886), IV, 71-2.

Chapter 2: *The Corsican Brothers*

1 Preface to *The Winter's Tale*, 28 April 1856, quoted J. W. Cole, *The Life and Theatrical Times of Charles Kean, F. S. A.* (London, 1859), II, 171-2.
2 Ellen Terry, *Memoirs*, edited by E. Craig and C. St. John (London, 1933), p. 13.
3 *Ibid.* p. 23.
4 For technical details see Appendix to *The Corsican Brothers*, Michael R. Booth, *English Plays of the Nineteenth Century* (Oxford, 1969), II, 71-5. Also MS. prompt-copy, Folger Shakespeare Library, Da 72.
5 G. H. Lewes, *The Leader*, 28 Feb. 1852.
6 C. E. Pascoe, *The Dramatic List*, p. 349.
7 John Colman, *Players and Playwrights*, I, 269.
8 *Ibid.*
9 Westland Marston, *Our Recent Actors*, p. 361.
10 C. E. Pascoe, *The Dramatic List*, p. 350.
11 W. M. Phelps and J. Forbes-Robertson, *The Life and Works of Samuel Phelps* (London, 1886), p. 208.

12 G. H. Lewes, *The Leader*, 28 Feb. 1852.

13 Westland Marston, *Our Recent Actors*, p. 124.

14 *Ibid.* p. 125.

15 G. H. Lewes, *On Actors and the Art of Acting* (London, 1875), pp. 13-18.

Chapter 3: Theatre of feeling

1 G. H. Lewes, *On Actors and the Art of Acting*, p. 39.

2 *Morning Post*, 1 March 1814, quoted G. Playfair, *Kean* (London, 1939, 1950 ed.), p. 106.

3 G. W. Taylor, 'The Just Delineation of the Passions: Theories of Acting in the Age of Garrick', *The Eighteenth Century English Stage*, edited by K. Richards and P. Thomson (London, 1972), pp. 52-72.

4 *Lichtenberg's Visits to England as Described in his Letters and Diaries*, translated by M. L. Mare and W. H. Quarrel (Oxford, 1938), p. 10.

5 Henry Fielding, *Tom Jones* (Everyman edition, 1962), II, 308.

6 John Hill, *Treatise on the Art of Playing; The Actor* (London, 1750).

7 *Whitehall Evening Post*, 17 Mar. 1779.

8 J. Donahue, *Dramatic Character in the English Romantic Age* (Princeton, 1970), p. 244.

9 W. Hazlitt, *Complete Works*, edited by P. P. Howe (London, 1903), V, 179.

10 L. Hunt, *The Examiner*, 26 Feb. 1815.

11 G. H. Lewes, *On Actors and the Art of Acting*, pp. 18-19.

12 W. C. Macready, *Reminiscences*, edited by F. Pollock (London, 1875), p. 51.

13 W. Hazlitt, *The Times*, 15 June 1817.

14 W. C. Macready, *Reminiscences*, pp. 101-2.

15 W. Hazlitt, *The Times*, 15 June 1817; *The Examiner*, 16 June 1816.

16 W. C. Macready, *Reminiscences*, p. 148.

17 W. Scott, *Quarterly Review*, XXXIV (1826), p. 219.

18 For Siddons's own analysis of the role, see S. Siddons, 'Remarks on the Character of Lady Macbeth', in T. Campbell, *Life of Mrs Siddons* (London, 1834), II, 10-34.

19 J. Boaden, *Memoirs of Mrs Siddons* (London, 1807), II, 134-5.

20 W. R. Alger, *Life of Edwin Forrest* (New York, 1877), II, 545.

21 F. W. Hawkins, *Life of Kean* (London, 1869), pp. 346-7.

22 W. Robson, *The Old Playgoer* (London, 1845), p. 114.

23 *The Thespian Preceptor; or, A Full Display of the Scenic Art* (London, 1810), pp. 33-42.

24 G. Grant, *The Science of Acting* (London, 1828), pp. 136-7.

25 H. Siddons, *Practical Illustrations of Rhetorical Gestures* (London, 1822), p. 3.

26 *Ibid.* pp. 14-17.

27 *Ibid.* pp. 307-8.

28 J. Donahue, *Dramatic Character*, p. 345.

29 J. R. Roach, *The Player's Passion* (Newark, 1985), pp. 58-68.

30 C. Bell, *Anatomy and Expression, as Connected with the Fine Arts* (London, 1804 [3rd ed. 1840]), pp. 190-8.

31 W. James, *Principles of Psychology* (London, 1890).

32 R. Cooter, *The Cultural Meaning of Popular Science* (Cambridge, 1984), p. 35.

33 G. Garcia, *The Actor's Art* (London, 1888), p. 112: P. Mantegazza, *Physiognomy and Expression* (London, n.d. [1885]), p. 43.

34 R. Cooter, *The Cultural Meaning of Popular Science*, p. 114.

35 Quoted *ibid.* p. 155.

36 George Raymond, *Memoirs of Robert W. Elliston* (London, 1846), II, 401-3.

37 Letter of Apr. 1820, quoted A. S. Downer, *The Eminent Tragedian*, pp. 62-3.
38 *Daily News*, 18 May 1820, quoted W. Archer, *William Charles Macready* (London, 1890)
39 *La Réunion*, 16 Apr. 1828, quoted A. S. Downer, *The Eminent Tragedian*, p. 114.
40 W. C. Macready, *Diaries*, II, 475 and 485.
41 *Ibid.* II, 487.
42 Edward Mayhew, *Stage Effect; or, The Principles which Command Dramatic Success in the Theatre* (London, 1840), p. 44, quoted M. Meisel, *Realizations* (Princeton, 1983), p. 29.
43 E. Mayhew, *op. cit.* pp. 50-2.
44 M. Meisel, *Realizations*, pp. 124-41.
45 K. G. Holmström, *Monodrama, Attitudes, Tableaux Vivants* (Stockholm, 1967), pp. 110-40.
46 *Art-Union*, IX (1847), quoted R. D. Altick, *The Shows of London* (Harvard, 1978), p. 348.
47 R. D. Altick, *op. cit.* p. 349.
48 Oxberry's 'Memoir', p. 14, quoted A. H. Saxon, *The Life and Art of Andrew Ducrow* (Hamden, Conn., 1978), p. 144.
49 *Edinburgh Evening Courant*, 15 Dec. 1827.
50 Quoted M. R. Booth, *English Melodrama* (London, 1965), p. 142.
51 Quoted A. H. Saxon, *Life of Ducrow*, p. 317.

Chapter 4: *Richelieu*

1 See Macready, *Diaries*, I, 476-92: *Reminiscences*, pp. 462-71: C. H. Shattock, *Bulwer and Macready* (Urbana, 1958), pp. 77-131: W. Marston, *Our Recent Actors*, pp. 25-36: also Introduction and Appendix to 'Richelieu' in M. R. Booth, *English Nineteenth Century Plays* (Oxford, 1969-73), I, 237-315.
2 Edward Bulwer-Lytton, *Pelham, or the Adventures of a Gentleman* (London, 1828), quoted in R. B. Henkle, *Comedy and Culture* (Princeton, 1980), p. 23.
3 *The Times*, 5 Jan. 1837.
4 Macready to Bulwer, 11 Jan.1838; Shattuck, *Bulwer and Macready*, p. 64.
5 Bulwer to Macready, 9 Sept. 1838; *ibid.* p. 84.
6 Bulwer to Macready, 16 Sept. 1838; *ibid.* p. 88.
7 Bulwer to Macready, 22 Feb. 1839; *ibid.* p. 120.
8 Bulwer to Macready, 18 Dec. 1838; *ibid.* p. 108.
9 *Ibid.*
10 *Ibid.* p. 109.
11 Bulwer to Macready, 17 Nov. 1838; *ibid.* pp. 94-5.
12 Macready, *Reminiscences*, p. 470.
13 *Ibid.* pp. 708-9.
14 J. Colman, *Players and Playwrights*, I, 50.
15 *Richelieu*, prompt-copy marked 'Oliver W. Doud' with cast list for 1861 production at Winter Garden, New York (Laurence Barrett as Richelieu), Harvard Theatre Collection.
16 Bulwer to Macready, 22 Feb. 1839; Shattuck, *Bulwer and Macready*, p. 121.
17 J. Colman, *Players and Playwrights*, pp. 48-9.
18 *The Examiner*, 9 Nov. 1850.
19 W. Marston, *Our Recent Actors*, pp. 33-4.
20 *The Examiner*, 22 Sept. 1815.

21 G. H. Lewes, *On Actors and the Art of Acting*, p. 40.
22 2 and 11 Jan, 1833; *Diaries*, I, pp. 1 and 5.
23 W. Marston, *Our Recent Actors*, p. 51.
24 *Letters of David Garrick*, edited by D. M. Little and G. M. Kahrl (London, 1963), I, 350.
25 W. Marston, *Our Recent Actors*, pp. 35 and 28.
26 *Ibid.* II, 363-4.
27 G. H. Lewes, *On Actors and the Art of Acting*, pp. 43-4.

Chapter 5: Comic acting

1   Michael Booth, *English Plays of the Nineteenth Century*, III, 61.
2   W. Robson, *The Old Playgoer* (London 1846), pp. 55-8.
3   *The London Magazine*, Oct. 1822.
4   *The London Magazine*, July 1824.
5   *Records of a Stage Veteran*, 1828; quoted W. C. Russell, *Representative Actors* (London, 1888), p. 323.
6   *Blackwood's Magazine*, 1840; quoted Russell, *Representative Actors*, p. 324.
7   *Examiner*, 18 May 1828.
8   *The Modern Drama*, 1862; quoted Russell, *Representative Actors*, pp. 385-6.
9   C. E. Pascoe, *The Dramatic List* (London, 1880), p. 71.
10 W. Marston, *Our Recent Actors*, pp. 246-7.
11 *Ibid.* pp. 382-4.
12 W. Marston, *Our Recent Actors*, p. 246.
13 Thomas Marshall, *The Lives of the Most Celebrated Actors and Actresses* (London, 1847), p. 106.
14 H. Morley, *Journal of a London Playgoer* (London, 1891), p. 62.
15 Quoted Walter Goodman, *The Keeleys, on the Stage and at Home* (London, 1895), pp. 157-9.
16 *Ibid.* pp. 150-1.
17 G. H. Lewes, *On Actors and the Art of Acting*, pp. 77-9.
18 Mrs Patrick Campbell, *My Life and Some Letters* (London, 1922), p. 116.
19 Sir Theodore Martin, *Helen Faucit, Lady Martin* (Edinburgh, 1900), p. 263.
20 *Ibid.*
21 C. W. Smith, *The Actor's Art* (London, 1872), pp. 6-7.
22 W. Marston, *Our Recent Actors*, p. 233.
23 G. H. Lewes, *On Actors and the Art of Acting*, pp. 62-3.
24 *The Times*, 22 May 1858.
25 G. H. Lewes, *On Actors and the Art of Acting*, pp. 69-70.
26 W. Marston, *Our Recent Actors*, pp. 299-300.
27 J. R. Planché, *Recollections and Reflections* (London, 1872; revised edition, 1901), p. 126.
28 See D. Mayer, *Harlequin in his Element* (London, 1969).
29 Mollie Sands, *Robson of the Olympic* (London, 1979), p. 17.
30 W. Davidge, *Footlight Flashes* (New York, 1866), pp. 56-7.
31 Dutton Cook, 'Frederick Robson' in *The Gentleman's Magazine*, June 1882, quoted M. Sands, *Robson*, p. 49.
32 *Morning Chronicle*, 21 Aug. 1853.
33 G. A. Sala, *A Sketch of Frederick Robson* (London, 1864), p. 20.
34 M. Sands, *Robson*, p. 46.

35 *Illustrated London News*, 30 April 1853.
36 *The Observer*, 1 May 1853.
37 M. Sands, *Robson*, p. 48.
38 *Illustrated London News*, 10 July 1853.
39 H. Morley, *London Playgoer*, p. 51.
40 M. Sands, *Robson*, pp. 58-9.
41 H. Morley, *London Playgoer*, p. 53.
42 J. R. Planché, *Recollections*, pp. 350-7.
43 G. A. Sala, *Atlantic Monthly*, June, 1864; quoted B. Matthews and L. Hutton, *Actors and Actresses* (New York, 1886), IV, pp. 205-6.
44 Charles Dickens, *Letters* (London, 1893), I, 451.
45 *The Times*, 28 Mar. 1857.
46 W. Marston, *Our Recent Actors*, pp. 363-6.
47 *Ibid.* p. 372.
48 *Uncle Tom's Cabin*, film, Thomas A. Eddison (New Jersey, 1903).
49 *The Times*, 3 July 1868.
50 Joseph Knight, *The Theatre*, Jan. 1880, quoted D. Mullin, *Victorian Actors and Actresses in Review* (Westport, Conn., 1983), p. 454.

Chapter 6: *Our American Cousin*

1 John Lester Wallack, *Memories of Fifty Years* (New York, 1889), pp. 159-60.
2 Joseph Jefferson, *Autobiography* (London and New York, 1889), p. 194.
3 Wallack, *Memories of Fifty Years*, p. 160.
4 T. Edgar Pemberton, *Memoirs of E. A. Sothern* (London, 1889), pp. 4 and 16.
5 *Oxford English Dictionary*.
6 Edward H. Sothern, *The Melancholy Tale of 'Me'* (New York, 1916), p. 173.
7 Joseph Jefferson, *Autobiography*, pp. 197-8.
8 Edward A. Sothern, *Birds of a Feather* (New York, 1878), p. 24, 68 and 57.
9 Edward H. Sothern, *The Melancholy Tale of 'Me'*, pp. 173-4.
10 'New York. Sept. 6', quoted B. Matthews and L. Hutton, *Actors and Actresses* (New York, 1886), V, 81.
11 MS YC.4997(32), Folger Shakespeare Library.
12 T. E. Pemberton, *Memoirs of E. A. Sothern*, p. 45.
13 MS YC.4997(37), Folger Shakespeare Library.
14 Edward A. Sothern, *Birds of a Feather*, pp. 117-20.
15 *Atheneum*, 16 Nov. 1861; quoted Pascoe, *Dramatic List*, p. 307.
16 J. Colman, *Players and Playwrights*, I, 231-2.
17 'Theatrical Types', quoted T. E. Pemberton, *The Life and Writings of T. W. Robertson*, (London, 1893), p. 95.
18 *Our American Cousin*, 'John Moore's' prompt-copy with MS additions, Folger Shakespeare Library, photocopy 018.
19 T. E. Pemberton, *Memoirs of E. A. Sothern*, p. 34.
20 *Ibid.*
21 H. Morley, *London Playgoer*, p. 233.
22 J.Oxenford, *The Theatre*, 1 Oct. 1878.
23 *New York Mirror* 12 Aug. 1882, cutting in Harvard Theatre Collection, extra illustrated edition, B. Matthews and L. Hutton, *Actors and Actresses*.
24 T. E. Pemberton, *Memoirs of E. A. Sothern*, pp. 51-2.
25 *Ibid.*

26 '2 Feb. 1908', Havard Theatre Collection, 'Cuttings; E. A. Sothern'.
27 MS addition to 'John Moore's' prompt-copy, Folger Shakespeare Library.
28 Macready to Barton, 14 Mar. 1866. MS AM16218, Princeton University Library.
29 T. E. Pemberton, *Memoirs of E. A. Sothern*, p. 31.
30 'Howard', *New York Herald* 6 Sept. nd., Havard Theatre Collection 'Cuttings; E. A. Sothern'.

Chapter 7: French naturalism and English ensemble

1 *Illustrated London News*, quoted R. Baldrick, *Life and Times of Frédérick Lemaître*, (London, 1959), p. 193.
2 H. Morley, *Journal of a London Playgoer*, p. 223.
3 My italics, *The Times*, 27 Oct. 1860, quoted Pascoe, *The Dramatic List*, p. 396.
4 *Ibid.* p. 398.
5 G. H. Lewes, *On Actors and the Art of Acting*, pp. 118-19.
6 Westland Marston, *Our Recent Actors* (London, 1888), pp. 318-19 and 361.
7 Pascoe, *The Dramatic List*, p. 384.
8 H. Morley, *Journal of a London Playgoer*, p. 220.
9 See Appendices, M. Baker, *The Rise of the Victorian Actor*, pp. 201-10.
10 C. Scott, *The Drama of Yesterday and Today* (London, 1899), I, 435-6.
11 J. Colman, *Players and Playwrights*, II, 154-5.
12 Title of chapter, C. Scott, *The Drama of Yesterday and Today*, I ,471.
13 A. Filon, *The English Stage* (London, 1892), p. 113.
14 For a full discussion of the 'originality' of the Robertsonians see E. B. Watson, *Sheridan to Robertson* (Cambridge, 1926), pp. 392-400, and M. Savin, *T. W. Robertson, His Plays and Stagecraft* (Providence, R.I., 1950).
15 S. and M. Bancroft, *The Bancrofts; Recollections of Sixty Years* (London, 1909), p. 39.
16 J. Colman, *Players and Playwrights*, I, 271-2.
17 A. Filon, *The English Stage*, p. 117.
18 See W. Tydeman, *Plays by Tom Robertson* (Cambridge, 1983), p. 3.
19 Quoted T. E. Pemberton, T*he Life and Writings of T. W. Robertson* (London, 1893), p. 178.
20 Pascoe, *The Dramatic List*, pp. 382-3.
21 S. and M. Bancroft, *Recollections of Sixty Years*, pp. 62-3.
22 M. Baker, *The Rise of the Victorian Actor*, p. 118.
23 S. and M. Bancroft, *Recollections of Sixty Years*, pp. 69-72.
24 M. Baker, *The Rise of the Victorian Actor*, p. 113.
25 Quoted S. and M. Bancroft, *Recollections of Sixty Years*, p. 75.
26 Ellen Terry's *Memoirs*, edited by E.Craig and C. St John (London, 1933), p. 110.
27 S. and M. Bancroft, *Recollections of Sixty Years*, p. 114.
28 T. E. Pemberton, *Introduction to 'Society' and 'Caste'*, quoted G. Rowell, *The Victorian Theatre* (London, 1978), p. 82.
29 Sidney Dark, *Stage Silhouettes* (London, 1901), p. 33.
30 T. E. Pemberton, *The Life and Writings of T. W. Robertson*, p. 200.
31 A. Filon, *The English Stage*, pp. 139 and 145.
32 Hamilton Fyfe, *Sir Arthur Pinero's Plays and Players* (London, 1930), p. 259.
33 I. Vanbrugh, *To Tell My Story* (London, 1948), p. 179.
34 W. E. Houghton, *The Victorian Frame of Mind* (Yale, 1957), pp. 154-6.
35 J. Colman, *Players and Playwrights*, II, 92.
36 S. and M. Bancroft, *Recollections of Sixty Years*, p. 249.

37 *The Times*, quoted M. Savin, *T. W. Robertson, His Plays and Stagecraft.*
38 H. James, *The Scenic Art*, edited by Allan Wade (London, 1949), pp. 147-8.

Chapter 8: *Caste*

1   S. and M. Bancroft, *The Recollections of Sixty Years*, p. 96
2   *Caste*, Act I, from W. Tydeman, *Plays by Tom Robertson* (London, 1982), p. 137.
3   Quoted M. Savin, *T. W. Robertson, His Plays and Stagecraft*, p. 86.
4   A. Filon, *The English Stage*, p. 120.
5   *Caste*, Act III.
6   S. and M. Bancroft, *Recollections of Sixty Years*, p. 95.
7   B. Matthews and L. Hutton, *Actors and Actresses* (New York, 1886), V, 31-2.
8   C. Pascoe, *The Dramatic List*, p. 27.
9   C. Scott, *The Drama of Yesterday and Today*, I, 525-6.
10 A. Derbyshire, *The Art of the Victorian Stage* (London, 1907), pp. 140-1.
11 H. James, *The Scenic Art*, edited by Allan Wade (London, 1949), p. 145.
12 *Ibid.* p. 144.
13 R. W. Emerson, *English Traits* (London, 1856), World Classics, pp. 62-4.
14 S. and M. Bancroft, *Recollections of Sixty Years*, p. 93.
15 H. James, *The Scenic Art*, pp. 148 and 110.
16 F. Benson, *My Memoirs* (London, 1930), p. 182.
17 *Daily News*, 8 Apr. 1867, quoted C. Pascoe, *op. cit.* p. 184.
18 S. and M. Bancroft, *Recollections of Sixty Years*, pp. 99-100.
19 *Ibid.* p. 17.
20 B. Matthews and L. Hutton, *Actors and Actresses*, V, 31.
21 Quoted T. E. Pemberton, *The Life and Writings of T. W. Robertson*, pp. 120-1.
22 A. Filon, *The English Stage*, pp. 116-17.
23 H. James, *The Scenic Art*, p. 109.
24 *Daily News*, 8 Apr.1867, C. Pascoe, *The Dramatic List*, p. 184.
25 G. B. Shaw, *Dramatic Opinions and Essays* (London, 1906), V, i, 280-2.

Chapter 9: The conventions of melodrama

1   J. L. Styan, *Drama, Stage and Audience* (Cambridge, 1975), p. 194.
2   J. L. Smith, *Melodrama* (London, 1973), pp. 9-10.
3   B. Sharratt, 'The politics of the popular' in D. Bradby *et al.*, *Performance and Politics in Popular Theatre*: p. 279; M. R. Booth, *English Melodrama* (London, 1965) p. 14.
5   B. Sharratt, '*The politics of the popular*', pp. 281-2.
6   Peter Brooks, *The Melodramatic Imagination* (New Haven, 1976), chapter 2, pp. 24-55.
7   Gilbert à Beckett, *Quizzology of the British Theatre* (London, 1846), p. 26.
8   E. G. Craig, *Henry Irving* (London, 1930), p. 61.
9   Peter Brooks, *The Melodramatic Imagination*, p. 14.
10 M. G. Lewis, 'The Captive', 1803, in M. Baron-Wilson, *Life and Correspondence of M. G. Lewis* (London, 1839).
11 R. M. Sillard, *Barry Sullivan and his Contemporaries* (London, 1901), I, 135.
12 C. Reade, 'A Dramatic Musician', *The Era*, reprinted *Readiana* (London, 1880), p. 29.
13 F. Corder, 'Recitation with Music', in H. Campbell *et al.*, *Voice, Speech and Gesture* :

Elocutionary Art (London, 1897), p. 214.

14 J. E. Murdoch, 'The Stage', quoted J. Colman, *Playwrights and Players*, I, 45-6.
15 T. Martin, *Helen Faucit* (Edinburgh, 1900), pp. 37-8.
16 J. A. Hammerton, *The Actor's Art* (London, 1897), p. 38.
17 H. Chance Newton, *Cues and Curtain Calls* (London, 1927), pp. 95 and 36-7.
18 S. Dark, *Stage Silhouettes* (London, 1902), p. 135.
19 R. Filippi, *Hints to Speakers and Players* (London, 1911), p. 24.
20 C. J. Plumptre, *King's College Lectures on Elocution* (London, 1883), p. 48.
21 R. Filippi, *Hints to Speakers and Players*, p. 5.
22 Richard Bebb (ed.), 'Great Actors of the Past', Argo record (1977).
23 *The Times*, 9 Oct. 1837, cited C. E. Pascoe, *The Dramatic List* (London, 1880), p. 87.
24 *Morning Chronicle*, 29 Jan. 1845, cited *ibid.* pp. 88-9.
25 *Atheneum*, 26 Apr. 1856, cited *ibid.* p. 119.
26 *Saturday Review*, 27 Sept. 1856, cited *ibid.* p. 120.
27 Westland Marston, *Our Recent Actors* (London, 1888), p. 308.
28 *Daily News*, 3 Jan. 1879, cited C. E. Pascoe, *The Dramatic List*, p. 372.
29 *The Era*, 23 Dec. 1882.
30 *Ibid.*
31 Unidentified cutting, 4 Sept.1899, Harvard Theatre Collection.

Chapter 10: *Jack Sheppard*

1 S. M. Ellis, 'Jack Sheppard in Literature and Drama' in H. Bleakley and S. M. Ellis, The Trial of Jack Sheppard (London, 1933), pp. 92-5: Keith Hollingsworth, The Newgate Novel (Detroit, 1963), pp. 39-45.
2 W. H. Ainsworth, Jack Sheppard (London, 1839), p. 244 and J. B. Buckstone, *Jack Sheppard* (London, 1839), Act III, Scene 2, p. 43.
3 S. M. Ellis, *The Trial of Jack Sheppard*, pp. 105-7: K. Hollingsworth, *The Newgate Novel*, pp. 145-7.
4 J. R. Stephens, *The Censorship of English Drama*, 1824-1901 (Cambridge, 1980), pp. 66-7: H. Chance Newton, *Crime and the Drama* (London, 1927), p. 67.
5 K. Hollingsworth, *The Newgate Novel*, p. 141.
6 J. R. Stephens, *Censorship of English Drama*, pp. 73-7.
7 Eric Hobsbawm, *Bandits* (London, 1969).
8 Kellow Chesney. *The Victorian Underworld* (London, 1970), chapters 4 and 5.
9 M. Meisel, *Realizations* (Princeton, 1983), pp. 265-79.
10 S. M. Ellis, *op. cit.* p. 85 reproduces a version of the same print from *Punch*, 11 Dec. 1841, representing Lord 'Jack' Russell, stading on the 'Treasury Bench', carving his name watched by Robert Peel, as Owen Wood, from behind some lumber labelled 'Timber Duties'.
11 W. H. Ainsworth, *Jack Sheppard*, p. 1.
12 *Ibid.* p. 22.
13 Westland Marston, *Our Recent Actors*, p. 13.
14 F. Rahill, *The World of Melodrama* (Penn State UP, 1967), pp. 208-9.
15 *The Times*, 10 Mar. 1855: C. E. Pascoe, *The Dramatic List*, p. 228.
16 G. H. Lewes, *On Actors and the Art of Acting*, p. 87.
17 C. Pearce, *Madame Vestris and her Times* (London, n.d.), p. 55.
18 J. Foster, *Life of Dickens*, edited by J. W. T. Ley (London, 1928), p. 668.
19 See D. Mayer, 'Sexuality in Pantomime', *Theatre Quarterly*, IV (1971).
20 S. M. Ellis, *The Trial of Jack Sheppard*, p. 116.

21 Walter Goodman, *The Keeleys, on the Stage and at Home* (London, 1895), pp. 15-16 and 73.
22 *Ibid.* pp. 62-3.
23 *Ibid.* p. 20.
24 *Ibid.* pp. 3 and 16-17.
25 J. B. Buckstone, *Jack Sheppard*, Act V.
26 *Letters of Charles Dickens*, edited by House and Storey (Oxford, 1965), I, 459-60.
27 W. Goodman, *The Keeleys*, p. 30.
28 *Ibid.* p. 36.
29 See. R. Fitzsimon, *The Charles Dickens Show* (London, 1970).
30 M. R. Booth *et al.*, *Revels History of Drama in English*, IV: 1750-1880 (London, 1975), p. 199.

Chapter 11: The psychology of acting

1 See above pp. 32-3.
2 Denis Diderot, *Paradoxe sur le comédien* translated by W. H. Pollock, 1883, reprinted *The Paradox of Acting and Masks or Faces?* (New York, 1957), p. 19.
3 J. R. Roach, *The Player's Passion* (Newark, 1985), chapters 4-6.
4 Francois Joseph Talma, Introduction to Lekain's *Memoirs* (Paris, 1825); quoted as 'Reflections on Acting' in *Papers on Acting*, edited by Brander Matthews (Columbia University, 1915).
5 Helen Faucit, *Some of Shakespeare's Female Characters* (Edinburgh, 1887), pp. 92-3.
6 *Ibid.* p. 146.
7 Diary entry, quoted Sir Theodore Martin, *Helen Faucit*, p. 25.
8 Diary entry, quoted J. C. Trewin, *The Journal of W. C. Macready* (London, 1967), p. 69.
9 Alan Downer, *The Eminent Tragedian*, pp. 193-4.
10 Helen Faucit, *Female Characters*, pp. 334-5.
11 *Ibid.* p. 166.
12 Theodore Martin, *Helen Faucit*, p. 49.
13 John Colman, *Players and Playwrights*, I, pp. 40-1.
14 G. H. Lewes, *On Actors and the Art of Acting*, pp. 91-7.
15 Charles Darwin, *On the Expression of Emotions in Man and Animals*, p. 239.
16 G. H. Lewes, *Problems of Life and Mind* (London, 1878), III, 441.
17 J. Roach, *The Player's Passion*, p. 190.
18 Constant Coquelin, *Art and the Actor* (Paris, 1880), published in *Papers on Acting*, edited by Branders Matthews (reprinted Columbia University, 1924), p. 26.
19 Constant Coquelin, 'Acting and Actors' *Harpers Monthly* (May, 1887), p. 891.
20 Ted Shawn, *Every Little Movement* (New York, 1954).
21 Moses True Brown, *The Synthetic Philosophy of Expression* (New York, 1886), p. 144.
22 Hugh Campbell *et al.*, *Voice, Speech and Gesture*, (London, 1897), pp. 125-6.
23 Ted Shawn, *Every Little Movement*, pp. 12-13.
24 Laurence Irving, *Henry Irving, the Actor and his World* (New York, 1952), pp. 452-3.
25 Henry Irving, *The Dramatic Addresses of Henry Irving* (London, 1893), pp. 55-6.
26 Dion Boucicault, 'Coquelin – Irving', *North American Review*, Aug. 1887.
27 R. D. Altick, *Victorian Studies in Scarlet* (New York, 1970), pp. 83-4.
28 H. Chance Newton, *Crime and the Drama* (London, 1927), p. 264.
29 For details of the text and Irving's performance, see *Henry Irving and 'The Bells'* edited by David Mayer (Manchester, 1980).
30 Eric Jones-Evans, quoted *ibid.* p. 82.

31 E. G. Craig, *Henry Irving* (London, 1930), pp. 58-61.
32 William Archer, *Henry Irving, Actor and Manager* (London, 1883), pp. 33-89.
33 Ellen Terry and G. B. Shaw, *A Correspondence*, edited by C. St. John (London, 1931), p. 88.
34 *Ibid*. p. 228.
35 *Ibid*. p. 173.
36 Ellen Terry, *Memoirs*, edited by E. Craig and C. St. John (London, 1933), p. 173.
37 E. G. Craig, *Henry Irving*, p. 54.
38 Clement Scott, *Yesterday and Today*, V, ii, 391.
39 James Thomas, *The Art of the Actor Manager; Wilson Barrett and the Victorian Theatre* (Ann Arbor, 1984), pp. 55-6.
40 *Ibid*. p. 62.
41 *The Theatre*, Oct. 1881.
42 A. Brereton, *Dramatic Notes* (London, 1885), pp. 55-6; quoted D. Mullins, *Victorian Actors and Actresses in Review*, p. 514.
43 G. R. Sims, 'To a Fashionable Tragedian', *Fun*, 1876, quoted L. Irving, *Henry Irving*, p. 271.
44 *The Idler*, quoted J. Thomas, *The Art of the Actor Manager*, p. 133.
45 *Ibid*. p. 134.
46 *Ibid*. p. 129.

Chapter 12: *Trilby*

1 George Du Maurier, *Trilby* (Everyman edition, London, 1931), p. 257.
2 Michael Booth, *Victorian Spectacular Theatre* (London, 1981), p. 160.
3 Henry James, *Harper's Monthly*, quoted Leonée Ormond, *George Du Maurier* (London 1969), p. 309.
4 See *The Nature of Hypnosis: Basic Reading*, edited by R. E. Shon and M. T. Orne (New York, 1965), pp. 3-7.
5 Maria M. Tatar, *Spellbound* (Princeton, 1978), p. 231.
6 *Ibid*. p. 243.
7 Hesketh Pearson, *Beerbohm Tree; His Life and Laughter* (London, 1956), p. 93.
8 *Manchester Guardian*, 9 Sept. 1895.
9 *The Era*, 2 Nov. 1895.
10 W. Archer, *The Theatrical World*, 1895, London (1896), p. 333.
11 Michael Sanderson, *From Irving to Olivier* (London, 1984), p. 331.
12 Max Beerbohm, *Herbert Beerbohm Tree*, p. 178.
13 *Ibid*. p. 185.
14 William Archer, *Theatre World*, 1895.
15 G. B. Shaw, *Saturday Review* 16 May 1896, in E. Wilson, *Shaw on Shakespeare*, (London, 1961), pp. 98.
16 *Saturday Review* 11 Feb. 1905, *ibid*. p. 142.
17 Max Beerbohm, *Herbert Beerbohm Tree*, pp. 242-3.
18 *Ibid*. pp. 223-6
19 *Ibid*. p. 72. See also Stanislavski, *My Life in Art* (London, 1924), pp. 403-7.
20 Max Beerbohm, *Herbert Beerbohm Tree*, p. 130.
21 Herbert Beerbohm Tree, 'The Imaginative Faculty', *Thoughts and Afterthoughts* (London 1913), pp. 95-7.
22 *Ibid*. pp. 98-100.
23 Stanislavski, *My Life in Art*, pp. 465-6.

24   J. R. Towse, *Sixty Years in the Theatre; an Old Critic's Memories* (New York 1916), pp. 446-7.
25   Hesketh Pearson, *Life of Oscar Wilde*, London (1946), p. 232.
26   Max Beerbohm, *Herbert Beerbohm Tree*, p. 259.

Chapter 13: Shakespearian interpretation

1   J. L. Styan, *The Shakespeare Revolution* (London, 1977), pp. 11, 17 and 25.
2   C. Lamb, 'On the Tragedies of Shakespeare' (1812) quoted G. Rowell, *Victorian Dramic Criticism* (London, 1971), p. 24.
3   Attributed to Mounet-Sully in E. Braun, *Meyerhold on Theatre* (London, 1969), p. 209.
4   E. Burke, *A Philosophical Enquiry into the Origins of our our Ideas of the Sublime and the Beautiful*, edited by J. T. Boulton (London, 1758), p. 39.
5   J. Hankey, *Othello: Plays in Performance* (Bristol, 1987), p. 119.
6   Tori Haring-Smith, *From Farce to Metadrama* (Westport, Conn., 1985), p. 18.
7   George Daniel, *The Taming of the Shrew*, edited by Cumberland (London 1830), p. 7.
8   J. R. Planché, *Recollections and Reflections* (London, 1872), p. 296.
9   *The Examiner*, 23 Mar. 1844.
10 See J. Macdonald 'The Taming of the Shrew at the Haymarket Theatre, 1844 and 1847', *Nineteenth Century British Theatre*, edited by K. Richards and P. Thomson, (London, 1971), pp. 164-7.
11 W. Marston, *Our Recent Actors*, pp. 288-9.
12 C. Scott, *The Theatre of Yesterday and Today*, II, 36.
13 Quoted; Macdonald, 'The Shrew at the Haymarket', p. 163.
14 W. Marston, *Our Recent Actors*, pp. 165-6.
15 Haring-Smith, *From Farce to Metadrama*, p. 48.
16 W. Graham-Robertson, *Life Was Worth Living* (New York, 1931), pp. 215-32; for the personal relationship between Daly and Rehan see Cornelia Skinner, *Family Circles* and M. Felheim, *The Theatre of Augustin Daly* (Harvard, 1956), p. 43.
17 Haring-Smith, *From Farce to Metadrama*, p. 56.
18 Graham-Robertson, *Life Was Worth Living*, p. 231.
19 C. Scott, *The Theatre of Yesterday and Today*, II ,415-16.
20 Ellen Terry, *Memoirs*, p. 224.
21 W. Winter, *Shakespeare on the Stage* (London, 1912), p. 520.
22 Ada Rehan, 'Katharine', Introduction to *Taming of the Shrew*, New York (1900), quoted Haring-Smith, *From Farce to Metadrama*, pp. 63-4.
23 C. Scott, *The Theatre of Yesterday and Today*, pp. 425-6.
24 Quoted J. F. Daly, *The Life of Augustin Daly* (New York, 1917), p. 466.
25 *Ibid.* p. 429.
26 F. C. Davis, 'These Our Actors', *Lippincott's Magazine*, Oct. 1885, quoted B. Hewlitt, *Theatre USA* (New York, 1959), pp. 242-3.
27 A. B. Walkley, *Playhouse Impressions* (London, 1892), p. 39.
28 E. Wilson, *Shaw on Shakespeare* (London, 1961), pp. 178-9.
29 *Ibid.* p. 180.
31 *Ibid.* p. 130.
31 Graham-Robertson, *Life Was Worth Living*, p. 231.
32 J. Colman, *Fifty Years of an Actor's Life* (London, 1904), p. 419. and see *New Variorum Edition of 'As You Like It'*, edited by R. Knowles (New York, 1977), pp. 636-7.
33 Helen Faucit, *Some of Shakespeare's Female Characters*, pp. 230-1.

34 T. Martin, *Helen Faucit, Lady Martin*, p. 65.

35 H. Faucit, *Female Characters*, p. 238.

36 C. Pascoe, *The Dramatic List*, pp. 140-1.

37 H. Morley, *Journal of a London Playgoer*, p. 286.

38 T. Martin, *Helen Faucit*, pp. 404-5.

39 *Ibid*. p. 362.

40 A. Downer, *The Eminent Tragedian*, pp. 193-4; and *The Journal of W. C. Macready*, edited by J. C. Trewin, pp. 146-58.

41 C. Pascoe, *The Dramatic List*, p. 138.

42 T. Martin, *Helen Faucit*, p. 362.

43 R. Lowe, in B. Matthews and L. Hutton, *Actors and Actresses*, III, 179.

44 H. Faucit, *Female Characters*, p. 243.

45 W. Hazlitt, *Complete Works*, edited by P. Howe (London, 1903), V, 179.

46 A. Jameson, *Shakespeare's Heroines* (London, 1833; 1898 ed.), p. 35.

47 G. C. D. Odell, *Shakespeare from Betterton to Irving* (New York, 1920), II, 295-6.

48 *Ibid*. p. 353; E. Terry, *Memoirs*, p. 21.

49 See Joy Melville, *Ellen and Edy* (London, 1987); Nina Auerbach, *Ellen Terry*, (London, 1987); J. Stokes, M. R. Booth and S. Bassnett, *Bernhardt, Terry, Duse*, (London, 1988).

50 E. W. Godwin, *The Architect*, 27 Mar. 1875, cited *Shakespeare Variorum Edition*, pp. 392-3.

51 M. Merchant, 'On Looking at *The Merchant of Venice*', *Nineteenth Century British Theatre*, edited by Richards and Thomson, pp. 174-5.

52 E. W. Godwin, in *Shakespeare Variorum Edition*, p. 387.

53 C. Scott, *Yesterday and Today*, I, 585-6.

54 D. Cook, *Nights at the Play*, pp. 71-2.

55 A. Comyns-Carr, *Reminiscences* (London, 1926), p. 31.

56 Hesketh Pearson, *Beerbohm Tree* (London, 1956), p. 11.

57 E. Terry, *Memoirs*, pp. 87-8.

58 D. Cook, *Nights at the Play*, p. 72.

59 C. Scott, *Yesterday and Today*, p. 586.

60 H. James, *The Scenic Art*, p. 109.

61 E. Terry, *Memoirs*, p. 86.

62 N. Auerbach, *Ellen Terry*, p. 172.

63 C. Cowden Clarke, *Shakespeare's Characters*, p. 401.

64 E. Terry, *Memoirs*, p. 128.

65 A. Hughes, *Henry Irving, Shakespearian* (London, 1981), pp. 224-41.

66 Cited *ibid*. pp. 238-9.

67 C. Cowden Clarke, *Shakespeare's Characters*, p. 407.

68 H. A. Jones, *The Shadow of Henry Irving*, cited A. C. Sprague, *Shakespearian Players and Performances* (London, 1954), p. 111.

69 *West End Review*, July 1898, cited A. Hughes, *Henry Irving, Shakespearian*, p. 239.

Chapter 14: *Hamlet*

1 W. Poel's *Diary*, 23 Feb. 1877, cited R. Speaight, *William Poel, and the Elizabethan Revival* (London, 1954), p. 32.

2 W. C. Macready, *Reminiscences*, I, 296-7.

3 E. Ransome, *The Terrific Kemble* (London, 1978), p. 215.

4 R. Speaight, *William Poel*, p. 46.

5   R. F. Lundstrom, *William Poel's Hamlets: Director as Critic* (Michigan, 1984), p. 15.
6   R. Speaight, *William Poel*, p. 50.
7   *The Standard*, 18 Apr. 1881, cited R. F. Lundstrom, *William Poel's Hamlets*, p. 28.
8   *The Stage*, 22 Apr. 1881, *ibid.*
9   *The Morning Post*, 17 Apr. 1881, cited B. L. Webb, *Poetry on the Stage; William Poel's Production of Verse Drama* (Salzburg, 1979), p. 111.
10 *The Academy*, 23 Apr. 1881, cited R. F. Lundstrom, *William Poel's Hamlets*, p.29.
11 For details see R. F. Lundstrom, *William Poel's Hamlets*, pp. 18-28.
12 'The Acting Editions of Shakespeare's Plays', *The Era*, 2 July 1881, reprinted in W. Poel, *Shakespeare in the Theatre* (London, 1913), pp. 158 ff.
13 *The Standard*, 20 Feb. 1890, cited R. Speaight, *William Poel*, p. 72.
14 *The Daily Chronicle*, 3 Sept. 1913, *ibid.* p. 90.
15 See B. L. Webb, *Poetry on Stage*, pp. 121-4.
16 N. Marshall. *The Producer and the Play* (London, 1957), p. 151.
17 *The Saturday Review*, 31 July 1909, cited R. Speaight, *William Poel*, p. 63.
18 Stokes, Booth and Basnett, *Bernhardt, Terry, Duse*, p. 32.
19 'On Acting and the Need for a Dramatic Academy', *Theatre*, May 1893, cited R. F. Lundstrom, *William Poel's Hamlets*, p. 44.
20 G. B. Shaw, *Dramatic Opinions*, I, 21.
21 C. Scott, *Some Notable Hamlets* (London, 1899), p. 154.
22 W. Winter, *Vagrant Memories* (New York, 1915), pp 350-1, quoted D. Mullin, *Victorian Actors and Actresses in Review*, p. 210.
23 J. Forbes Robertson, *A Player Under Three Reigns* (London, 1925), p. 164.
24 K. T. Gielgud, *A Victorian Playgoer* (London, 1980), p. 30.
25 W. Archer, *The Theatre for 1895* (London, 1896), pp. 286-8.
26 Cited M. Peters, *Mrs Pat* (London, 1984), p. 114.
27 K. T. Gielgud, *A Victorian Playgoer*, p. 32.
28 M. Peters, *Mrs Pat*, pp. 112-15.
29 *Ibid.* pp. 52-3.
30 J. Forbes Robertson, *A Player Under Three Reigns*, pp. 84-5.
31 R. Findlater, *The Player Kings* (London, 1957), p. 157: A. E. Wilson, *The Lyceum* (London, 1952), p. 123.
32 W. Archer, *The Theatre for 1895*, pp. 254-6.
33 J. T. Grein, *Dramatic Criticism* (London, 1899), p. 189.
34 E. Wilson, *Shaw on Shakespeare*, pp. 82-7.
35 K. T. Geilgud, *A Victorian Playgoer*, p. 62.
36 E. Wilson, *Shaw on Shakespeare*, p. 90.

Plate I — Long-run machinery

The Corsican Brothers by Dion Boucicault: Princess Theatre, 24 February 1852
The ghost of Louis dei Franchi appears to his brother Fabien pointing to the vision of his death. Charles Kean acted both brothers, and ingenious trap-work was needed for him to play the ghost while doubles stood in for Fabien and the corpse

Plate II — The classical image

(a) An idealised portrait of Macready in *Virginius* by Sheridan Knowles: Covent Garden, 17 May 1820
(b) A more realistic portrait of Macready in the light of John Colman's description (p. 56)
(c) Helen Faucit as Antigone, *c.* 1846. She first played Virginia with Macready in 1837

Plate III — A versatile mimic

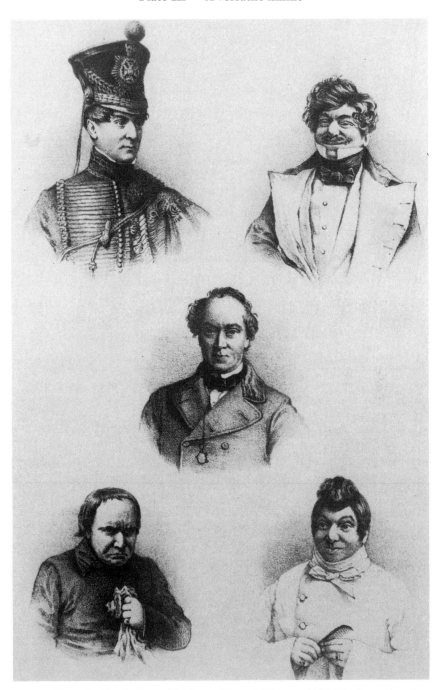

Patter v Clatter by Charles James Matthews: Olympic Theatre, 1836. Matthews played four characters, changing from one to the other almost instantaneously

Plate IV — A traditional comic costume

(a) and (b) *Paul Pry* by John Poole
    John Liston in the original Haymarket Theatre production, 1826
    J. L. Toole played the role from 1854 until into the 1890s
(c) An unknown actor as Marks in the film of *Uncle Tom's Cabin*, 1903

Plate V — The Yankee and the Toff

Our American Cousin by Tom Taylor: Laura Keen's Theatre, 15 October 1858
(a) Joseph Jefferson as Asa Trenchard
(b) E. A. Sothern as Lord Dundreary

Plate VI — Cup-and-saucer ensemble

Caste by Tom Robertson: The Prince of Wales's Theatre, 6 April 1862
(a) Marie Wilton and John Hare as Polly Eccles and Sam Gerridge
(b) In Act III the Marquise offers to bring up Esther's child. Each character responds to the suggestion in their own way

Plate VII — Cross-dressing in melodrama

(a) Mrs Louise Keely; sternly naturalistic in *Jack Sheppard* by J. B. Buckstone: Adelphi Theatre, 28 October 1839

(b) Madame Celeste; rather more provocative in *The Arab Boy*: Adelphi Theatre, *c.* 1840

Plate VIII — Sacred or profane?

The Sign of the Cross by Wilson Barrett, Princess Theatre, 1896
Marcia (Maud Jefferies), doomed to be eaten by lions in the Colosseum, inspires the
devotion of her persecutor, Marcus Superbus (Wilson Barrett)

Plate IX — La vie bohémienne

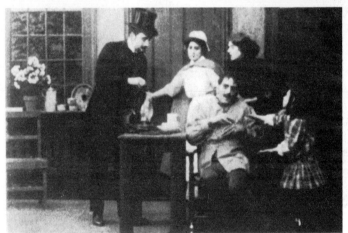

(a) and (b) *Trilby* by Paul Potter: Haymarket Theatre, 30 October 1895
Dorothea Baird as Trilby
Herbert Beerbohm Tree as Svengali
(c) A still from the film *The Drunkard*, Thomas Edison, 1903. The unknown actor follows
the business and gestures of Charles Warner, who created the role of Copeau in *Drink* by
Charles Reade, after Zola's *L'Assommoir*, 1879

Plate X — Shakesperian heroines

(a) Ellen Terry as Portia, Lyceum Theatre from 1879
(b) Ada Rehan as Katharine, the Shrew, 1887

Plate XI — 'Elizabethan' settings

(a) J. R. Planché's *Taming of the Shrew*, Haymarket Theatre, 1844
(b) William Poel's second First Quarto *Hamlet*, Carpenter's Hall, 1900. Ofelia's [sic] 'Mad Scene'

Plate XII — *Hamlet*, Lyceum, 11 September 1897

(a) Johnston Forbes Robertson as Hamlet
(b) Mrs Patrick Campbell as Ophelia
(c) The 'Play Scene', Act III. This scenery was originally designed for Irving's 1878 production

Further reading

The analysis of acting methods of the past is a relatively recent study. Pioneer historian Arthur Colby Sprague, *Shakespeare and the Actors* (1944) and *Shakesperean Players and Performances* (1954), listed variations in business and character interpretation without differentiating the actors' basic assumptions about the purpose or practice of their art. Bertram Joseph's *The Tragic Actor* (1959) gave more consideration to changes in physical and vocal technique, but still did not place the actors in their social and cultural context. Contemporary critics were quoted without question. Of course they do provide essential eye-witness evidence, and Victorian critics had the luxury of commenting at a length that modern journalists could never dream of. I have made much use of such critics, but I hope not unquestioningly. The most useful *collections* of critical writing include: C. E. Pascoe, *The Dramatic List* (1880); Branders Matthews and Laurence Hutton, *Actors and Actrresses of Great Britain and the United States* (1886); George Rowell, *Victorian Dramatic Criticism* (1971); Donald Mullin *Victorian Actors and Actresses in Review* (1983). The one Victorian critic whose collected criticism ought to be read as a whole, in that he develops a clear philosophical argument as to the nature of acting, is George Henry Lewes, *On Actors and the Art of Acting* (1875), though of course Hazlitt, Leight Hunt, William Robson, Henry Morley, Westland Marston, Dutton Cook, Clement Scott, William Archer, Joseph Knight, Henry James and Bernard Shaw should all be recognised as having very personal views on the nature and function of theatre.

In an attempt to penetrate the subjectivity of the critics, I have made considerable use of technical books written by, or for, actors. They reveal more baldly than the eloquent critics the aesthetic and psychological assumptions of the profession. There are few modern reprints of this material, but the following may be traceable in libraries: Henry Siddons, *Practical Illustrations of Rhetorical Gesture and Action* (1807); Leman T. Rede, *The Way to the Stage* (1827); C. W. Smith, *The Actor's Art* (1873); Gustave Garcia, *The Actor's Art* (1882): C. J. Plumptre, *The King's College Lectures on Elocution* (1883); Hugh Campbell (ed.) *Voice, Speech and Gesture; Elocutionary Art* (1897); Rosina Filippi, *The Speaker* (1911). An essential study of the psychology of acting is William Archer's *Masks or Faces?* (1888), while Branders Matthews, *Papers on Acting* (1924) contains several essays by actors themselves. I have read many actors' memoirs and contemporary biographies – most are so anecdotal there is little need to warn against their subjectivity – but there are several modern biographies and critical monographs that are are both informative and pereceptive. I found the following particularly valuable: Laurence Irving, *Henry Irving, the Actor and his World* (1951); Alan S. Downer, *The Eminent Tragedian, William Charles Macready* (1966); Shirley S. Allen, *Samuel Phelps, and Sadler's Wells* (1971); David Mayer, *Henry Irving and 'The Bells'* (1980); Alan Hughes, *Henry Irving, Shakespearian* (1981); Margot Peters, *Mrs Pat* (1984); Nina Auerbach, *Ellen Terry* (1987); John Stokes, Michael R. Booth and Susan Bassnett, *Bernhardt, Terry, Duse* (1988).

Finally there is a handful of crucial modern works of criticism, which attempt to interpret the contemporary evidence to reveal underlying aesthetic, cultural, psychological or sociological developments. I must acknowledge that all of the following have been inspirational for my own study: Joseph Donahue, *Dramatic Character in the English Romantic Age* (1970); Michael Baker, *The Rise of the Victorian Actor* (1978); W. B. Worthen, *The Idea of the Actor* (1981); Martin Meizel, *Realizations* (1983); and Joseph Roach, *The Player's Passion* (1985).

The play texts used for synopses in the chapters of detailed analysis were:

Dion Boucicault, *The Corsican Brothers*, in M. R. Booth, *English Plays of the Nineteenth Century* (Oxford, 1969), vol. 2.

Edward Bulwer-Lytton, *Richelieu*, in M. R. Booth, *English Plays of the Nineteenth Century* (Oxford, 1969), vol. 1.

Tom Taylor, *Our American Cousin*, Samuel French (New York, 1869).

T. W. Robertson, *Caste*, in William Tydeman, *Plays by Tom Robertson*, British and American Playwrights series, Cambridge University Press (Cambridge, 1982).

J. B. Buckstone, *Jack Sheppard*, Webster & Co. (London, 1839).

Paul Potter, *Trilby*, in M. Kilgariff, *The Golden Age of Melodrama* (London, 1974).

Shakespeare, *Hamlet*, First Folio from Furness Variorum edition (Philadelphia, 1877), vol 2.

Index

Academy of Dramatic Art (RADA), 128, 170
Adelphi Theatre, 16, 17, 123, 134, 138-9, 142-3
Ainsworth, Harrison, 135-9, 152
Aldridge, Ira, 176
Alexander, George, 104, 193
Altick, Richard, 153
Anderson, James, 5-6
Anne Blake (Marston), 28
Archer, Frank, 101
Archer, William, 20, 110, 153, 156, 167, 169, 201, 202
Astley's Amphitheatre, 14, 47
As You Like It, 183-6
Atkins, Robert, 173

Bain, Alexander, 148
Baird, Dorothea, 167
Baker, George Pierce, 202
Baker, Michael, 7-8, 10, 17, 101
Bancroft, Marie (Wilton), 98-102, 106-7, 108, 112, 113-16, 141, 200
Bancroft, Squire, 96, 98-9, 101, 106, 110, 112, 113, 116, 200
Barker, H. Granville, 172, 173, 198, 203
Barnum, P. T., 85, 92
Barrett, Wilson, 44, 131-3, 158-61, 164, 193
Bateman, Kate and Ellen, 92
Bedford, Paul, 68, 75, 139-40
The Beggar's Opera (Gay), 140
Belasco, David, 150
Bell, Sir Charles, 41
The Bells (Lewis), 78, 121, 154-6, 158, 166
Belphegor, 99, 130

Benson, Frank, 113, 193-4, 197
Bergson, Henri, 67
Bernhardt, Sarah, 101, 164
Betty Martin, 140
Booth, Edwin, 4
Booth, Michael, 120, 164
Boucicault, Agnes (Robertson), 98
Boucicault, Dion, 8, 15-16, 20, 21, 23, 25, 117, 152
Box and Cox (Morton), 66-7, 110
Brereton, Austin, 151
Breuer, Josef, 166
Bridges-Adams, W., 173
Britannia Theatre, 16, 136
Brooke, Gustavus, 176
Brooks, Peter, 121, 124
Brown, Ford Madox, 193
Brown, Moses True, 150
Buckstone, John Baldwin, 12, 65-9, 79, 84-5, 90, 96, 99, 102, 134-43
Bulwer-Lytton, Edward, 18, 43, 52-61, 97
Bunn, Alfred, 11
Burke, Edmund, 176
Byron, H. J., 90, 98-9

Calvert, Charles, 200
Campbell, Mrs Patrick, 69-70, 164, 169, 172, 193, 200-2, 203-4
The Captive (Lewis), 49
Caste (Robertson), 100-1, 108-18
Cato (Addison), 36
Cecil, Arthur, 96, 101
Celeste, Mme, 16, 129-30
censorship, 136-8
Chambers, E. K., 197
Child of the Wreck (Planché), 129

Index

Chippendale, W. H., 4, 12, 117

Cibber, Colley, 38

Cinq Mars (de Vigny), 56

Clarke, John S., 106

Clive, Kitty, 177

Coal Hole Tavern, 47

Coberg Theatre, 14, 17, 136 (*see also* Old Vic)

Coghlan, Charles, 101, 188-90

The Colleen Bawn (Boucicault), 8-9, 160

Colman, George, 11

Colman, John, 3, 26, 27, 56, 97, 105, 126, 147

Combe, George, 42-3

Comédie Française, 199

commedia dell' arte, 1

Comyns-Carr, Alice, 189

Cons, Emma, 197

Cooke, George Frederick, 35, 127

Cooke, T. P., 90

Cooter, Roger, 42-3

Coquelin, Constant, 149-52, 154, 199

Corder, Frederick, 126

Coriolanus, 35-6, 193

The Corsican Brothers (Boucicault), 23-9, 72, 92, 124

The Courier of Lyons (Reade), 125

The Court Theatre, 72, 101, 104

Covent Garden Theatre, 7, 10, 11, 13-15, 53, 106, 124, 146

Cowden-Clarke, Mary, 186

Cox and Box (Bernand and Sullivan), 66

Craig, Edward Gordon, 122-3, 155, 157, 170, 172, 199, 201

Cromwell (Bulwer-Lytton), 53, 56

Cruikshank, George, 47, 135, 138

The Crushed Tragedian (H. J. Byron), 90

Cymbeline, 193

Daddy Hardacre (Simpson), 77-8

Daly, Augustin, 179-83

Darwin, Charles, 105, 127, 148

David Garrick (Robertson), 90

Davidge, William, 17, 74

Delsarte, François, 149-52, 156

Descartes, René, 41

Dickens, Charles, 17, 53, 68, 77, 97, 114, 142-3, 152, 194

Diderot, Denis, 33, 144-5, 147, 149, 152

Dillon, Charles, 4, 99, 130-1

The Doll's House (Ibsen), 180

Dolmetsch, Arnold, 197

Donahue, Joseph, 33, 40

Don Giovanni in London, 141

Donne, William, 137-8

Drew, John, 181

Drink (Reade), 93, 131

The Drunkard, 227

Drury Lane Theatre, 10-11, 30

The Duchess de la Vallière (Bulwer-Lytton), 53

Ducrow, Andrew, 47-50, 129, 149

Dumas, Alexandre, 25, 159

Du Maurier, Gerald, 172

Du Maurier, George, 162-7

The Dumb Man of Manchester (Rayner), 49

Duncan, Isadora, 150

Duse, Eleonora, 128

Egan, Pierce, 138

Elizabethan Stage Society, 170, 198

elocution, 126-9

Ellis, Edwin, 125

Elliston, Robert, 2, 43, 46

An Enemy of the People (Ibsen), 169-70

Engle, J. J., 39

Evans, Edith, 198

Evans, Patrick, 167

Farren, Nellie, 138, 141

Farren, Percy, 126, 146, 183

Farren, William, 16, 69-70, 74, 76, 90, 116, 145

Faucit, Helen, 13, 53, 92, 126, 145-7, 183-6, 189

Fechter, Charles, 93-5, 196

Filippi, Rosina, 128, 198

Filon, Augustin, 97, 102-3, 110, 116

The Flying Dutchman (Fitzball), 123-4, 129

Fogerty, Elsie, 198

Foote, Lydia, 113

Foote, Samuel, 11

Forbes-Robertson, Johnson, 101, 192, 200-4

Forrest, Edwin, 37

Forster, John, 58, 97

Freud, Sigmund, 152, 166

Furness, H. H., 197

Furnivall, Dr. F. J., 195, 197

Gall, F. J., 42-3

A Game at Speculation (G. H. Lewes), 72

Garcia, Gustave, 42, 128

Garrick, David, 30-2, 60, 127, 177, 182

Gertrude's Cherries, 26

Gilbert, W. S., 71, 76, 103-4, 105

Godwin, E. W., 187-90

Index

The Golden Fleece (Planché), 71-2
Grant, George, 38-9
Grant, James, 9
The Great Exhibition, 7
The Grecian Saloon, 74
The Green Bushes (Buckstone), 129-30
Greenwood, Thomas, 18-19
Greet, Ben, 193, 202
Greg, W. W., 197
Grein, J. T., 201
Grimaldi, Joseph, 73
Grundy, Sidney, 98
Guthrie, Tyrone, 173

Hamilton, Lady Emma, 47
Hamlet, 1, 4-5, 60, 93-5, 96, 127, 128, 170, 172, 192-204
Hare, John, 96, 99, 101-2, 106, 113, 116-17, 168, 193
Haring-Smith, Tori, 177, 179
Harley, John Pritt, 66-7
Harris, Augustus, 5
Harvard University, 151, 202
Haymarket Theatre, 6, 10-14, 66, 84, 104-7, 116, 168, 177
Hazlitt, William, 34-5, 59, 64, 187
Henry IV, 169, 200
Henry V, 24
Henry VIII, 19, 24, 164, 193
Her Majesty's Theatre, 101, 167
Herod (Phillips), 172
Hicks, 140
Hill, John, 32-3, 144
His House in Order (Pinero), 104
Holcroft, Thomas, 42
Hollingsworth, John, 200
Hollingsworth, Keith, 136, 138
Honey, George, 101, 113
Honner, Mrs, 140
Hoodless, Richard, 197
Horton, Precilla, 13
Hoskins, W., 1
Howe, Henry, 12
Hunt, Holman, 189
Hunt, Leigh, 34

Ibsen, Henrik, 96, 105, 118, 181
The Iron Chest (Colman), 2, 121, 194, 195
Irving, Henry, 1, 4-5, 20, 78, 96, 101, 104, 128, 133, 151-2, 154-8, 164, 189, 191, 194, 200, 202
Jack Sheppard (Buckstone), 134-43
James, Henry, 106, 111-13, 117, 152, 165, 166
James, William, 42, 148
Jameson, Mrs Anna, 186
Jefferson, Joseph, 81-3
John Bull (Colman), 63
Jones, Henry Arthur, 98, 103, 159, 180, 191
Jordan, Mrs Dorothy, 183
Le Juif Polonaise (Erckmann and Chatrian), 154

Katharine and Petruchio (Garrick and Kemble), 177-8
Kean, Charles, 3-4, 16-20, 23-9, 63, 75, 94, 102, 119, 187, 191, 196
Kean, Edmund, 2, 4, 11, 17, 24, 26, 29, 30-1, 33-7, 40, 45, 58, 63, 75, 133, 176, 186-7, 194
Kean, Mrs Ellen, 3-4, 25
Keeley, Mrs Mary, 140-3
Keeley, Robert, 16, 67-9, 140
Keeley Worried by Buckstone (Lemon and Webster), 68
Keene, Laura, 81-2
Keller, Prof., 47
Kelly, Charles, 96
Kemble, Charles, 14, 99, 128, 146
Kemble, Fanny, 92, 194
Kemble, John Philip, 11, 26, 30, 35-6, 106, 175, 177
Kendal, Mrs Madge (Robertson), 98, 106
Kendal, William, 96, 101, 106, 200
King Lear, 24, 158, 193
Knight, Joseph, 79
Knowles, Sheridan, 18, 37, 44, 174

The Lady of Lyons (Bulwer-Lytton), 13, 53, 146-7
Lamb, Charles, 63-4, 173-5
Langtry, Lily, 172
Larkin, Sophie, 113
Lavater, J. K., 42
Lee, Sidney, 197
Lemaître, Frédérick, 92-3
Leslie, Fred, 138
Lewes, George Henry, 26, 27-9, 43, 59, 60, 69, 71-2, 94-6, 113, 147-8, 199
Lichtenberg, G. C., 31
Liston, John, 12, 63-5, 73, 79
Little Dorrit (Dickens), 77
Little Jack Sheppard, 138, 141
London Assurance (Boucicault), 15-16, 178
Love's Labour's Lost, 15
Lyceum Theatre, 5, 12, 101, 104, 193, 200, 202

Index

MaCarthy, Lillah, 198

Macbeth, 5-6, 19, 36-7, 158, 175, 184, 193, (burlesqued: Talford) 75

Mackaye, Steele, 149-50

Macnamara, Mrs, 66

Macready, Mrs Kitty (Atkins), 45

Macready, William Charles, 3, 11, 12-14, 17-18, 26, 30, 36, 44-6, 50, 52-61, 63, 70, 90, 92, 97, 119, 126, 127-8, 133, 145, 147, 174, 176, 185, 194

The Maid and the Magpie (H. J. Byron), 114, 141

Malibran, Madame, 11, 128

Maria Martin, 136

The Marriage of Figaro (Beaumarchais), 140

Marston, Westland, 12, 26, 28, 52, 58-9, 65, 67, 72, 78-9, 130, 139, 178

Martin, Theodore, 183-4

Mathews, Charles James, 14-16, 70-2, 82, 85, 90, 97, 194

Mayhew, Edward, 46

Measure for Measure, 198

Medea (burlesqued), 77

Meiningen Company, 102, 105

Meisel, Martin, 47, 138

The Merchant of Venice, 60-1, 158, 186-91, (burlesqued), 75

Merivale, Herman, 184

Mesmer, F. A., 165-6

A Midsummer Night's Dream, 182, 193

Mitchell, John, 92

Money (Bulwer-Lytton), 13-14, 106

Morley, Henry, 16, 18, 67, 75-6, 87, 93, 96

Morris, David, 11

A Most Unwarrantable Intrusion (Morton), 68

MP (Pinero), 102, 106

Much Ado About Nothing, 200

Munden, Joseph, 63-4

Murray, Leigh, 116

music hall, 7-8, 10, 74, 107

musical accompaniment, 123-6

Neilson, Julia, 193

Neville, Henry, 150

Nicholas Nickleby (Dickens), 2 (play: Stirling), 142-3

Nicholson, 'Baron' Renton, 47

Nisbett, Louisa, 16, 178-9, 183-4

The Notorious Mrs Ebbsmith (Pinero), 200

Old Vic Theatre (Royal Victoria), 197, 199

Oliver Twist (Dickens), 136-7

Olympic Revels (Planché), 73

Olympic Theatre, 10, 14-16, 19, 27, 70-2, 73-8, 92, 100

O'Neill, Eliza, 40

Osbaldiston, D. W., 17

Othello, 94, 122, 158, 176

Our American Cousin (Taylor), 80-91

Oxenford, John, 87

Paganini, 11

Partridge, Bernard, 196

Paterson, Peter, 9

Patter versus Clatter (Mathews), 71

Paul Clifford (Bulwer-Lytton), 136

Pauline (Oxenford), 28

Pauline, Madame, 47

Paul Pry, 12, 79, 106

Pauncefort, Georgiana, 5

Pelham (Bulwer-Lytton), 53

Phelps, Samuel, 1, 10, 13, 17-20, 63, 186, 200, 204

Phillips, Mrs Alfred, 75

The Phrenologist (Webb), 43

phrenology, 42-3

physiognomy, 42

Pinero, Arthur, 98, 99, 101, 104-5, 180, 201

Pizarro (Sheridan), 6

Planché, J. R., 14, 71-3, 76, 177-8

Plot and Passion (Taylor), 76, 92, 125

Plumtre, Dr. Charles, 127-8

Poel, William, 127, 170, 192-9

The Poor Idiot (Ducrow), 49-50

poses-plastiques, 47

Potter, Paul, 162-4, 167

Prince of Wales's Theatre, 72, 97-103, 106, 108, 187, 189-90

Princess Theatre, 5, 16, 18, 23, 93, 193

Pygmalion (Shaw), 169

Quizzology of the British Drama (à Beckett), 122

Rachel, 92, 199

Reade, Charles, 20, 93, 105, 125

Rede, Leman, 10, 48

Rehan, Ada, 179-83

Ribot, Theodule, 152

Richard II, 169, 172

Richard III, 34

Richelieu (Bulwer Lytton), 18, 51-61, 183

[236]

Index

Ristori, Adelaide, 77
Roach, Joseph, 41, 144, 148
Robertson, Tom, 20, 85, 97, 98, 99-100, 102-3, 105, 108-18
Robson, Frederick, 72-8, 79, 131, 141
Robson, William, 37, 63
Rogers, Miss, 140
Romeo and Juliet, 201
Royalty Theatre, 198
Ryder, John, 25

Sadler's Wells Theatre, 1, 10, 18-20, 105
St Denis, Ruth, 151
St George's Hall, 195
St James's Theatre, 72, 92, 96, 101, 104, 106
Salome (Wilde), 172
Salvini, Thomaso, 176, 199
Sardanapalus (Byron), 3
Sardou, Victorien, 159
Saville, E. F., 140
The School for Scandal (Sheridan), 44, 62, 69
Scott, Clement, 96-7, 105, 111, 153, 158, 178, 180
Scott, James, 194
The Sea Captain (Bulwer-Lytton), 13
The Second Mrs Tanqueray (Pinero), 163, 200
The Settling Day (Taylor), 95
The Shakespeare Reading Society, 197
The Shakespere Society, 195-7
Sharratt, Bernard, 120-1, 140, 141
Shaw, George Bernard, 118, 153, 156-7, 169, 172, 182, 197, 203-4
Shawn, Ted, 149, 151
Sheridan, Thomas, 127
She Stoops to Conquer (Goldsmith), 62
Siddons, Henry, 39-40
Siddons, Sarah, 11, 26, 30, 36-7, 133, 175, 176
The Sign of the Cross (Barrett), 160-1
Silsbee, Joshua, 181
The Silver King (Jones), 131-3, 158-9
Sims, George R., 159
Smith, Henry, 55
Smith, O., 16, 139-40, 142
Society (Robertson), 97-100, 116
Sothern, Edward Askew, 79-91, 96, 98, 110, 119
Sothern, Edward H., 83
Steele, Joshua, 127

Stanislavski, K. S., 152, 169-71, 186
Sticotti, Arturo, 144
Still Waters Run Deep (Taylor), 27, 92
Stirling, Edward, 2, 194
Stoker, Bram, 151
Stratford Memorial Theatre, 194, 200
The Streets of London (Boucicault), 117
The String of Pearls; or the Fiend of Fleet Street (Dibdin Pitt), 136
Styan, J. L., 119-20
Sullivan, Barry, 4
Surrey Theatre, 14, 16, 17, 18, 19, 135-6

Taglioni, Marie, 11
A Tale of Mystery (Holcroft), 124-5
Talford, Thomas Noon, 18
Talma, 95, 127, 145, 147, 157
The Taming of the Shrew, 177-82, 198
Taylor, Tom, 8, 20, 84-5, 92, 117
Tempest, Marie, 193
The Templar (Slous), 28
Terriss, William, 96, 101
Terry, Ellen, 24-5, 102, 157, 164, 180, 187-91, 202
Terry, Kate, 190
Theatre Regulating Act (1843), 10, 16-18
The Thespian Preceptor, 38
Through Fire and Water (Gordon), 79
The Ticket of Leave Man (Taylor), 92, 117
Tom Jones (Fielding), 31-2
Toole, J. L., 78-9, 102
Tree, Herbert Beerbohm, 162-72, 189, 193
Tree, Iris, 168
Tree, Mrs Maud (Holt), 168, 196
Tree, Viola, 168
A Trick to Catch the Old One (Massinger), 37
Trilby (the novel: Du Maurier), 162-4 (the play: Potter), 162-172

Uncle Tom's Cabin, 79
Up at the Hills (Taylor), 96

Vanbrugh, Irene, 104
The Venetian Brothers, 1
Vestris, Madame Eliza, 13-16, 70-3, 98, 99, 141
Vezin, Herman, 128, 200, 204
Vezin, Mrs Herman, 98
Virginius (Knowles), 18, 44-7, 54, 174

Wallack, Lester, 81-2
The Wandering Minstrel (Mayhew), 74-5
Ward, Genevieve, 200

Index

Warner, Charles, 93, 131
Warner, Mrs Mary Amelia, 18
Warton, Madame, 47
Watts, G. F., 187, 189
Webster, Ben, 11-14, 16-17, 96, 142, 177, 179
Wigan, Alfred, 26-8, 76, 92-3, 95-6, 111
Wigan, Mrs Alfred, 95, 98
Wigan, Horace, 8, 95, 100
Wilde, Oscar, 98, 158, 164, 165
Willard, E. S., 159
William Tell (Knowles), 3
The Winter's Tale, 24, 147, 152

A Woman of No Importance (Wilde), 163
The Woodland Players, 193
Woodward, Henry, 177
Woolgar, Sara Jane, 16
Wright, Edward, 68-9
Wyndham, Charles, 96, 172, 193

Yates, Frederick, 139-40, 142
The Yellow Dwarf (Planché), 76-7
Younge, Frederick, 110-11

Zola, Emile, 93, 105, 117, 131, 159